Outdoor Lighting: **Nudes**

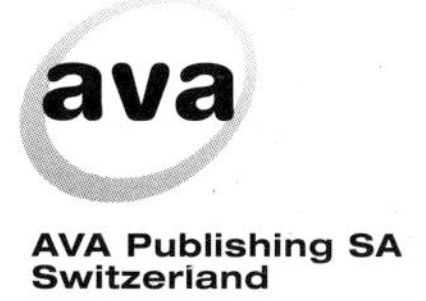

AVA Publishing SA
Switzerland

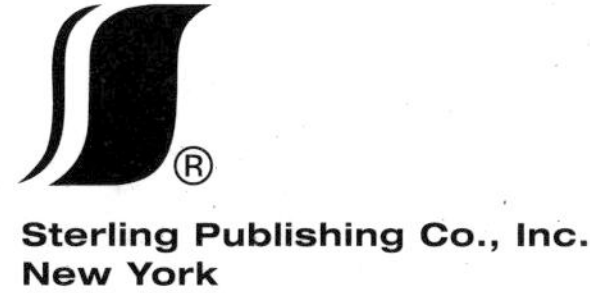

Sterling Publishing Co., Inc.
New York

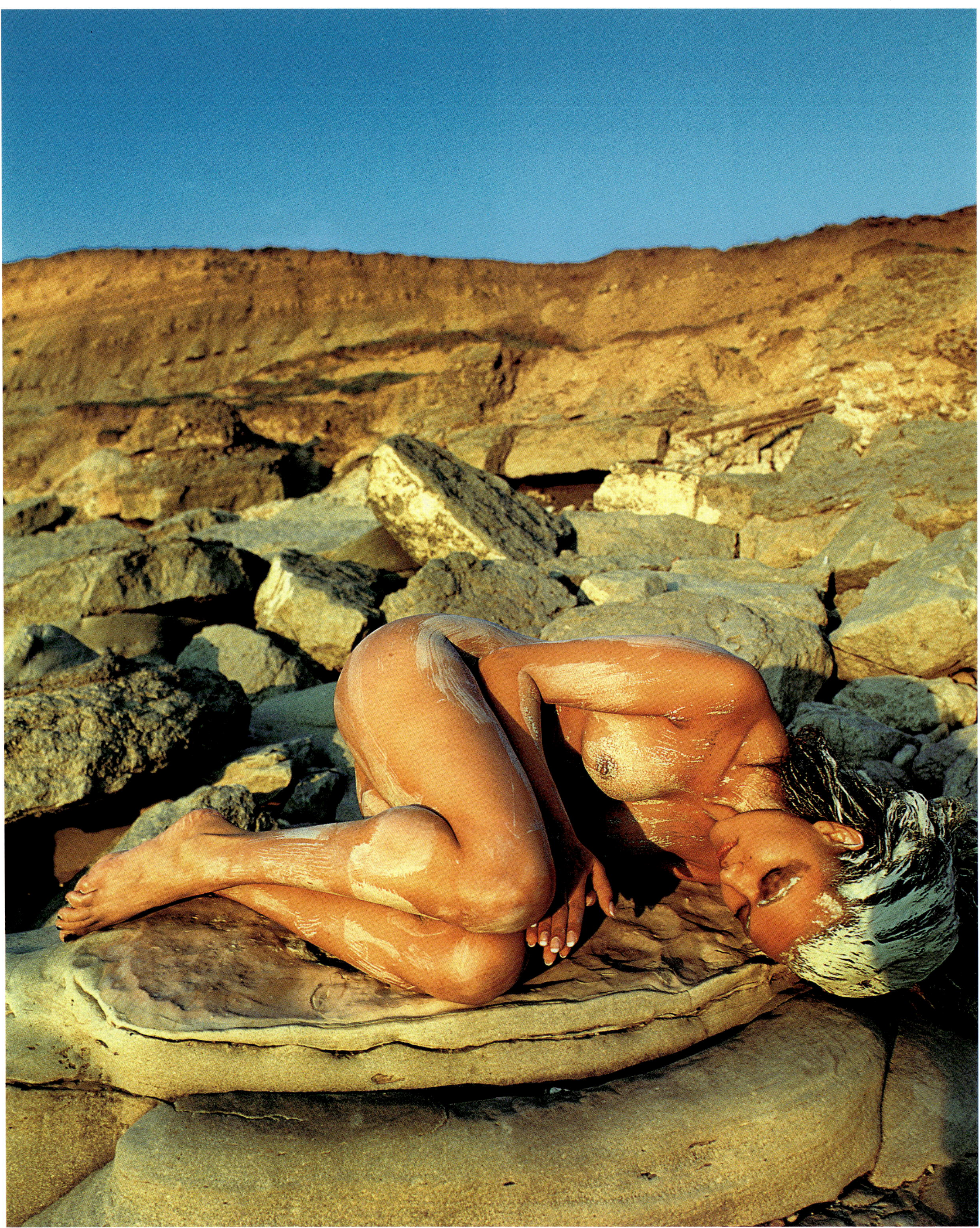

Cathy Joseph

Outdoor Lighting: **Nudes**

Published by AVA Publishing SA
rue du Bugnon 7
CH-1299 Crans-près-Céligny
Switzerland
Tel: +41 786 005 109
Email: enquiries@avabooks.ch

Distributed by Thames and Hudson (ex-North America)
181a High Holborn
London WC1V 7QX
United Kingdom
Tel: +44 20 7845 5000
Fax: +44 20 7845 5055
Email: sales@thameshudson.co.uk
www.thamesandhudson.com

Distributed by Sterling Publishing Co., Inc.
in USA
387 Park Avenue South
New York, NY 10016-8810
Tel: +1 212 532 7160
Fax: +1 212 213 2495
www.sterlingpub.com

in Canada
Sterling Publishing
c/o Canadian Manda Group
One Atlantic Avenue, Suite 105
Toronto, Ontario M6K 3E7

English Language Support Office
AVA Publishing (UK) Ltd.
Tel: +44 1903 204 455
Email: enquiries@avabooks.co.uk

ISBN 2-88479-038-1

10 9 8 7 6 5 4 3 2 1

Design by Gavin Ambrose

Production and separations by AVA Book Production Pte. Ltd., Singapore
Tel: +65 6334 8173
Fax: +65 6334 0752
Email: production@avabooks.com.sg

Acknowledgements

A very big thank you to all the photographers for contributing their wonderful pictures and being unfailingly helpful and patient in giving insights into how they work and sharing their expertise. Many thanks also to Brian Morris, Laura Owen and Natalia Price-Cabrera at AVA, Sarah Jameson for finding the pictures and Gavin Ambrose for the design. Finally to my husband Giles for his advice and enthusiasm.

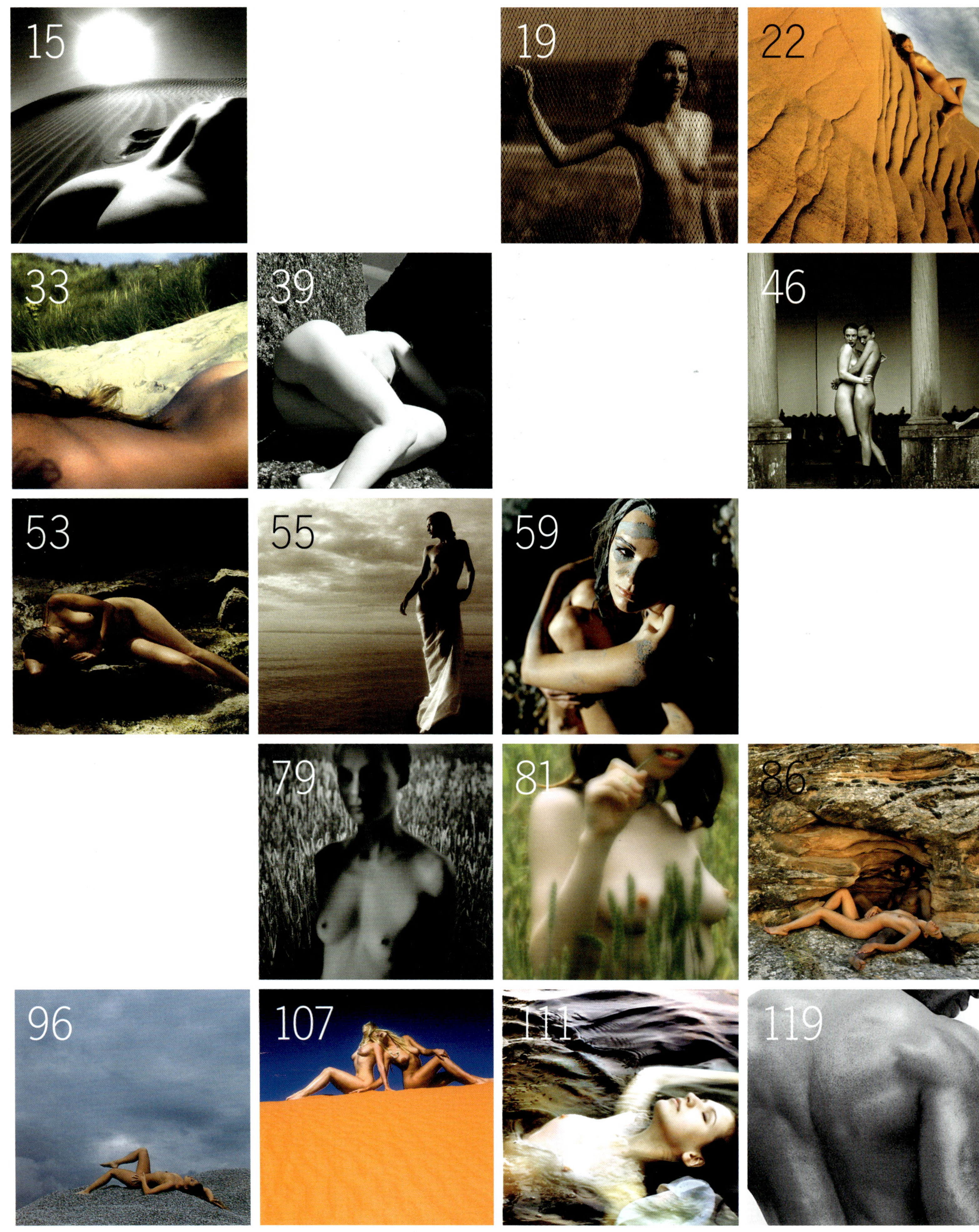

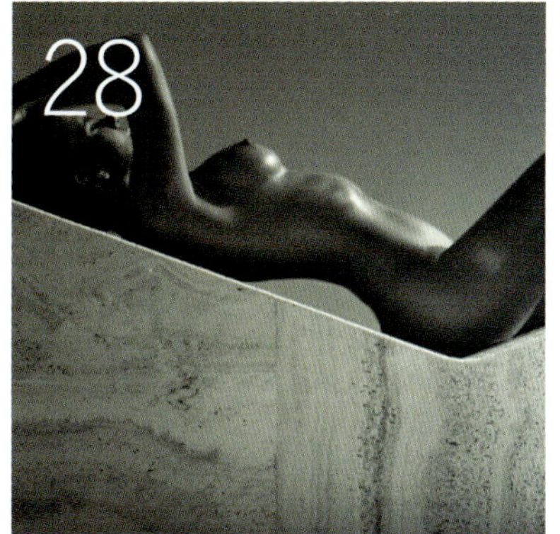

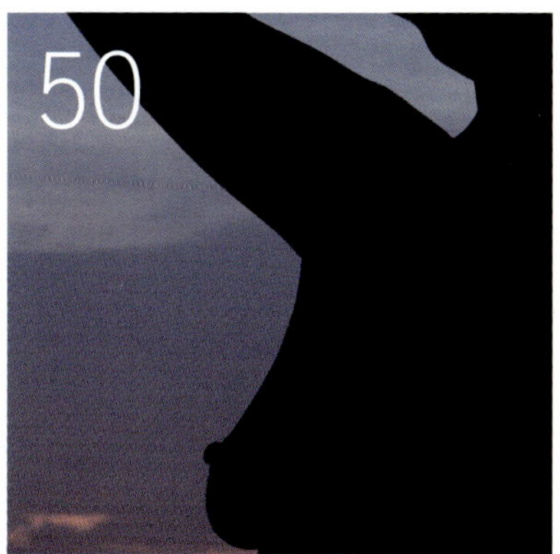

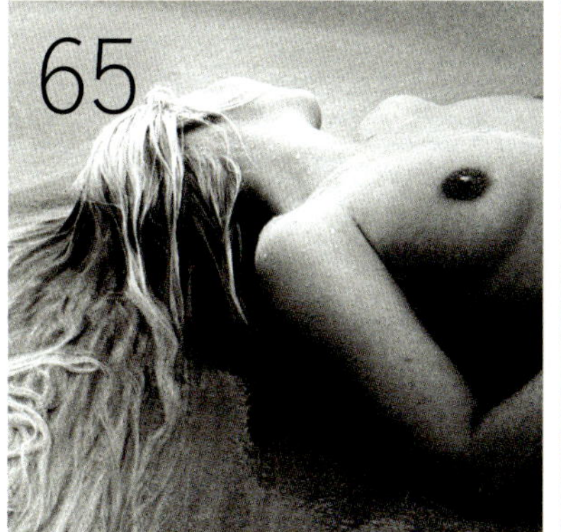

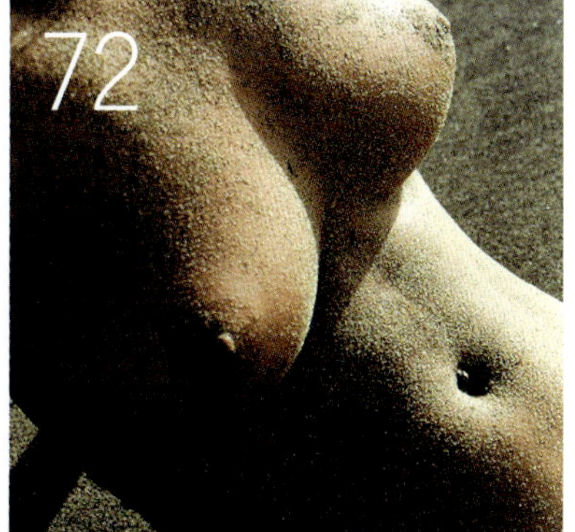

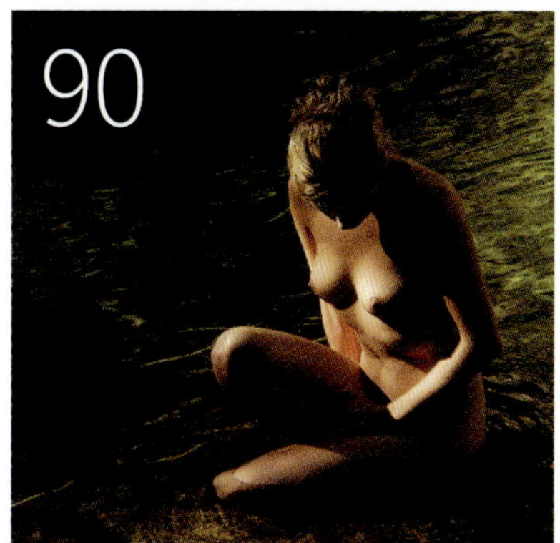

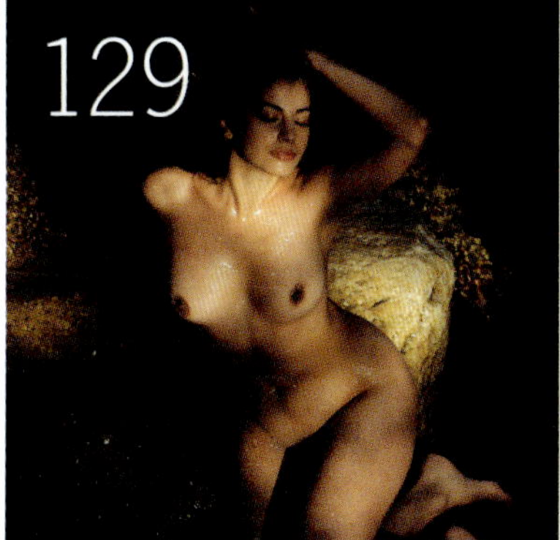

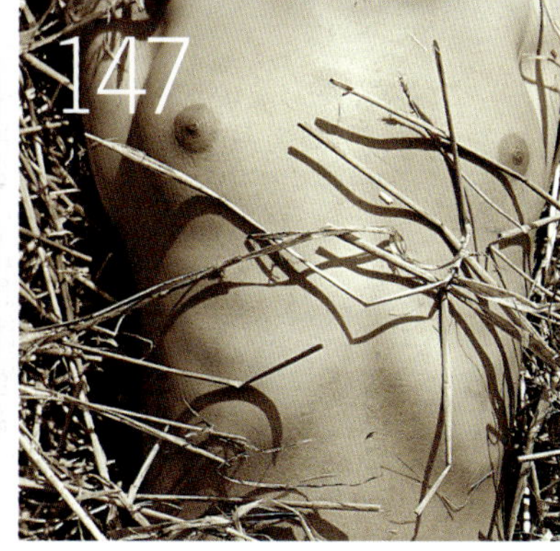

Contents

Introduction

Just like painters and sculptors before them, photographers have always been interested in the human body. In the early years of the camera, they were rather coy about the whole thing – Victorian society was easily shocked, or at least the public face of it was. Nude photography was very much an indoor pursuit; something best carried out privately in settings that resembled the boudoir. The misty-looking ladies were described as life studies and made to look like paintings as far as possible, to lend them an air of respectability.

All that changed during the last century when masters like Edward Weston and Bill Brandt revelled in the graphic accuracy of the lens. They showed that the nude body could be portrayed in terms of shape and form – a sensual and beautiful real-life subject at ease with nature, and not a risqué means of titillating the viewer.

Arguably some of Weston's best nudes were photographed in sand dunes in the 1930s, and they have been much copied since. It no longer seems strange to take nude photographs outside, although an audience is probably undesirable. This is one area of photography where a trust and rapport between model and photographer is not just beneficial, it's pretty much essential.

The lighting is every bit as important to the success of a nude photograph. It has a bearing on every aspect of the image – the location, the pose, the composition and the whole mood and feeling it conveys. There are no right and wrongs here and no textbook templates. Outdoor lighting is anything but predictable.

The purpose of this book is not to lay down any law, but to show what a wide range of possibilities this subject has to offer. The images have been selected from the work of a number of international photographers for their individual impact, variety and the way they have used daylight, in its many guises. Some pictures demonstrate the effectiveness of keeping things simple and often the only 'tool' found necessary was a 35mm camera. Others were more complex to set up, perhaps requiring more than one flash unit or several reflectors to adapt or supplement the light from the sun.

Whatever the equipment used, there are many choices to be made: overcast sky, strong, direct sun or open shade? Should the body be evenly lit or given a sculptural form through areas of highlights and shade. Is the mood of the shot to be quiet and mysterious or bold and erotic? It's a challenging area of photography because there is a fine line between a nude that will engage or move the viewer in some way, and a portrait of a person without any clothes on.

While this book is not an instruction manual, it does aim to inform. The background to each image is explained so you can understand what the photographer set out to achieve and exactly how he, or she, went about it. We look at why the location was chosen and how it affects the shot as well as compositional elements that contribute to its success. Most importantly, the lighting is examined – the position and strength of the sun, any additional equipment used and how all this has an influence on the final result.

Nude photography is a loose term, and we do not attempt to define it any further here. Within these pages you'll find a wide range of stylistic differences from extreme close-ups to full-length shots, the use of both colour and black and white, male nudes as well as female.

The purpose of the images differs, too. Some have been used commercially, in advertising or editorial, as public attitudes to nude imagery have relaxed over recent years. Others were taken for personal reasons, for the photographer, model or both. There is also a market for fine art nude photographs – that is those destined to hang on the wall of a gallery or of a private collector. Each presents its own difficulties and rewards, which the photographers describe in their own words here.

Whether you are a professional, student or amateur photographer, this book is designed for you to dip in at any point, as a source of inspiration, for reference or to help in the understanding of a particular aspect of outdoor nude photography.

Rene de Haan / Sylvie Blum / Philippe Pache

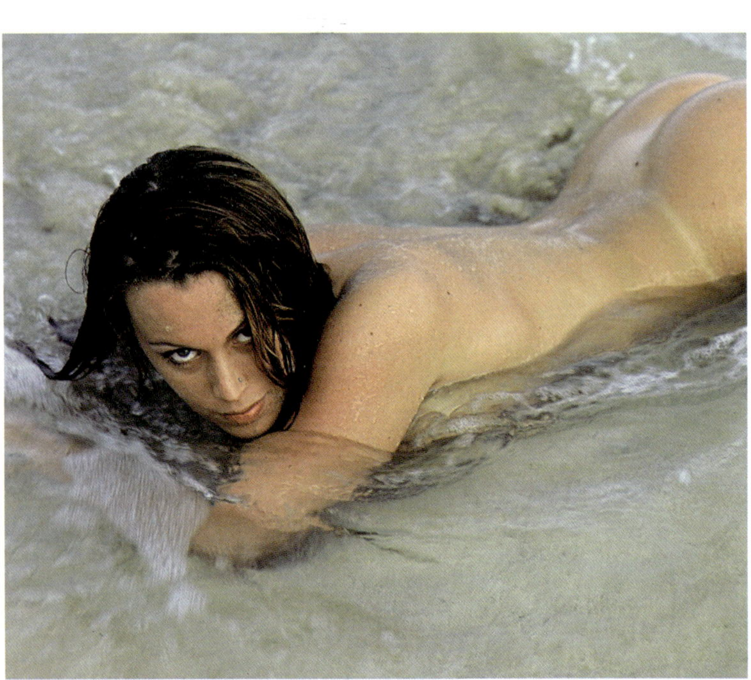

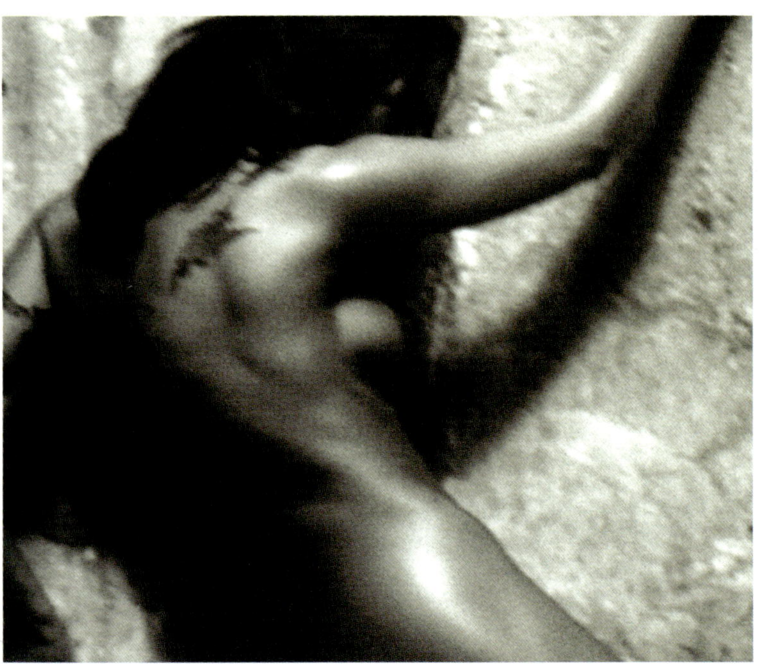

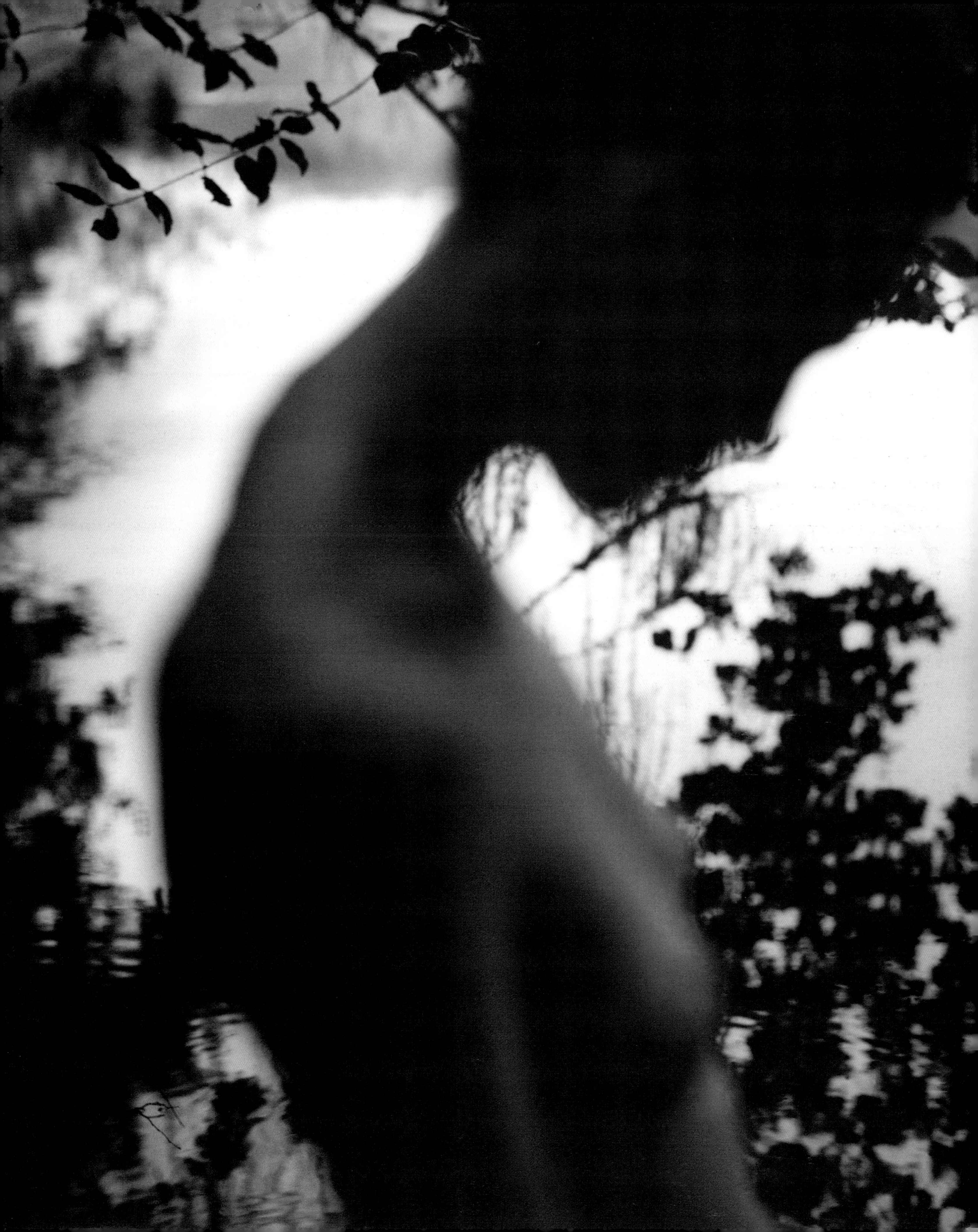

How to get the most out of this book

Divided into six chapters, this book sets out how to get great results when shooting nude photography outdoors. Read in its entirety, it covers all the ways in which light can be used and manipulated to best effect, from choosing the time of day to adding artificial lights and creating mood through filtration and reflection. Alternatively you can dip into the book at any point. Each spread is self-contained, concentrating on a particular aspect of outdoor lighting. As such, the book can be used as a problem solver for specific areas of interest, for example, how to effectively balance flash with daylight.

The text

The main (or, in some cases, sole) picture on each spread is accompanied by four paragraphs of text, with the headings, The brief, The location, Composition and Lighting and technique. These explain the background to the picture and the thought process of the photographers as he or she set out to achieve it. The image is analysed to pinpoint its strengths, look at compositional devices and see how the location was chosen and used to best effect. The technique and lighting employed are described in straightforward easy-to-understand language, with specific photographic terms explained in the glossary at the back of the book.

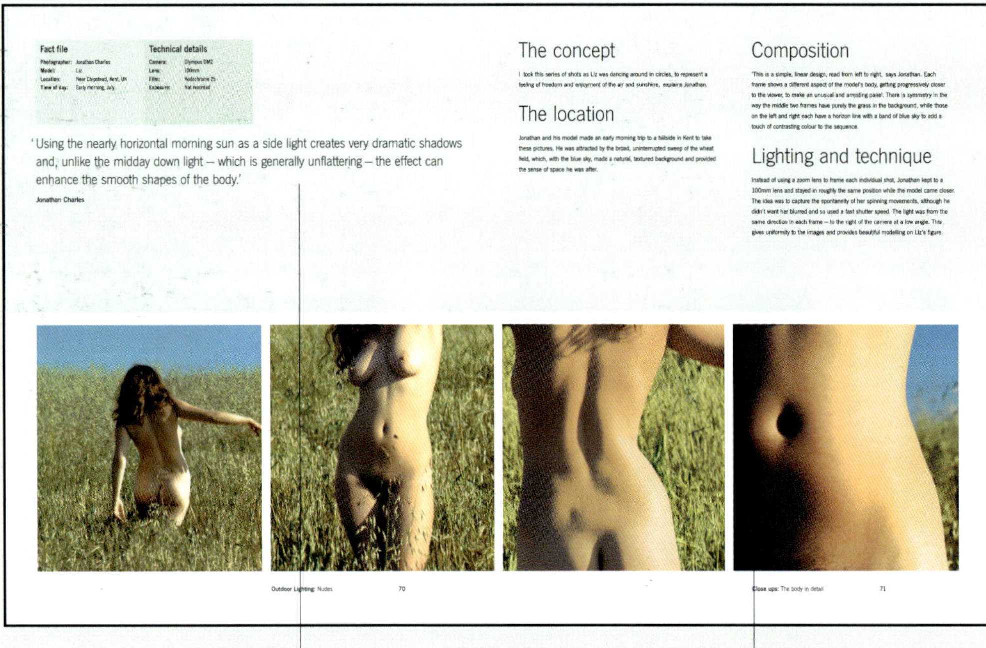

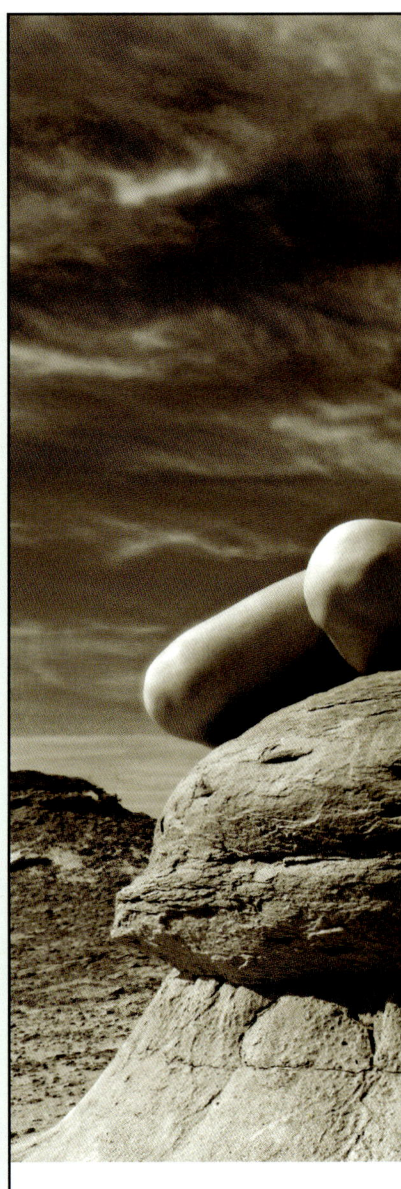

Quotations

The photographers' own words refer to their picture and explain what they were trying to achieve, any problems they encountered and tips they can pass on.

The pictures

Each spread is illustrated with one or more images, by the same or different photographers. The images have been chosen not only for their impact and quality but because they illustrate a particular technique or aspect of lighting.

Inspiration

The pictures are intended to provide a source of inspiration and ideas and can be enjoyed in their own right by professionals, students and all followers of nude photography who appreciate quality imagery.

Information

The written information explains how the pictures were achieved, thus giving the reader the background knowledge and confidence to try a similar effect for themselves.

Technical details

Camera, lens, film and exposure are included in a panel alongside every picture. This helps the reader understand how the choice of equipment may affect the result.

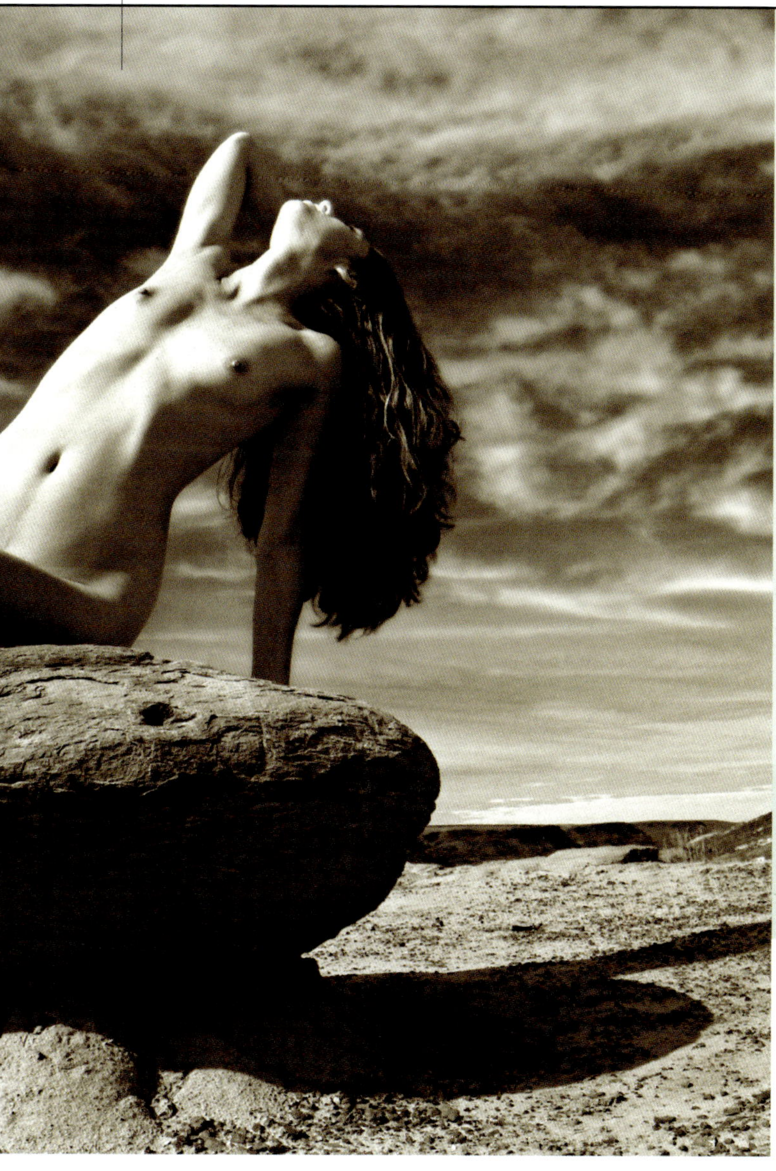

The concept

I was leading a photography workshop and we were working with three models — two females and one male. I split the groups into three, so each model had only two photographers, explains Darwin. 'We were looking to get photos of the nude form in landscapes that were r aw and element al, so rocks, sky, earth and water.'

The location

Darwin had taken his group to this spot near Drumheller, Alberta, Canada because he knew there were excellent rock formations that would fit the feel of the imagery they were going for. Drumheller is famous worldwide for its stark Badlands '.

Composition

The rock formation or hoodoo was the starting point for the composition. Wiggett set up the shot with the rock in the foreground and asked the model to sit on it. 'We tried out various poses and this is the one we liked best, as it seemed to f low with the natural elements in the scene, he explains. I placed the rock and the girl slightly to the left, so that the shadow would form a strong compositional element leading into the rest of the scene.'

Lighting and technique

The scene was strongly side lit, with the light coming from the left-hand side and slightly to the front of the model. This helps to bring out the shape of the model's figure and emphasise the texture of the rock formation and landscape. A polarising filter on the lens darkened the sky to contrast with the wonderful clouds passing overhead. Darwin used a wide-angle lens (35mm in 645 format is the equivalent of 20mm in 35mm format) to distort the size of the rock in relation to the surroundings. He had to rest the camera on the ground and prop the lens up with small rocks to hold the camera steady. He couldn't get his eye to the camera at this angle so used a right angle finder attached to the viewfinder.

Fact file		Technical details	
Photographer:	Darwin Wiggett	Camera:	Mamiya 645 Pro
Model:	Jamie	Lens:	35mm f/3.5
Location:	Drumheller, Alberta, Canada	Film:	Ilford XP-2 400
Time of day:	9am, August	Exposure:	1/250sec at f/9.5

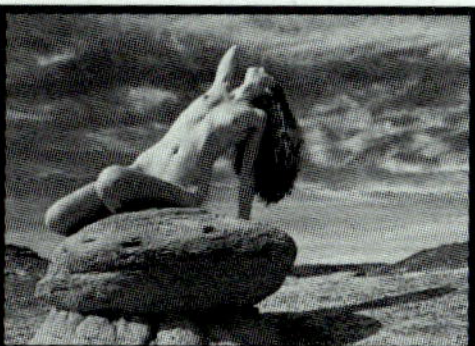

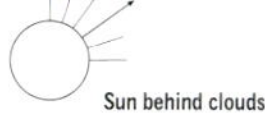

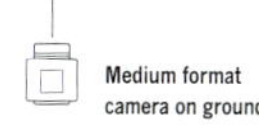

' I am foremost a landscape photographer and for me this shot is as much about the landscape as it is about the nude form.'
Darwin Wiggett

Fact file

Information in this panel includes the photographer, the client, location and timing of the shot. It accompanies every picture in the book.

Diagrams

These show the direction of the sun, position and type of camera and any additional equipment that was used, such as reflectors and flash or tungsten lighting units.

Nic Tucker

Chapter 1: **Light & form**

What is it about the nude form that people find so appealing? For many, it's not just a matter of sensuality. The lines and curves of the human body are beautiful in themselves, fascinating as pieces of living sculpture. But a sculpture has the advantage over a photograph – you can feel its shape and see it from every angle. To present the three-dimensional human form as a two-dimensional image you have to suggest the shape to the viewer. It's a challenge that has faced artists for centuries and those who have succeeded have done so by mastering the effect of light.

All the pictures on the following pages have been taken with a single light source – the sun. It's through using light and shade that an impression of form is created. Shadows can be soft and subtle, hard and clearly defined or somewhere in between. They can be created by the body itself or cast by nearby structures, man-made or natural. They should never be ignored, but used and manipulated to enhance the desired effect.

The unique properties of the skin can also be set off by surrounding or immediately adjacent contrasting textures. Sharp, angular or soft curving features in the landscape may be used to similar effect against the shape of the body. This section looks at some of the different possibilities.

The concept

'The nude in nature is always an interesting subject and Death Valley provided a perfect setting for me,' explains Felix Tian. 'The similarity in the form of the human body and nature is so harmonious, while the contrast in texture between them is very intense.'

The location

Death Valley has always been Felix's favourite place for photography. 'I love its harsh, rough, varied landscape and its silent and desperate atmosphere. Every time I drive nearby, I always make a detour through it. This picture was taken on the way as I was driving to Las Vegas.'

Composition

In order to express the vastness of the landscape and exaggerate the shape of the nude, Felix used a fish-eye lens, enabling him to include both the sun in the sky and the model in the foreground. 'This composition seemed perfect until later on, when I was doing an enlargement in the darkroom and I found several flares on the bottom of the picture. They fell on the model's body and were visually annoying, so I cropped the image into a square.'

Lighting and technique

At around 7am, the sun was low above the horizon and the light was not too strong. Felix faced the sun and positioned the model in front of him, so the contours of her body were outlined by areas of shadow. 'I carefully obtained many meter readings from each important part of the frame, using a spot meter, and decided on the reading from the model's back,' he explains. 'Knowing that the infrared film would give me some glowing effect on the skin, I was concerned it would overexpose and so I bracketed.'

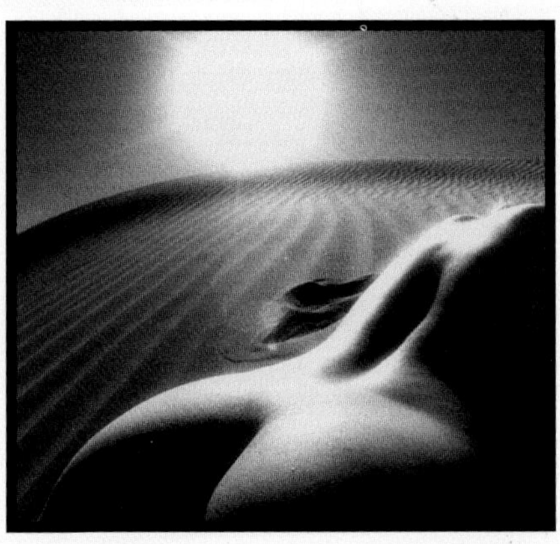

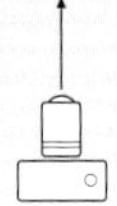

35mm camera with fish-eye lens

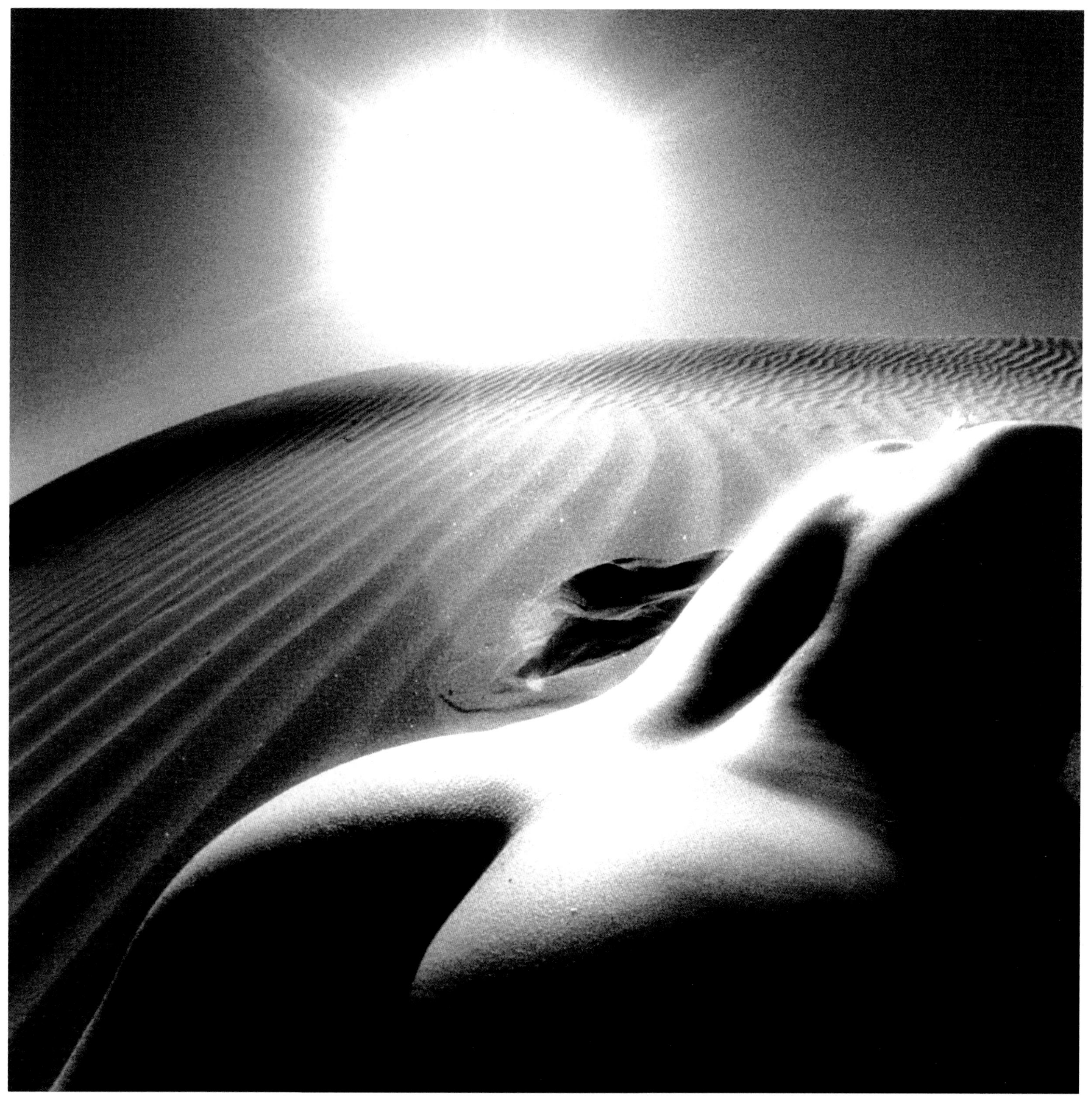

'The final print turned out just as I had pre-visualised. The model's skin didn't glow too much because there was not much infrared light at this time of day. In fact, it wouldn't have made much difference if I had used normal black-and-white film instead of infrared.'

Felix Tian

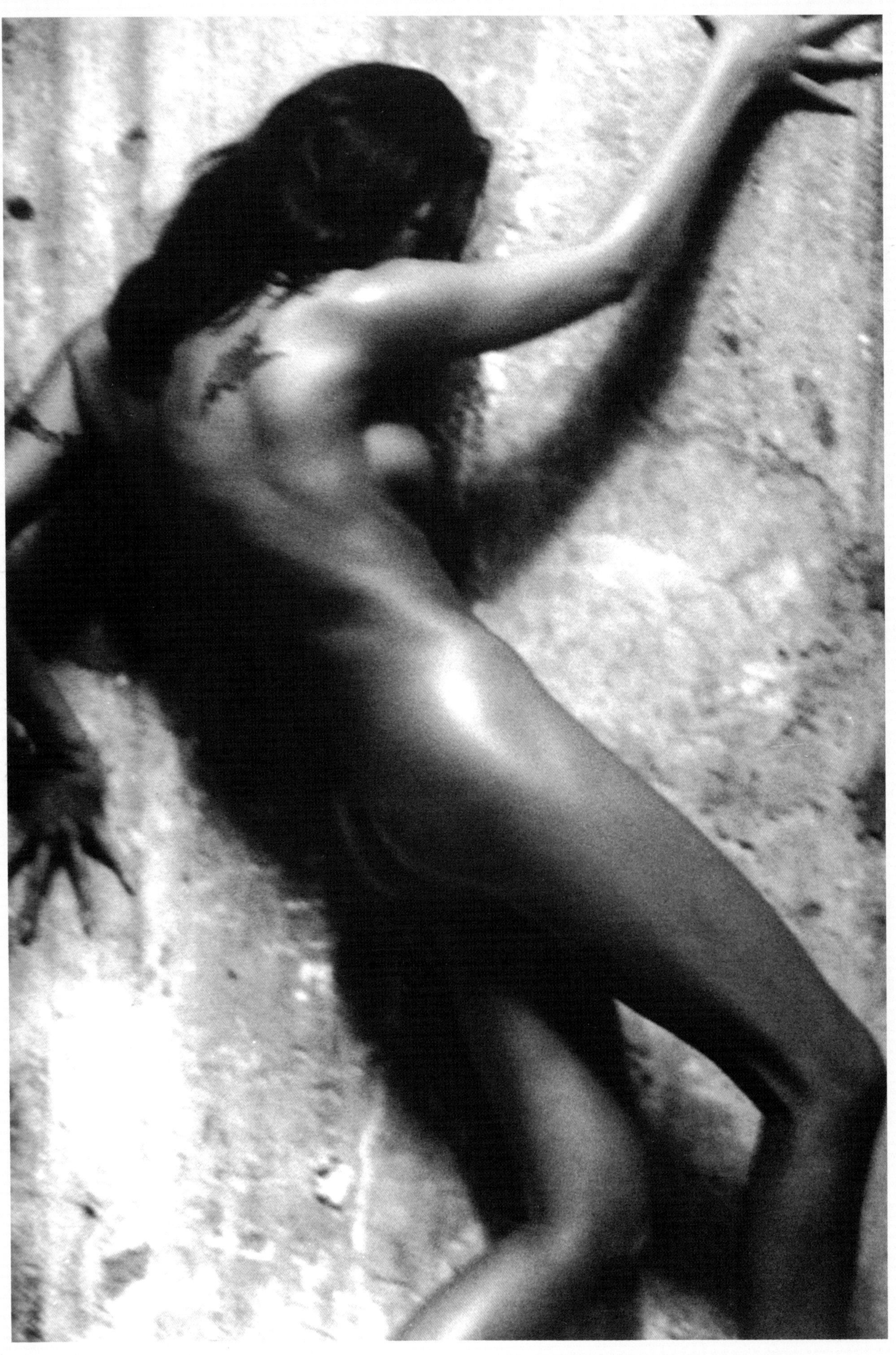

The concept

Sylvie Blum's work is not commissioned but she sells her images as signed, limited edition fine art prints. She had the idea for this shot when she first saw the wall, outside her studio. 'I liked the contrast between the hard texture of the wall and the smoothness of the model's skin,' she says.

The location

There could hardly be a more convenient outdoor location than on the doorstep of the photographer's studio. In images like this, where the model is the principal focus of attention, a suitable setting can be found almost anywhere, so long as the tone, texture and light are complimentary to the composition.

Composition

Sylvie wanted the model's body language to be expressive and quite feline, in fact her pose and outstretched fingers give the impression that she is about to climb the wall. 'It's a kind of homage to the film noir period,' adds Sylvie. 'The corny, and slightly unsharp character of this picture are what makes it interesting to me.' The shadows on the body and the wall contribute to the rather eerie atmosphere of the image.

Lighting and technique

The summer sun was high and strong when this shot was taken, but the overhanging roof of the building meant the model was in shade. Sylvie used a large white reflector to the right of the camera to throw a little more light on to that side of the model's body to separate it sufficiently from the wall.

Fact file

Photographer: Sylvie Blum
Model: Aysa
Location: Mannheim, Germany
Time of day: 3pm, July

Technical details

Camera: Nikon F4
Lens: 80–200mm
Film: Ilford FP4
Exposure: Not recorded

'I spend a lot of time helping the model to pose. I watch her move and give instructions for her facial expression and every inch of her body.'

Sylvie Blum

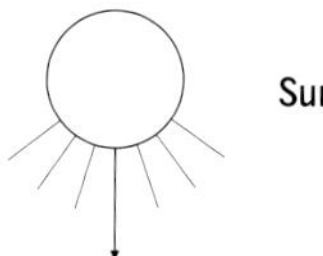

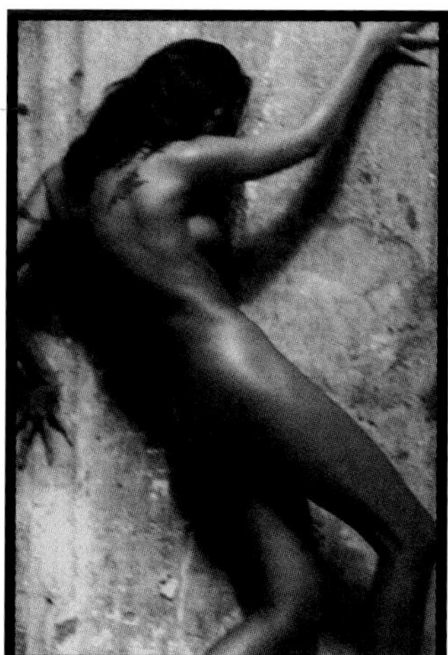

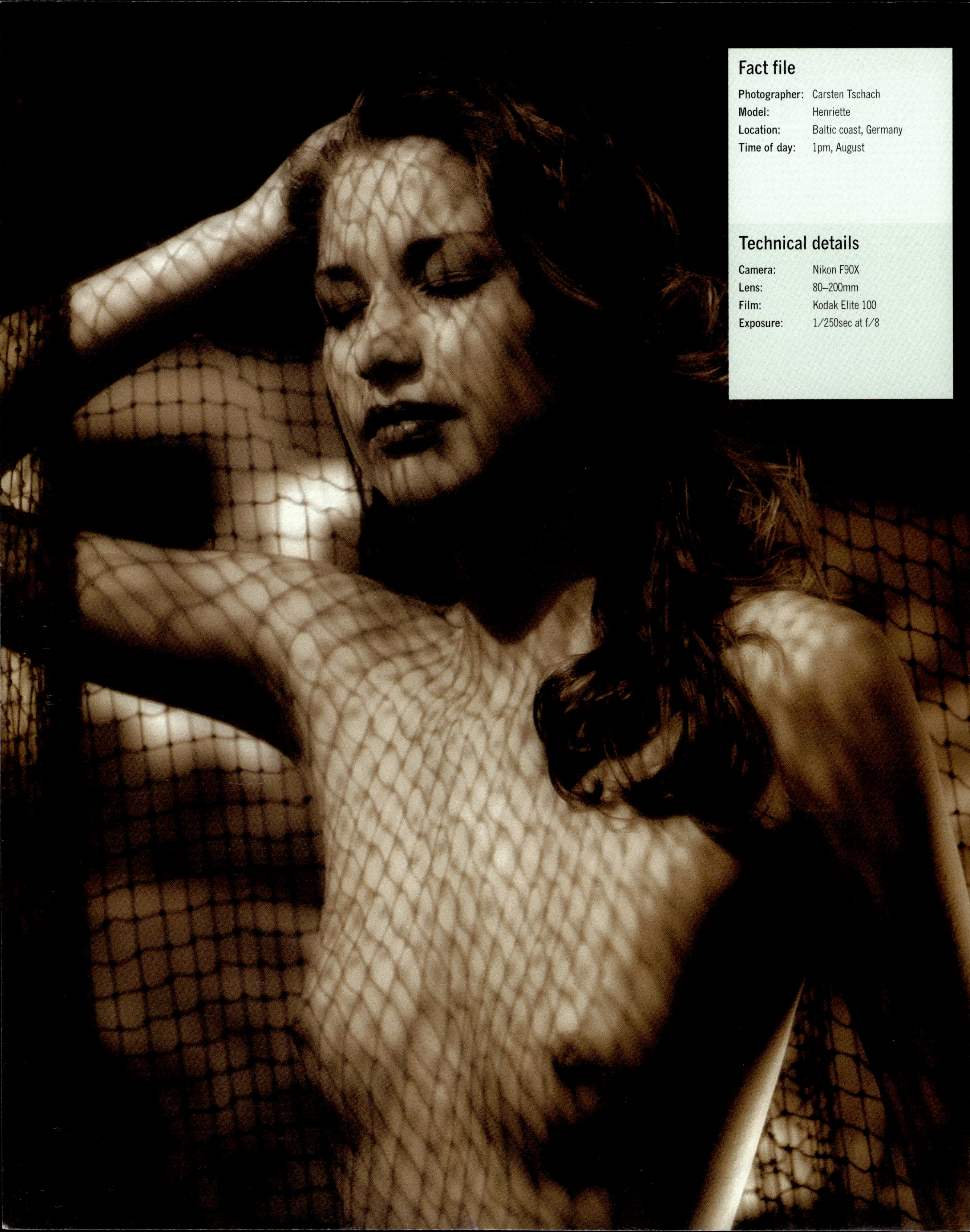
Fact file

Photographer: Carsten Tschach
Model: Henriette
Location: Baltic coast, Germany
Time of day: 1pm, August

Technical details

Camera: Nikon F90X
Lens: 80–200mm
Film: Kodak Elite 100
Exposure: 1/250sec at f/8

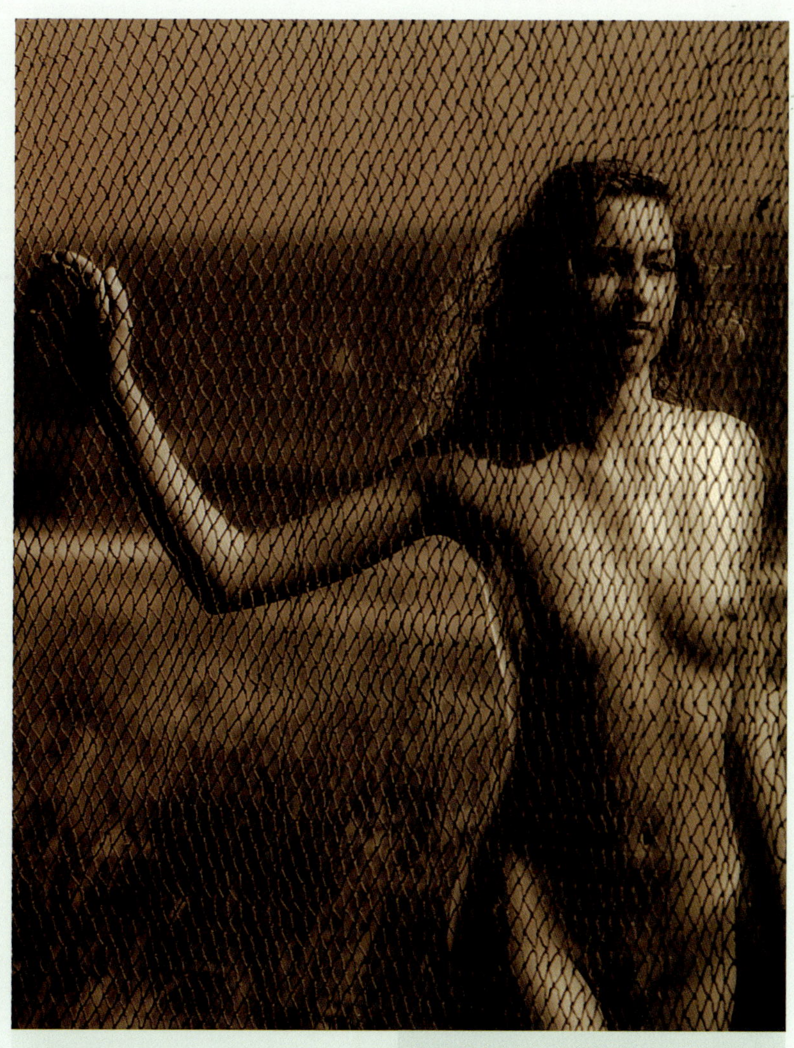

Fact file

Photographer:	Carsten Tschach
Model:	Henriette
Location:	Baltic coast, Germany
Time of day:	2pm, August

Technical details

Camera:	Nikon F90X
Lens:	80–200mm
Film:	Kodak Elite 100
Exposure:	1/250sec at f/8

For this alternative version, the model stood behind the net so the pattern is real rather than reflected. The sun was to the right of the camera, with a gold reflector placed to the left of it to fill in the deep shadows.

The concept

As often happens, this turned out to be a totally different shoot than the one Carsten Tschach had planned. 'We went to take some shots on the beach for our portfolios, but when I saw these fishing nets hanging up, I got the idea for these images,' he explains. 'If you have no client to satisfy, it's worth starting off with two or three ideas and then taking your time to find different inspiration.'

The location

'The German Ostsee (Baltic Sea) is a beautiful location and we went there to do something that looked like we'd been to the Mediterranean,' recalls Carsten. 'The fishing nets were hanging in the dunes for repair and cleaning and they turned out to be the perfect accessory for these images.'

Composition

Carsten spotted the way the net projected shadows on the sand and thought it would be interesting to capture a similar effect on the body. He positioned the model accordingly and used his zoom lens to try out a number of different compositions. The intriguing criss-cross pattern of the shadows, as well as the net itself in the background, add the illusion of texture and a sense of mystery to the image.

Lighting and technique

The sun was high in the sky and shining from the left of the camera, through the net which was to the side and behind the model. Carsten used a gold reflector, positioned on her other side to lighten up this shaded area. The image was taken on colour slide film, scanned into the computer and sepia-toned using tritone mode in Photoshop. It was then softened using a second layer with guassian blur. 'This could have been done with a soft-focus filter, but you get much more control using a computer afterwards,' he says.

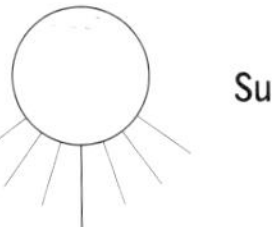

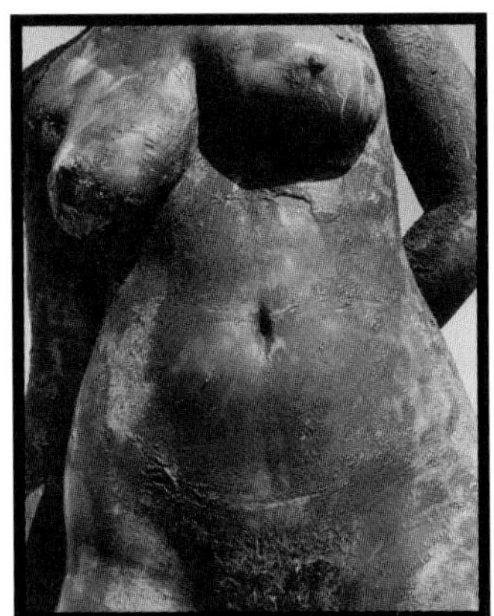

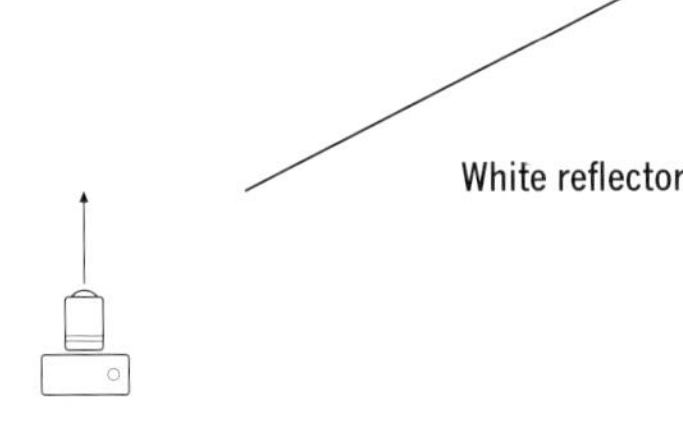

‘The mud on Ilana is the mildly radioactive and therapeutic Dead Sea mud. Applying it was the easy part but taking it off again with just a few gallons of water proved a harder task for her!’

Dejan Dizdar

The concept

‘This wasn't commissioned, but part of a big body of images I have been working on over the years about the nude as an element and a part of Geia (Mother Earth)’, explains Dejan Dizdar. The shot was pre-planned to some extent. He knew he wanted an extreme close-up using the texture of the mud, although the final composition evolved during the shoot.

The location

Dejan chose to shoot in the desert because he wanted to combine the idea of human life with a seemingly barren landscape. In this image, the background plays a minor role compared to the figure.

Composition

This image looks almost more like a sculpture than a photograph of a real person. The model's pose, the white background and the close-up concentration on the torso shot from a low angle, all give the model a statuesque quality. Using a 28mm wide-angle lens has given a slight distortion to the form of the body, making it appear more imposing, and it also allowed Dejan to keep the subject in focus from a very close range.

Lighting and technique

In December, the desert sunlight was still very harsh and strong, though not as hot as in summer. The sun was above Ilana, casting deep shadows on parts of her body. Dejan used a round 110cm white reflector about two metres away to try to fill in the shadow area under her breast. In retrospect, he feels the reflector should have been nearer to do this more effectively, but the dark patches are actually useful to add form through contrast and there is sufficient light on the body to show the texture of the mud on the skin.

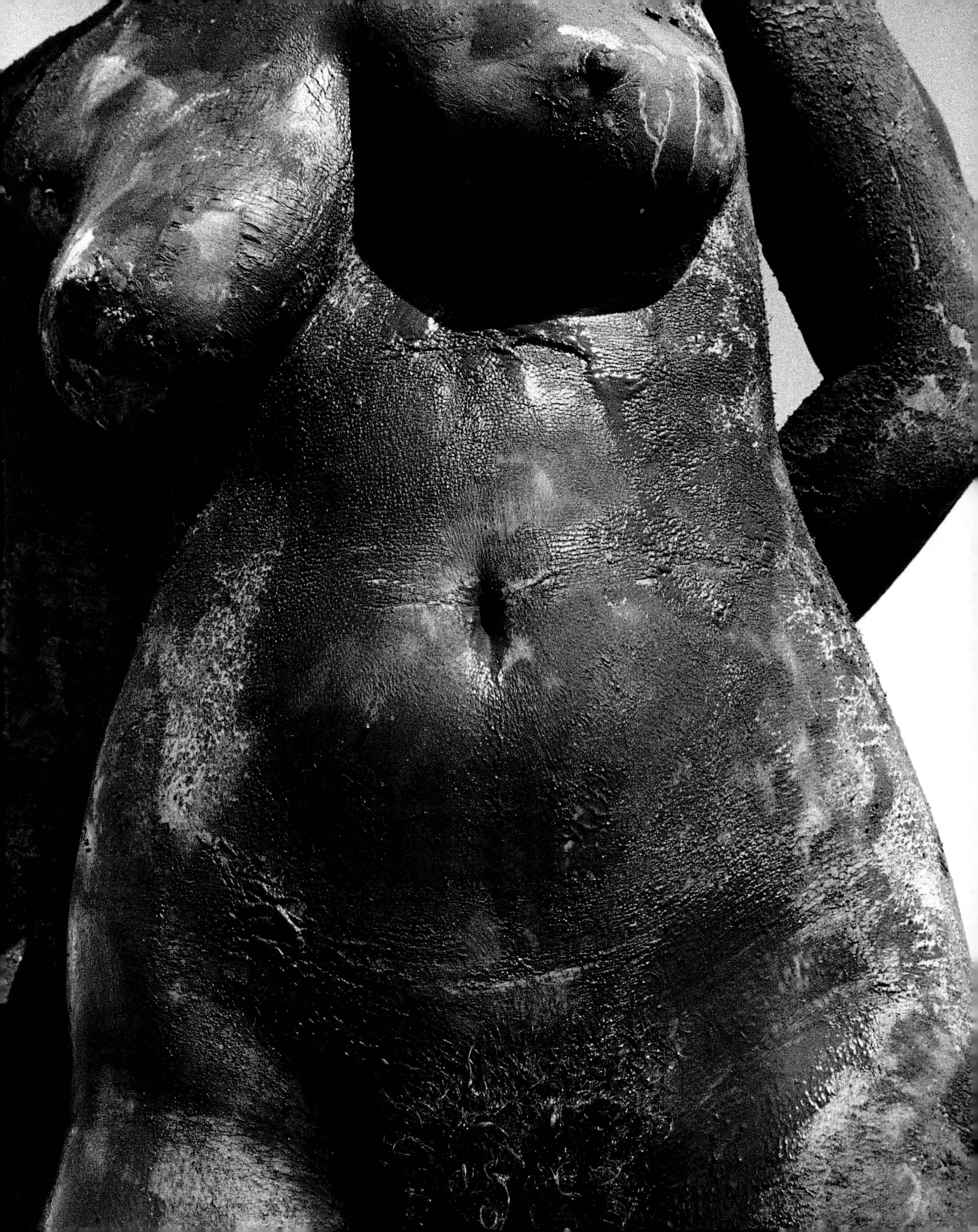

'I was particularly happy that the skin tones of the model and the rock formation were so similar in value, visually, one looked to be part of the other.'

Darwin Wiggett

Fact file

Photographer: Darwin Wiggett
Model: Jamie
Location: Alberta, Canada
Time of day: Late afternoon, August

Technical details

Camera: Mamiya 645 Pro TL
Lens: 45mm f/2.8N
Film: Fuji Velvia
Exposure: f/22 speed unrecorded

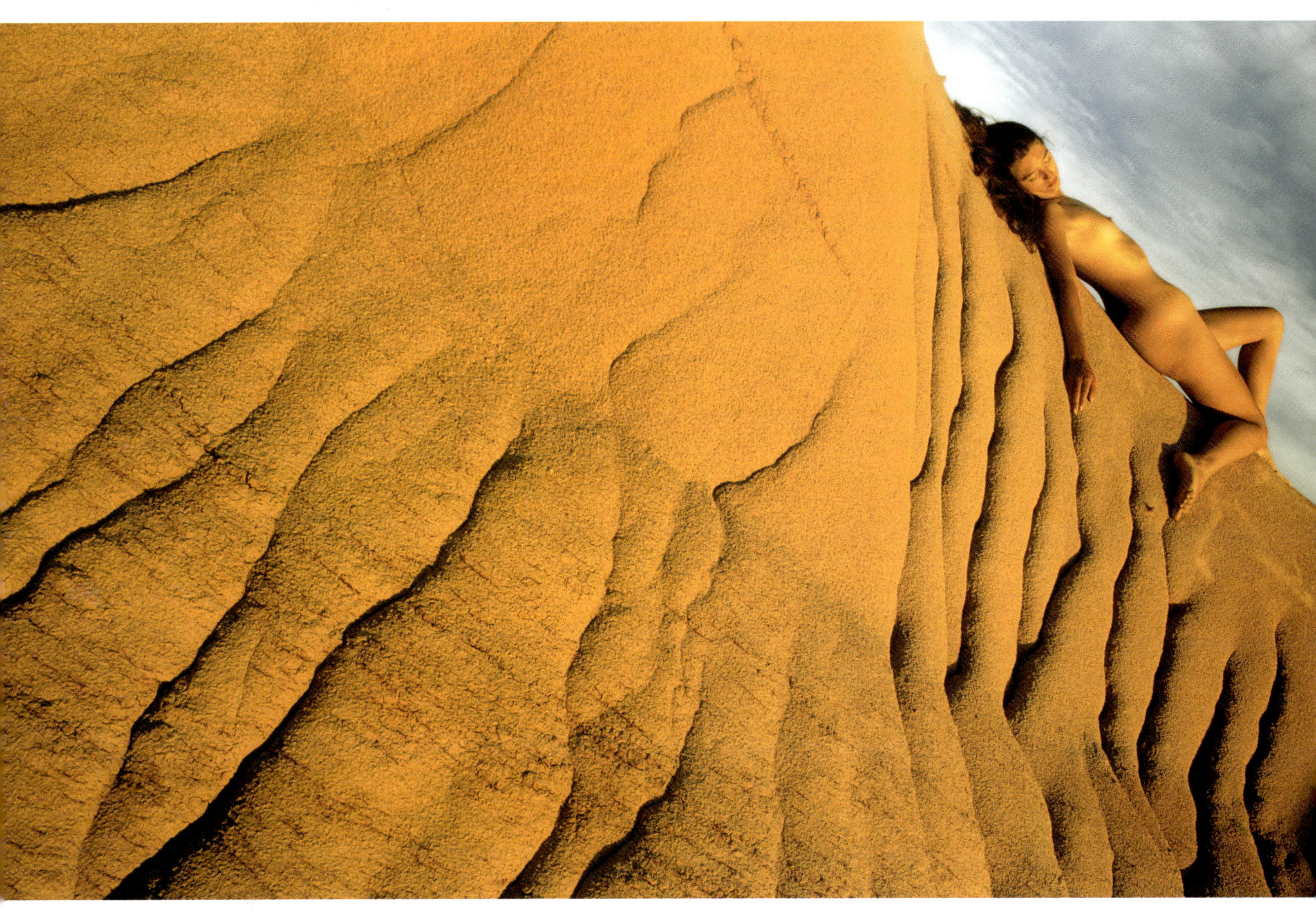

The concept

Darwin Wiggett's aim here was to integrate the human form into the natural rock formation so that the two elements of the image combined seamlessly together as a whole.

The location

Dinosaur Provincial Park in Alberta, Canada, is famous for its patterned and textured rock formations which, when the light is right, almost resemble giant folds of skin. It offers lots of potential for both landscape and nude photography and is a favourite location for Alberta-based Darwin.

Composition

'I wanted a composition that had dynamic tension,' explains Darwin. 'By tilting the camera so the rock formation and the girl were leaning to the right, I was able to add dynamic flow to the entire image. Also, by keeping the sky to a minimum, I was able to add more emphasis to the foreground lines of the rock formation. These lines were further enhanced by the use of a wide-angle lens. The converging lines of the rock formation lead the viewer's eye to the model.'

Lighting and technique

The late afternoon light was from the right-hand side and about 30 degrees from the horizon. Darwin used a Singh-Ray warm-toned polarising filter to reduce reflective glare and increase colour saturation. It also had the effect of darkening the blue sky and further enhancing the already warm light.

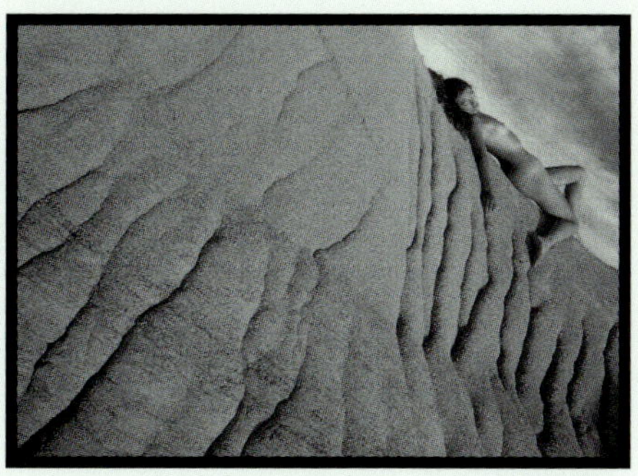

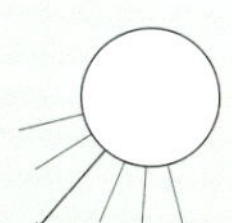

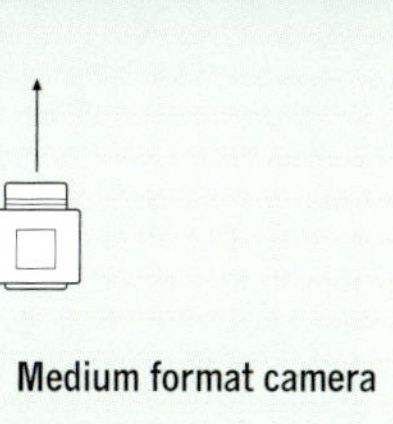

Medium format camera

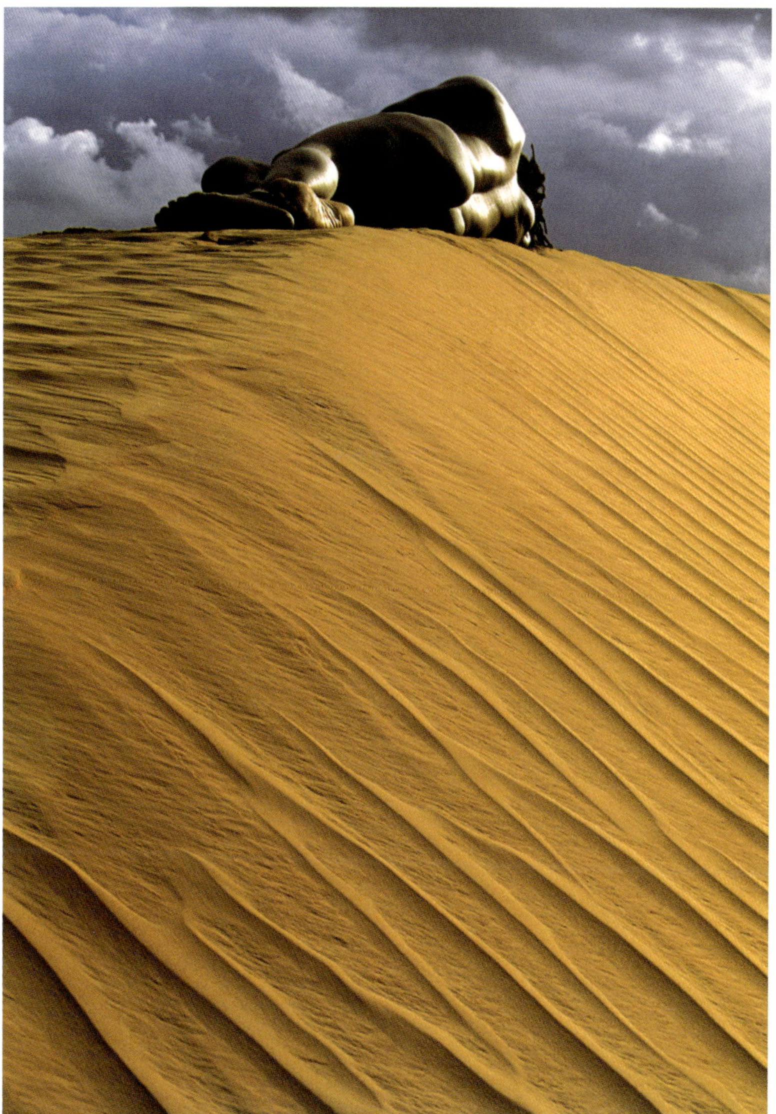

Fact file

Photographer: Darwin Wiggett
Model: Saphyre
Location: Arches National Park, Utah
Time of day: 30 minutes before sunset, June

Technical details

Camera: Canon EOS 1n
Lens: 70–200mm f/4
Film: Fuji Velvia
Exposure: 1/4sec at f/22

Taken during a photography workshop, the stormy sky and flat light was producing unsatisfactory, textureless photos. 'We were about to call it a day when the clouds broke on the horizon and started to give us strong, low, directional light,' explains Darwin. 'I wanted to contrast the lines of the male model with the lines in the dune, and the side lighting was perfect to do that.' ▲

The concept

The inspiration for this picture came from a piece of silk voile material, which has been used to dramatic effect. As quite often with his fine art nude work, this image has a classical feeling to it, and Trevor Yerbury's wife, Faye, gave the model's hair a Grecian style. 'I find the classical look to be appealing to a broad marketplace,' he says.

The location

Trevor often uses this particular beach, not far from Edinburgh in Scotland. 'You tend to be able to work with little interference there, but more important is the uninterrupted quality of light, the reflective qualities of the sand and water, and the fabulous textures available on the beach.'

Composition

The piece of voile is a simple touch but has a dramatic impact on this image. Its fine texture and translucency make a sensuous screen for the model and the shapes it created add interest to the composition. 'The voile was placed over Alison's head and we asked her to move her hands and body until we saw the best position,' explains Trevor. The sea in the background adds another subtle texture to the image and contributed to the sense of flowing movement.

Lighting and technique

In early evening, the sun was coming from above and to the right of the camera and the warmth of the light at this time of day made the voile seem to shine. Trevor added to this warm effect by printing on to Kodak Ektalure paper, then selenium toning followed by a short sepia tone of Trevor's own concoction. The image was cropped down from the square format of the Hasselblad camera because placing her to the left edge of the image increased the emphasis on the flowing voile.

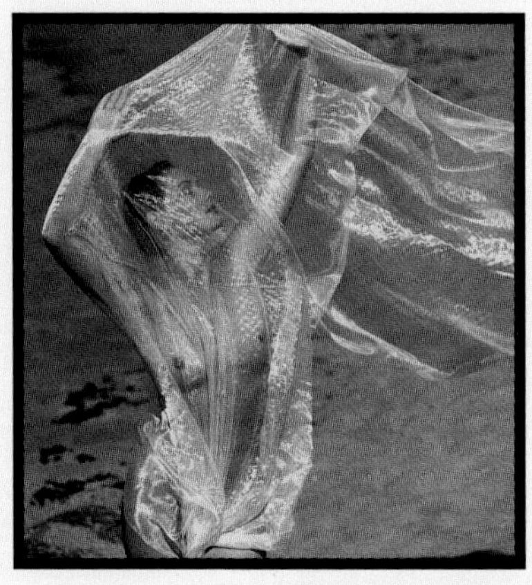

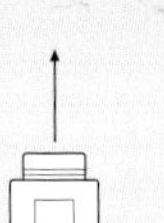

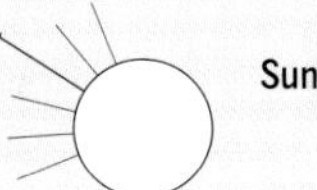

Medium format camera

'This was a classic example of the model helping me to interpret my ideas, and indeed improving on them.'

Trevor Yerbury

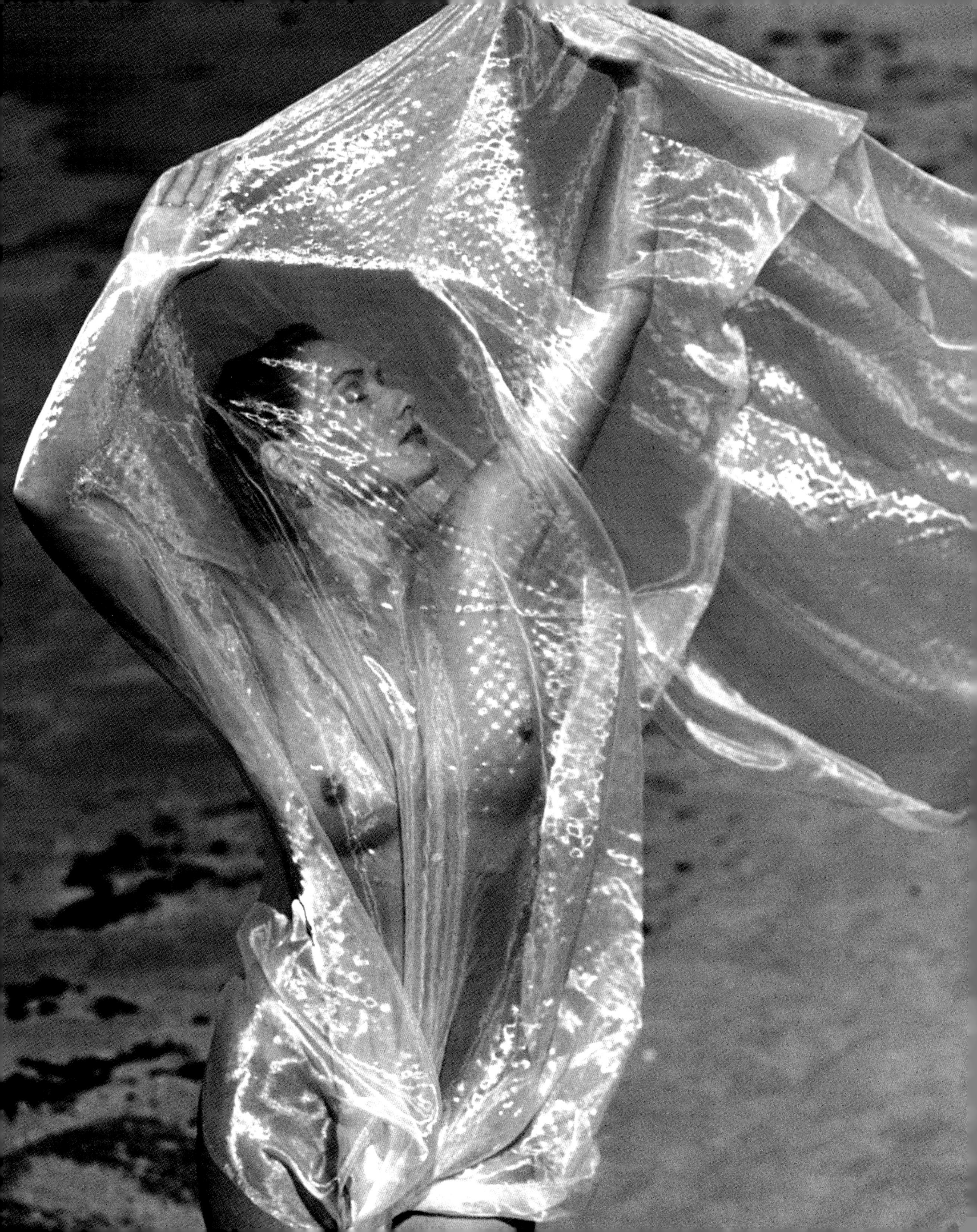

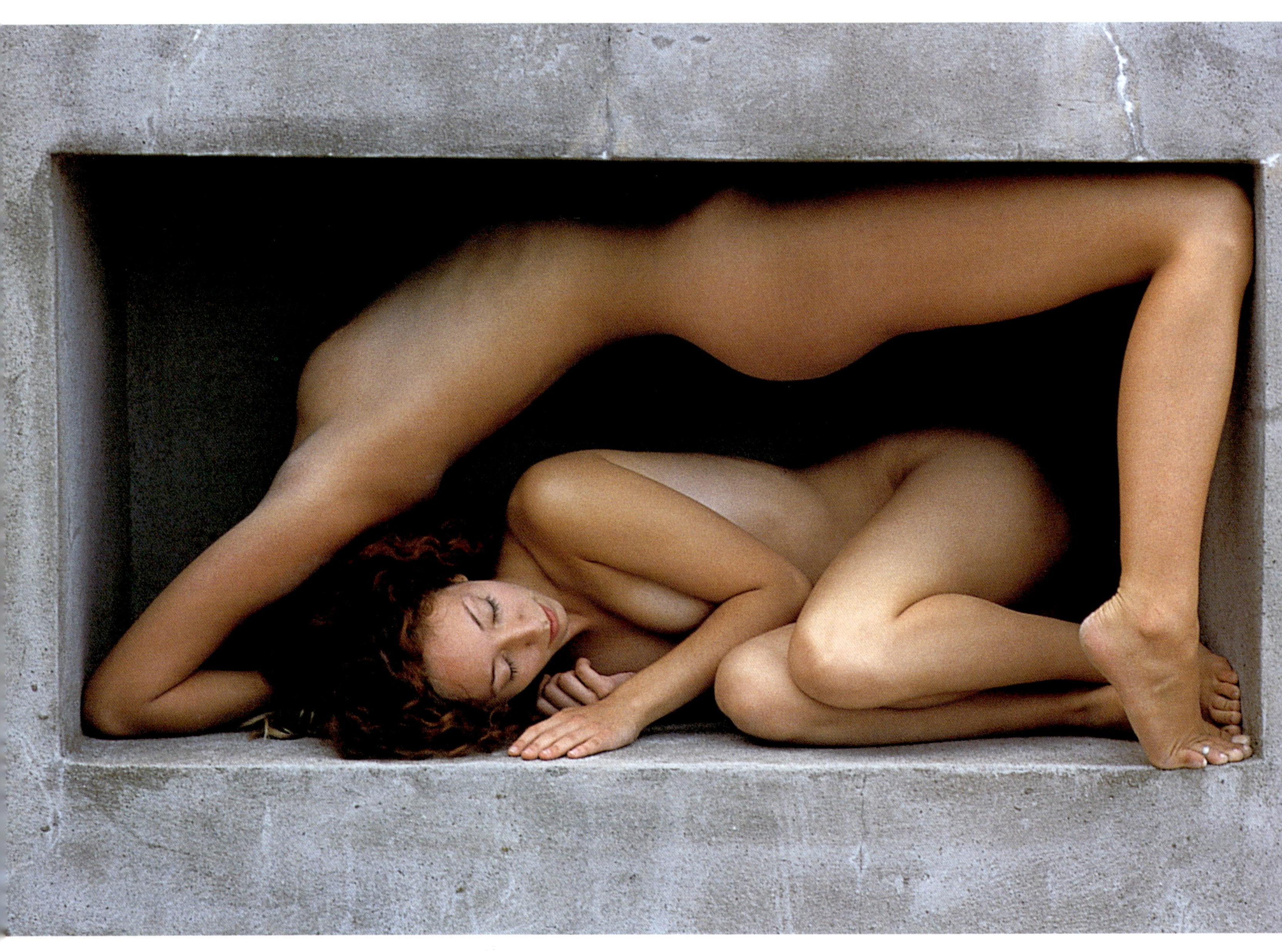

'After a couple of less successful compositions, this image came into shape, and was immediately recognised as distinct.'

Eric Boutilier-Brown

The concept

'This picture came about because of an earlier nude I made with a single model in this space,' explains Eric Boutilier-Brown. 'On this occasion, two friends were working together and I suggested we see what could be done with the concrete box.'

The location

'The 19th-century military fort where this image was produced is relatively remote and on early mornings during the week is often empty of visitors. It's full of concrete ruins and abandoned buildings, which offer great possibilities, especially on sunny days, when contrast is an issue.'

Composition

This is a really quirky image which Eric and the models have carried off extremely well. You have to admire the flexibility of the girl on top – if she had looked at all awkward or uncomfortable the shot would never have worked. Eric often uses medium format cameras but the image ratio of 35mm film is particularly suitable here.

Lighting and technique

The day was bright and sunny but this image is full of a soft quality of light. The figures were lit by both the open blue sky and the sun reflecting off grey concrete below the wall, giving a beautiful roundness to the figures in the box.

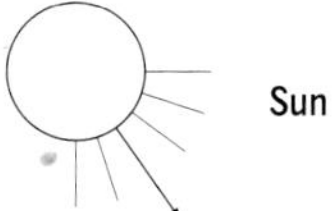

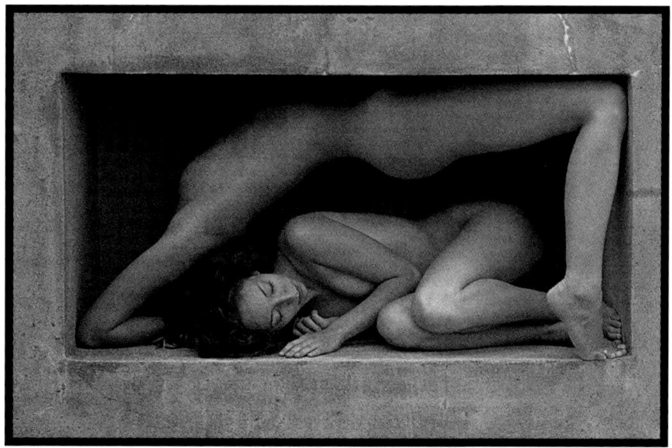

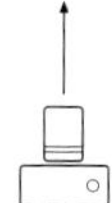

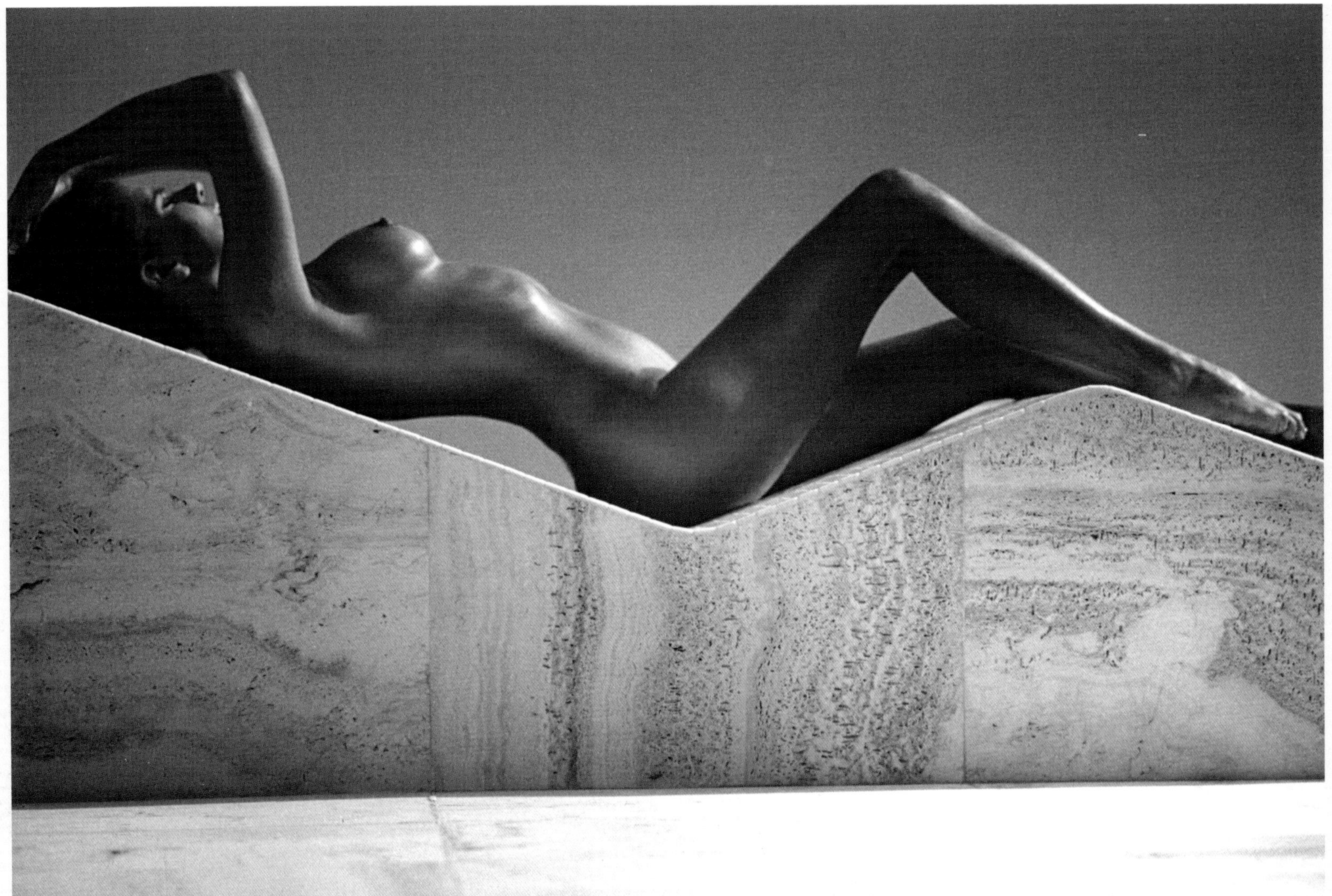

The concept

'I wanted to blend the body with the stone wall to make it look like a piece of sculpture, but with a real human figure,' says Sylvie.

The location

Sylvie was at a friend's house in Miami when she saw this wall which was part of the landscaping of the garden. The shape of it immediately appealed to her and she could see its potential as a striking foil for a nude.

Composition

This is a very strong, graphic image with no unnecessary details to distract from the clean lines within it. While it looks beautifully simple, Sylvie has taken great care to make sure the model's pose is exactly right in relation to the wall she is lying on. The angle of the arm, for example, acts as a frame round her head and is echoed by the angle of the leg, through which you can see a triangle of sky. The curves of the model's torso contrast with these geometric shapes, and the arch of the back is an important touch.

Lighting and technique

The sun was to the right of the camera and not too high in the sky at this time of day in November, creating highlights round the edge of the body. The stone of the ground was a pale grey marble, which reflected some light on to the shaded parts of the wall and the model.

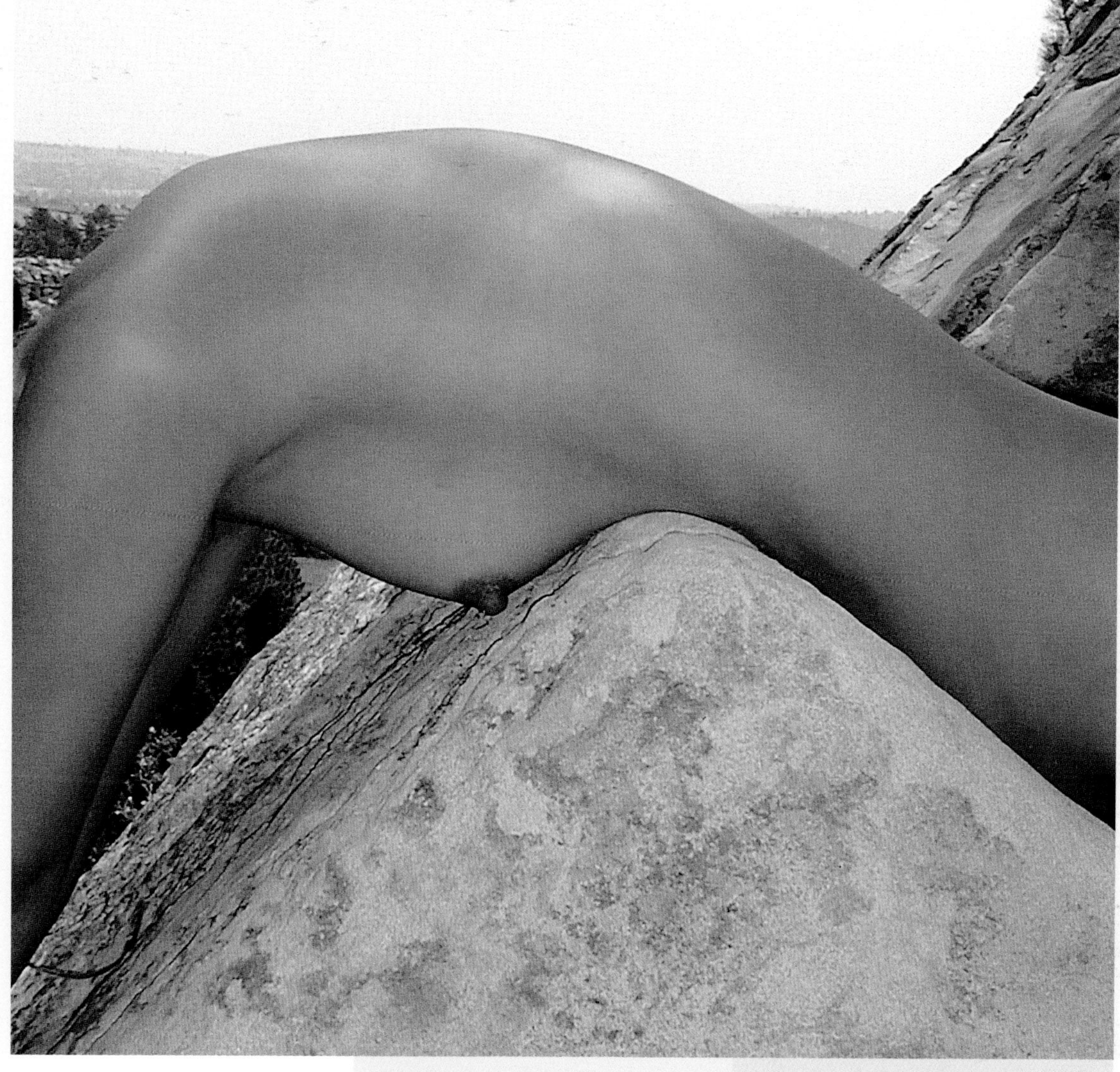

'I love the geometric lines of the wall combined with the curved beauty of the model.'

Sylvie Blum

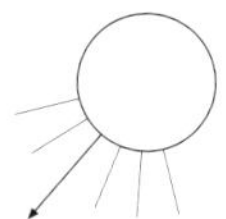
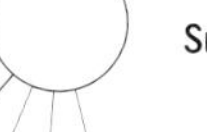
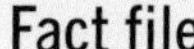

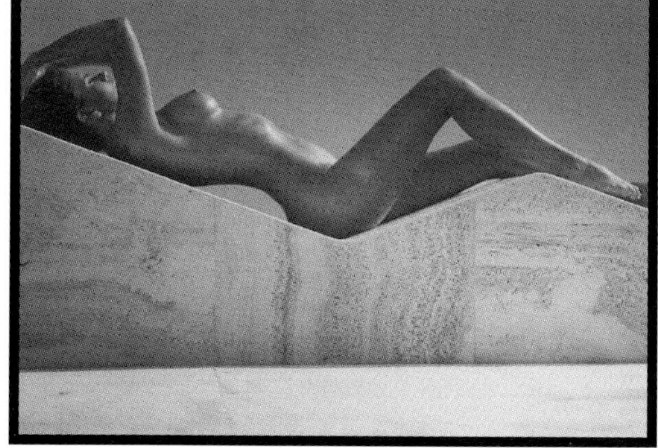

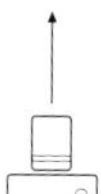

Blake White came across this angular rock while wandering around looking for locations in a city park. There was intermittent cloud cover and he waited for a moment when the bright sun was partly obscured to soften the lighting. The camera's flash was set to fill-in mode to lift and even out the tones further. ▲

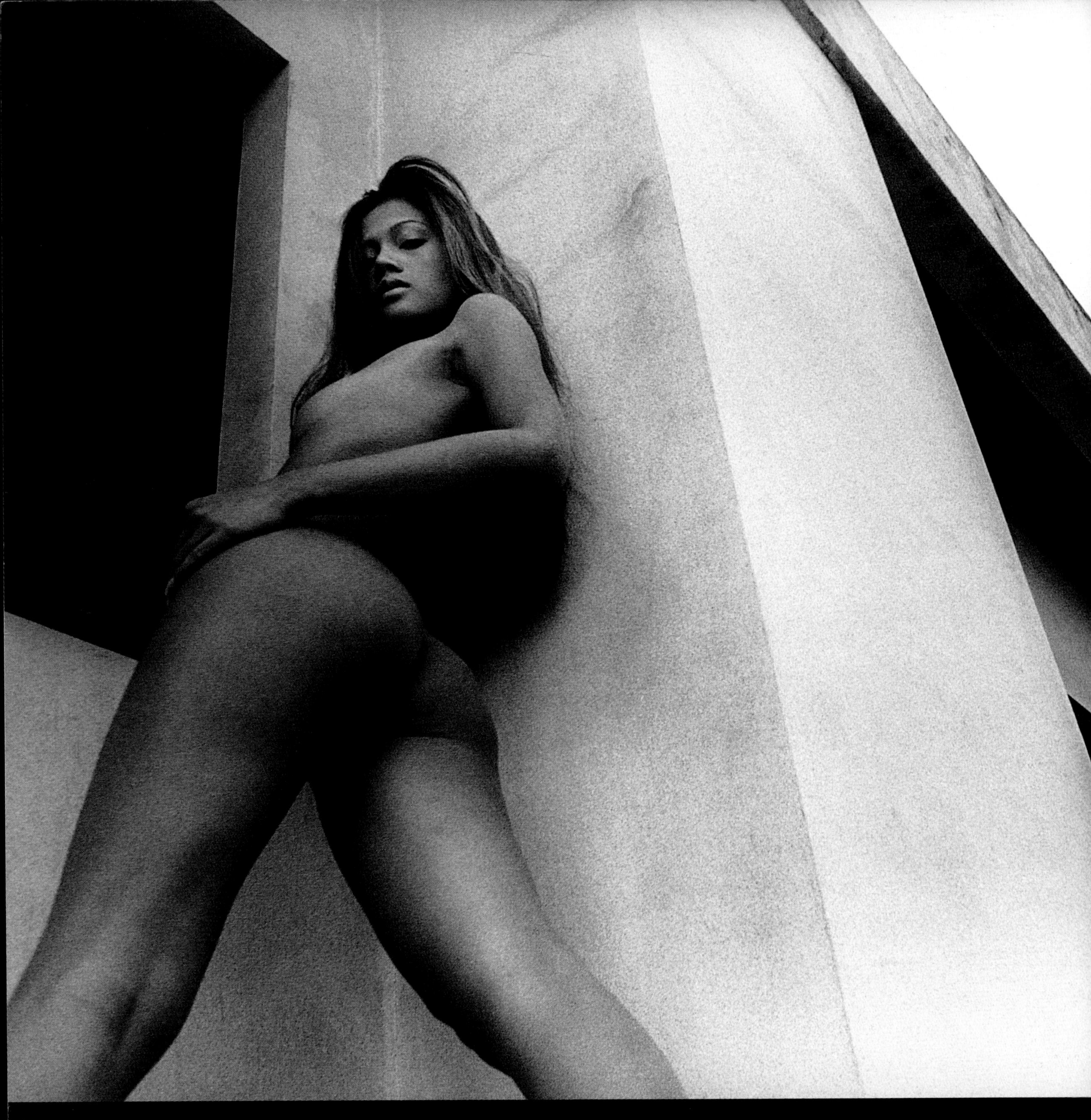

'What works well for me are the many different shapes and tonalities that can be seen throughout the image.'

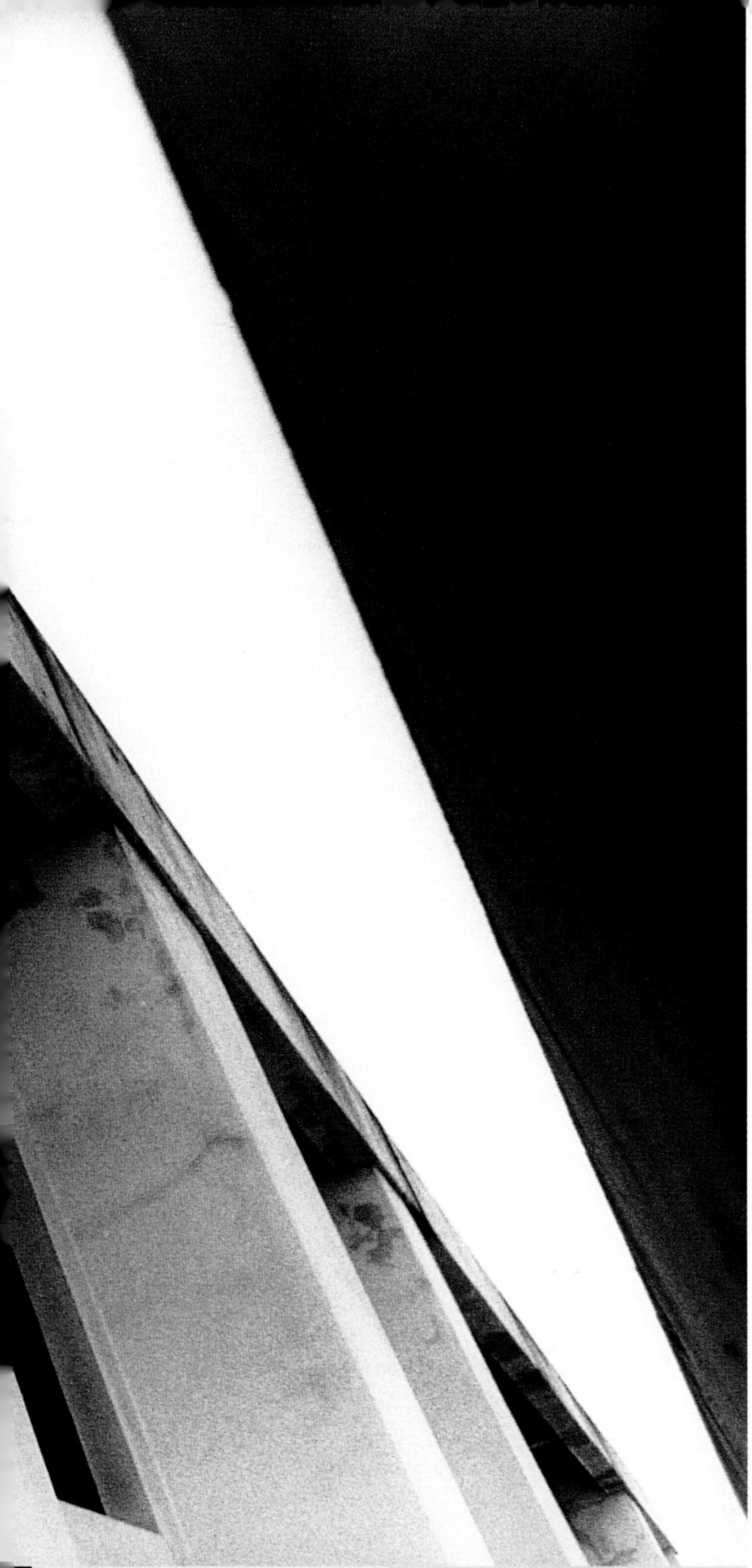

The concept

'I met Thitima and photographed her in Thailand. My aim was to try and get a compelling image on the other side of the planet,' says Kenn Litchenwalter. 'I have often travelled in Europe and the United States, but never to Asia. Consequently I really wanted to create something that could add to my collection of images from around the world.'

The location

'We had just begun wandering around Chiang Mai in an effort to find an interesting location. I just happened to notice this huge abandoned structure just off of the main street. We managed to get around a fence and worked our way inside.'

Composition

'I'm always on the look-out for sharp angles and graphics and I found this perspective by lying on the ground underneath a ledge shooting up towards Thitima and the backdrop,' recalls Kenn. 'I'm drawn most to this image by the triangle in the background mirroring the triangle created between Thitima's legs. I also like her strong, confident pose.'

Lighting and technique

Late in the morning, the sun was very bright, but fortunately it was striking the other side of the building. The model was in shadow here but plenty of light bounced off the white walls of an adjacent building so Kenn didn't need any additional reflectors or fill-in flash to provide even lighting on the model and background.

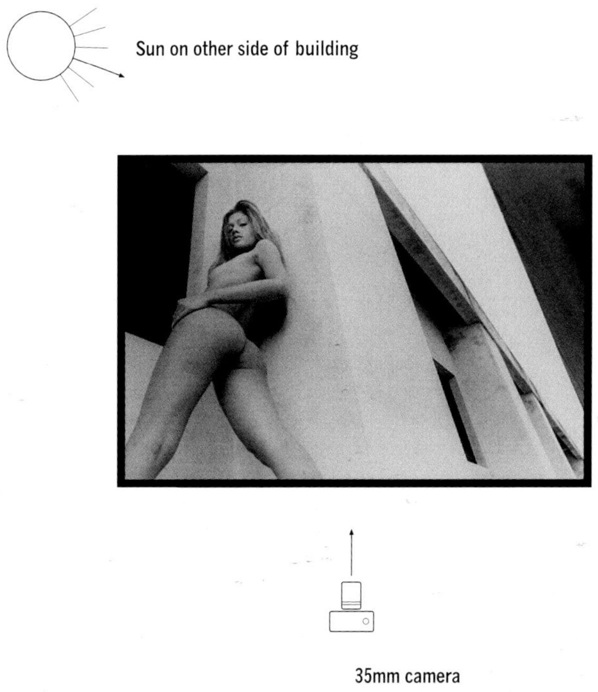

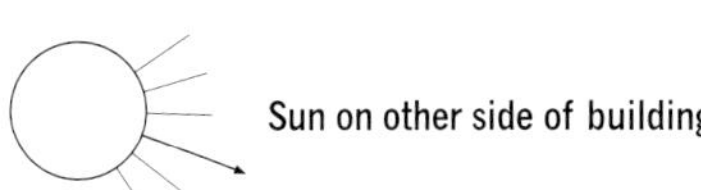

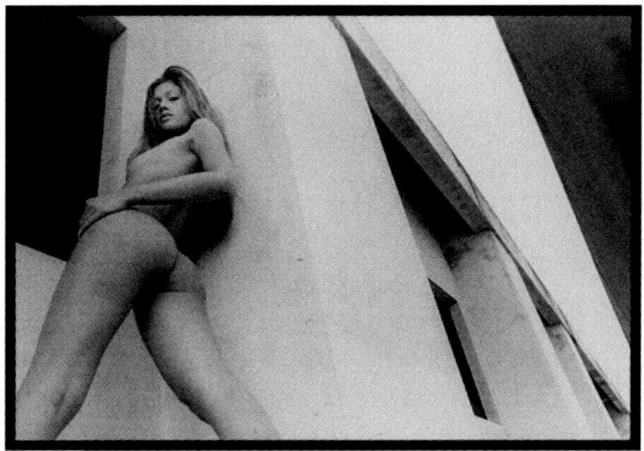

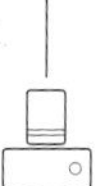

Fact file

Photographer:	Kenn Lichtenwalter
Model:	Thitima
Location:	Chiang Mai, Thailand
Time of day:	Late morning, February

Technical details

Camera:	Leica R6.2
Lens:	28mm
Film:	Ilford HP5 Plus
Exposure:	1/125sec at f/8

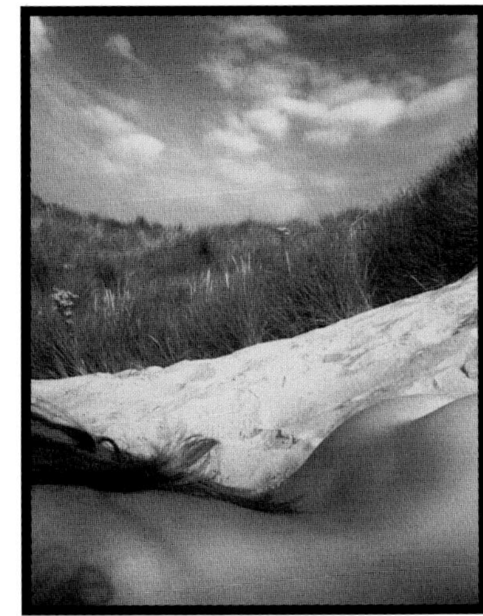

'By shooting close up, or selectively cropping afterwards, you can shoot in bright, direct sunlight and avoid unwanted areas of harsh shadow.'

Jonathan Charles

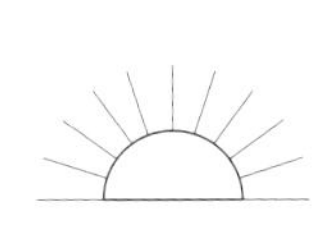

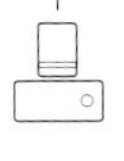

The concept

'This was a totally unposed shot,' recalls Jonathan. 'We were lying on the sand reading after having a swim when I looked over and noticed the wonderful series of layers of different colours and textures. I grabbed the camera and took the photo without moving, accidentally getting my own shadow on her shoulder.'

The location

Shell Bay, on the Dorset coast, is a favourite place of Jonathan's. 'It's owned by the National Trust and so the surroundings are wild and unspoilt,' he explains. On this occasion, he went there with his partner to relax, rather than take photographs, but he always takes his camera with him just in case.

Composition

Jonathan carefully framed the image to give equal emphasis to each 'layer', then exaggerated the wide angle perspective using Photoshop. The effect is almost like that of a fish-eye lens where the sky meets the grass and this curve beautifully echoes the curved form of the model. 'When you look up from the ground, your eye tends to see in this rounded perspective,' he explains. 'The camera cannot capture that so I wanted to re-create the scene as I actually saw it.'

Lighting and technique

'The direct sun, which was behind me, produced strong shading on the body,' says Jonathan. 'This gives a three-dimensional effect, which is emphasised by the close-up, wide angle perspective.' Kodachrome 25 is his favourite film because he finds it gives very accurate, rich colours, particularly if it's underexposed. 'Colour slide film has a wide, dynamic range, so you can print with detail in shadows and highlights and increase the contrast.'

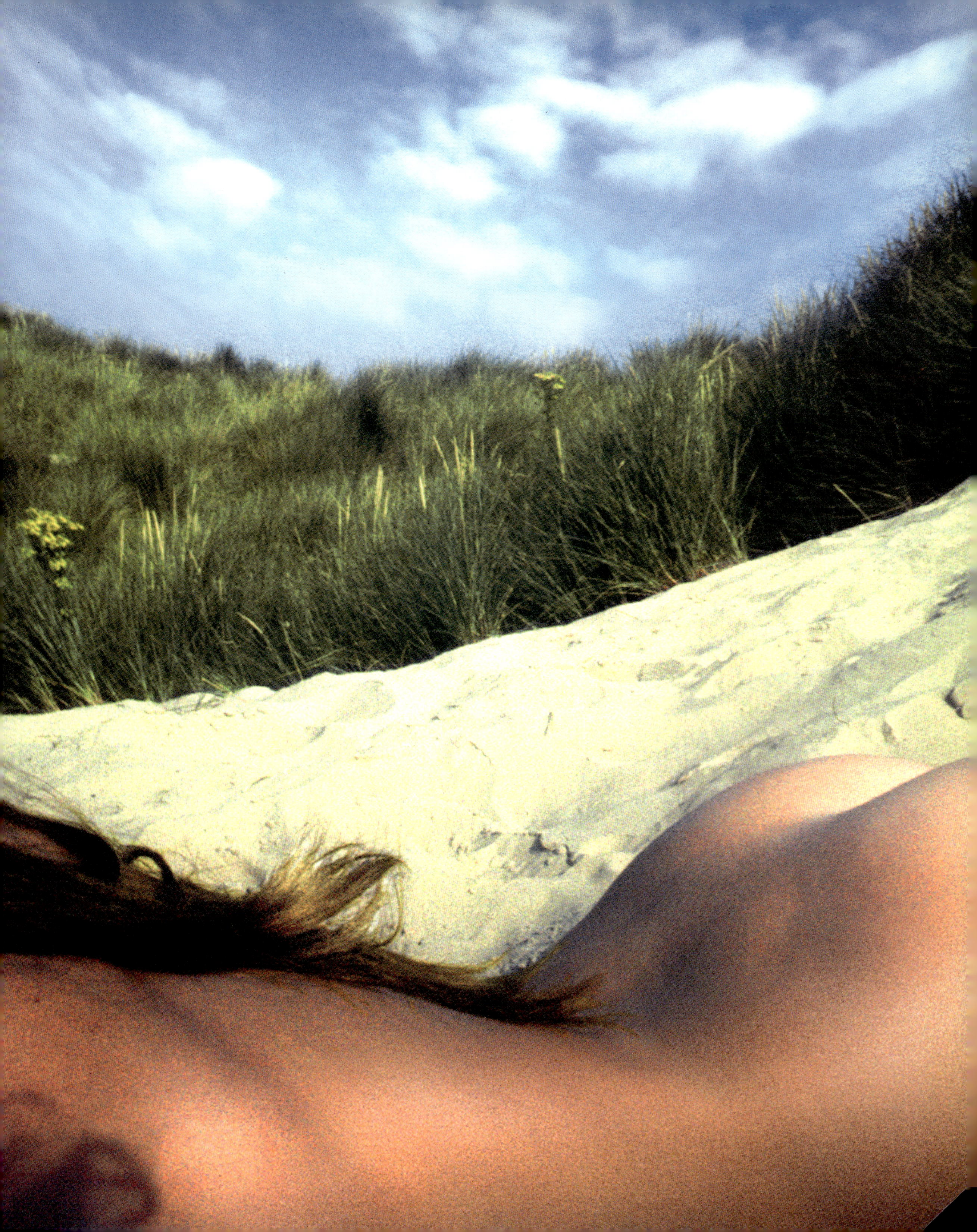

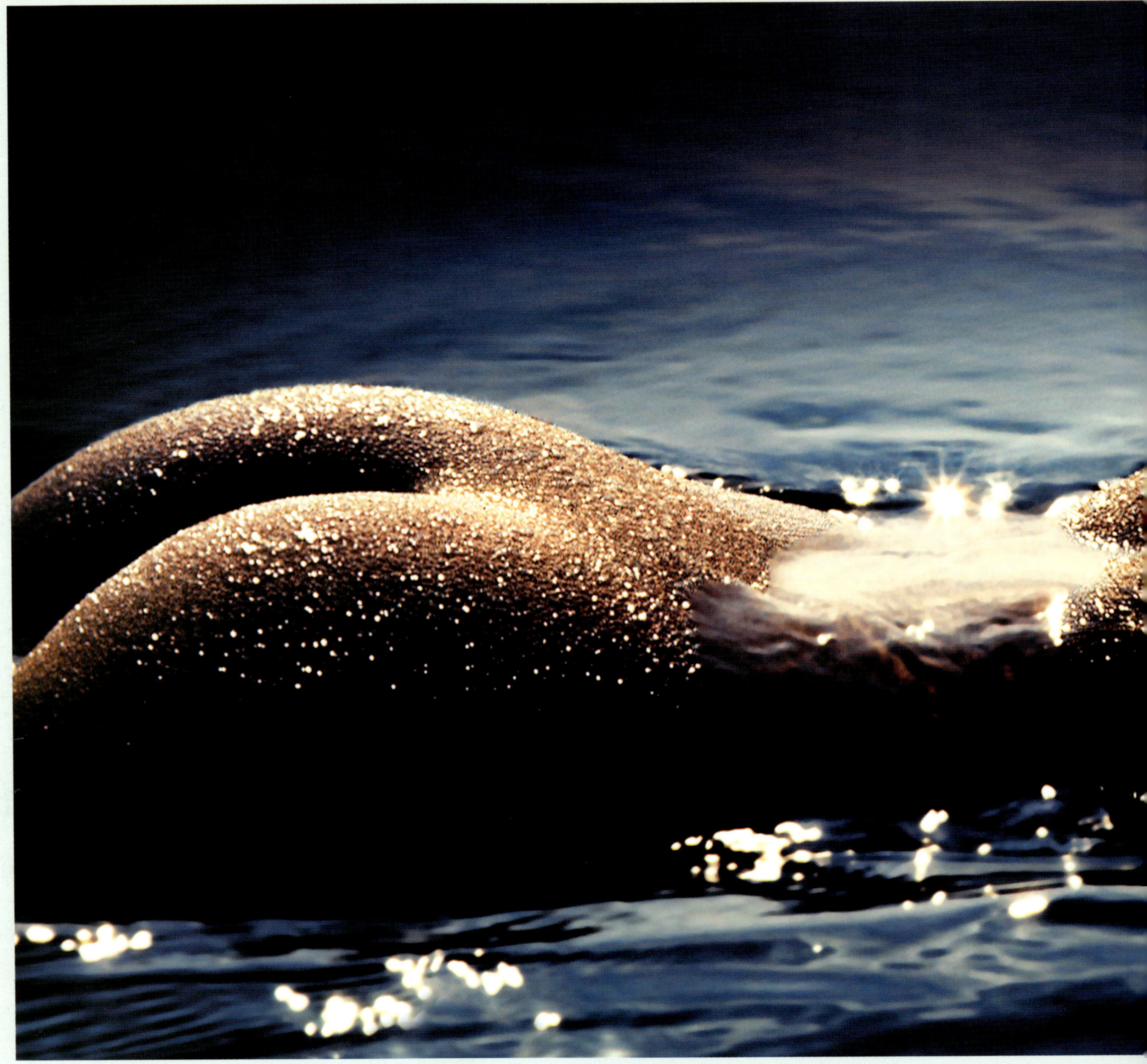

' It almost looks as though I've used a starburst filter but it's purely the very bright reflection of the early morning sun in the lens. The timing was critical – later in the day the whole scene would have been illuminated.'

Jonathan Charles

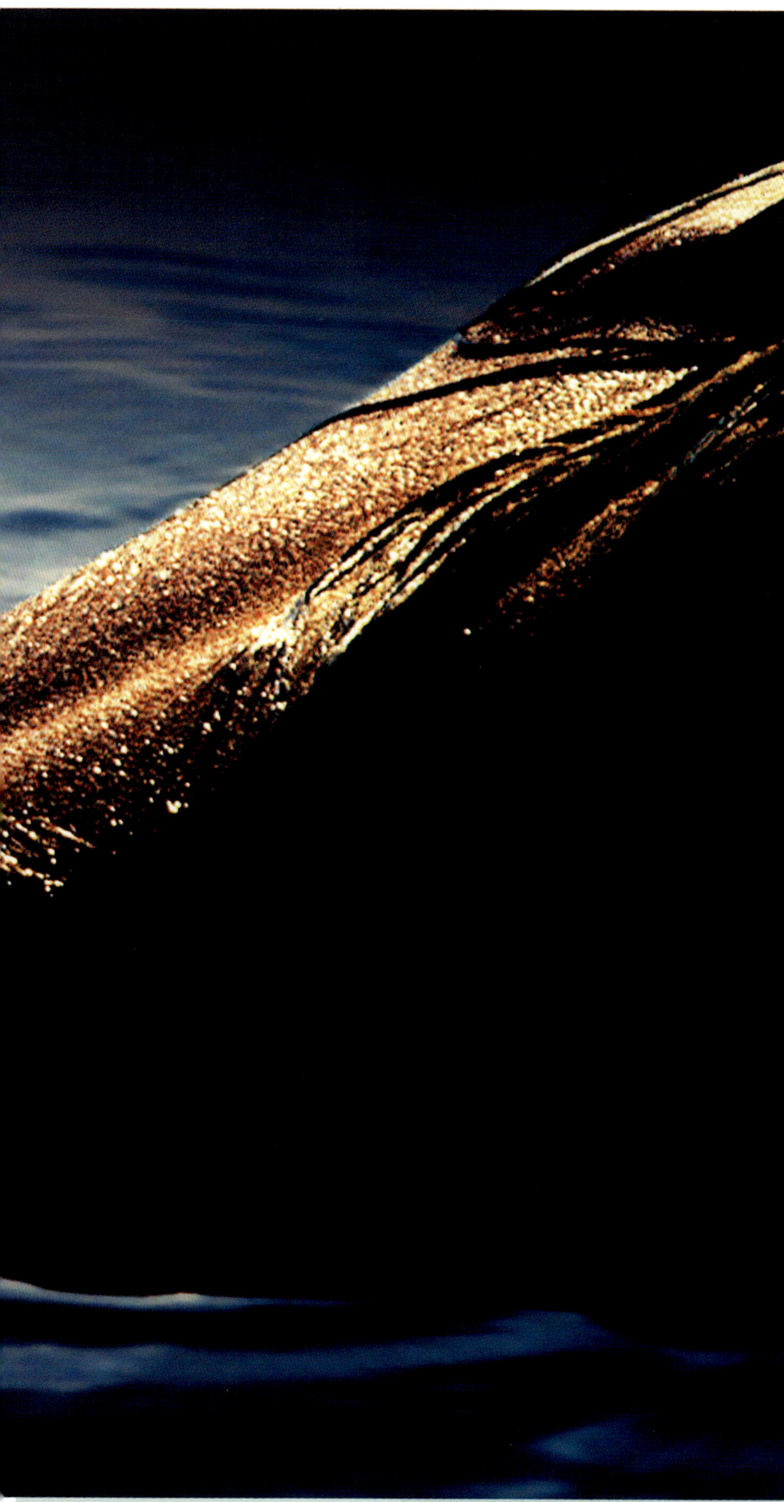

The concept

'This was an appreciation of the beautiful relationship between warm skin and cool sea,' says Jonathan.

The location

Jonathan and his girlfriend, Marie, had been walking by this beach near Bournemouth and noticed how beautiful the calm sea looked with the sun on its surface. They went back very early the next morning with this image in mind and Marie, rather bravely, agreed to pose in the chilly sea.

Composition

With Marie lying in the shallows, Jonathan stood right at the water's edge to get close enough with a 28mm lens. It's a classic composition, creating an almost symmetrical design using the curves of the body and the hotspot of the sun's reflection in the centre.

Lighting and technique

Taken directly into the early morning sun and its reflections, the *contre-jour* lighting enhances the texture of the skin and the water droplets, as well as the wet hair. Jonathan used very slow ISO 25 film, which he underexposed to saturate the colours and boost contrast.

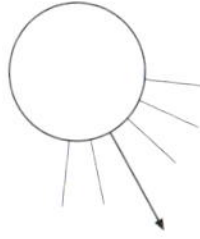

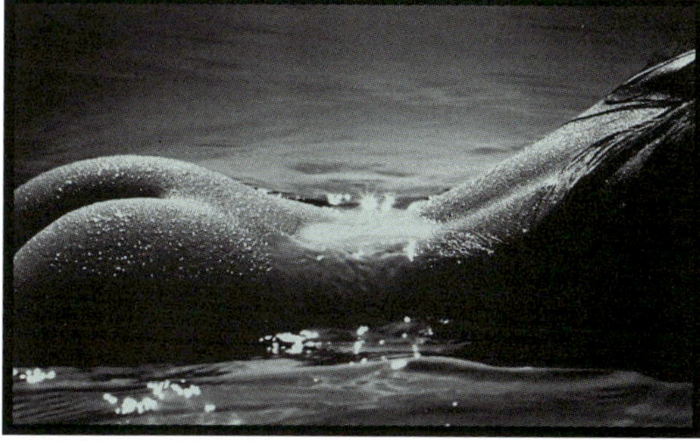

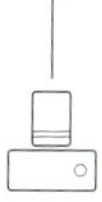

Fact file

Photographer:	Jonathan Charles
Model:	Marie
Location:	Hampshire, UK
Time of day:	Early morning, August

Technical details

Camera:	Olympus OM2
Lens:	28mm
Film:	Kodachrome 25
Exposure:	Not recorded

Chapter 2: **Creating a mood**

Brazenly erotic, subtly sensual, dark and dreamy, soft and romantic...the nude photograph can convey many different moods, each one evoking a different feeling and response from the viewer. The look and pose of the individual model and your choice of location will have an obvious bearing on this, but neither will be effective in inappropriate lighting and so all these elements of the composition should be considered together.

The mood you attempt to put across is dependent on your personal approach and preferences. Some photographers, for example, would never dream of shooting in harsh, midday light, opting instead for the softer effect of the sun later in the day. Others find that hard shadow and strong highlights define the body and give strength and impact to an image.

The look of the model and her surroundings can be completely transformed by the light in a matter of a few hours – and sometimes minutes – thus changing the message you are giving to the viewer. Consider carefully what you want that to be and time your shoot accordingly, or be prepared to adapt your preconceived ideas if nature won't oblige.

Fact file

Photographer:	Nana Sousa Dias
Model:	Vera
Location:	Gêres National Park, Northern Portugal
Time of day:	Afternoon, May

Technical details

Camera:	Fuji Finepix 6900Z
Lens:	35–210mm (equivalent)
Film:	Digital
Exposure:	1/125sec at f/8

' I love to photograph the human body. The smoothness of the curves and skin texture are incredibly beautiful with the appropriate light and I love to mix them with the hard, natural elements of the landscape.'

Nana Sousa Dias

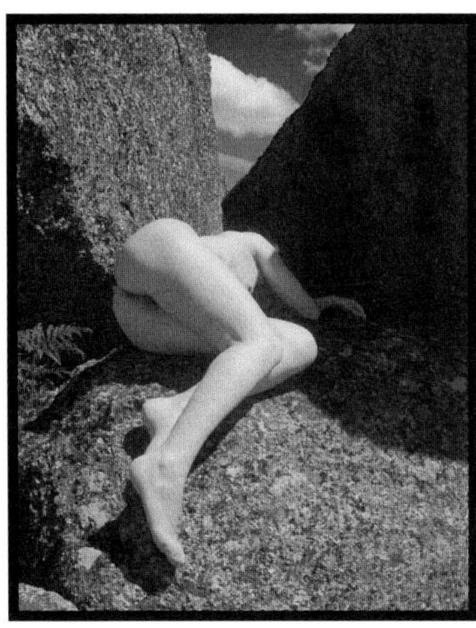

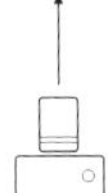

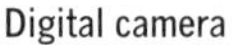
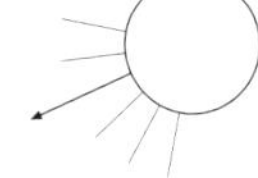

Digital camera   Sun

The concept

This was part of a study on outdoor nudes for Nana's portfolio. Some of them show the nude within architectural settings but here it was the imposing scale of the natural landscape that attracted him.

The location

Gêres National Park is a beautiful mountain region in the north of Portugal with rivers, cascades and lakes and is Nana's favourite place for landscape photography. He chose this spot, 500 metres from the road, for the large rock formations and also because it's extremely quiet – perfect for nude photography when a relaxed rapport between model and photographer is required.

Composition

Nana's starting point here was the two contrasting wedges of rock in the background, one showing its texture as it is lit by the sun, the other in deep shadow, with a triangle of sky in the middle. He placed the model to echo these angular structures, using the bright light falling on her to differentiate between the smoothness of her body and the hardness of her surroundings.

Lighting and technique

The sun was to the right of the camera and very bright, creating the hard light Nana was after to emphasise the contrast in texture and form between the soft skin of the model and the irregular rocks. No flash or reflectors were required but Nana used an orange filter on the lens to boost the contrast between the clouds and the sky. He usually uses a digital camera to make decisions about filters, viewpoint, the light and so on before taking the final image with a Pentax 645 medium format camera. In this case he preferred the digital image, taken with a 35mm focal length. 'The 45mm lens on the Pentax – equivalent to a 28mm in 35mm format – caused a bit of unflattering distortion,' he explains. 'This shot also had the cloud formations I wanted which, despite waiting for ages, didn't appear when I later used the Pentax.'

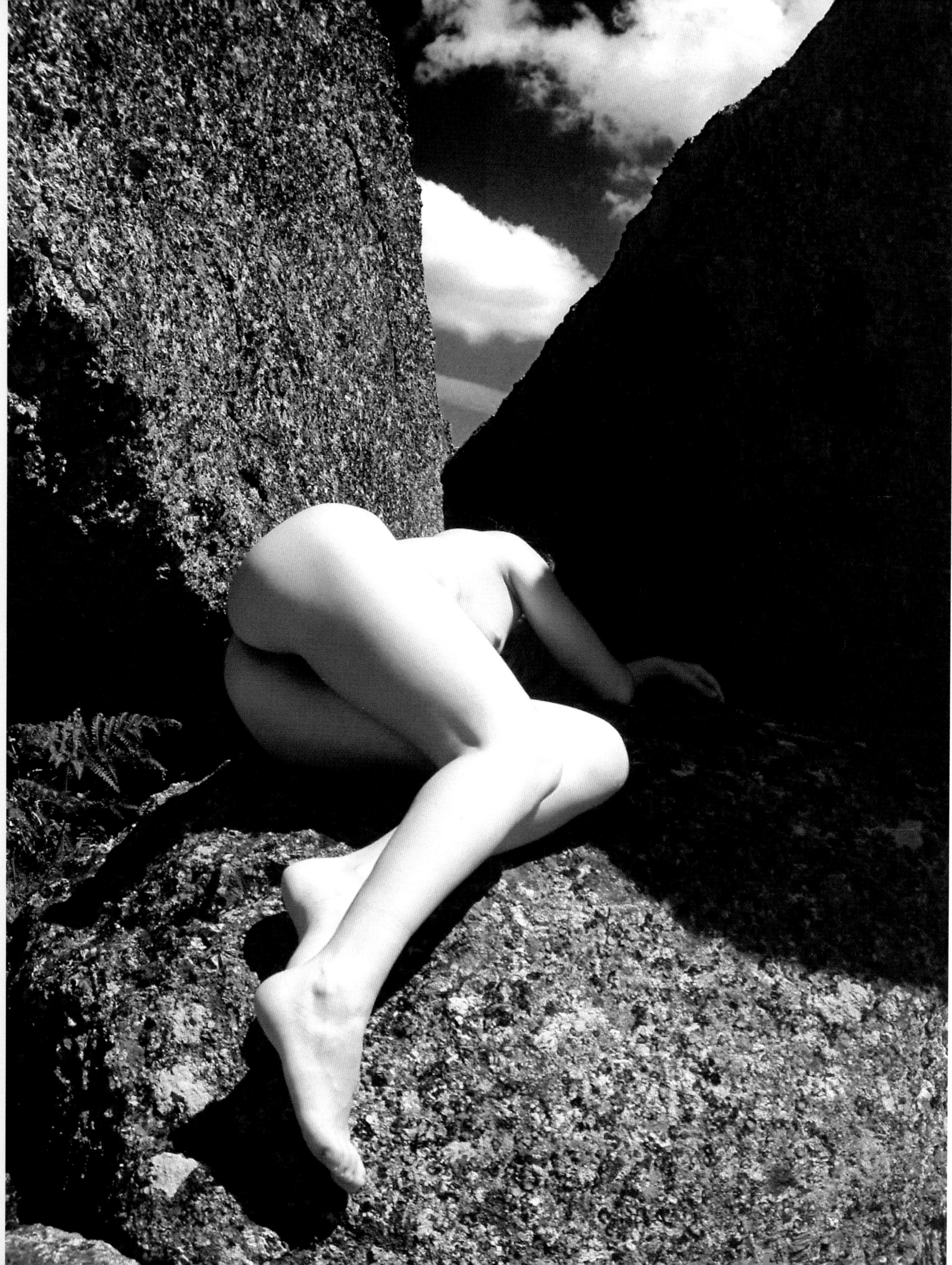

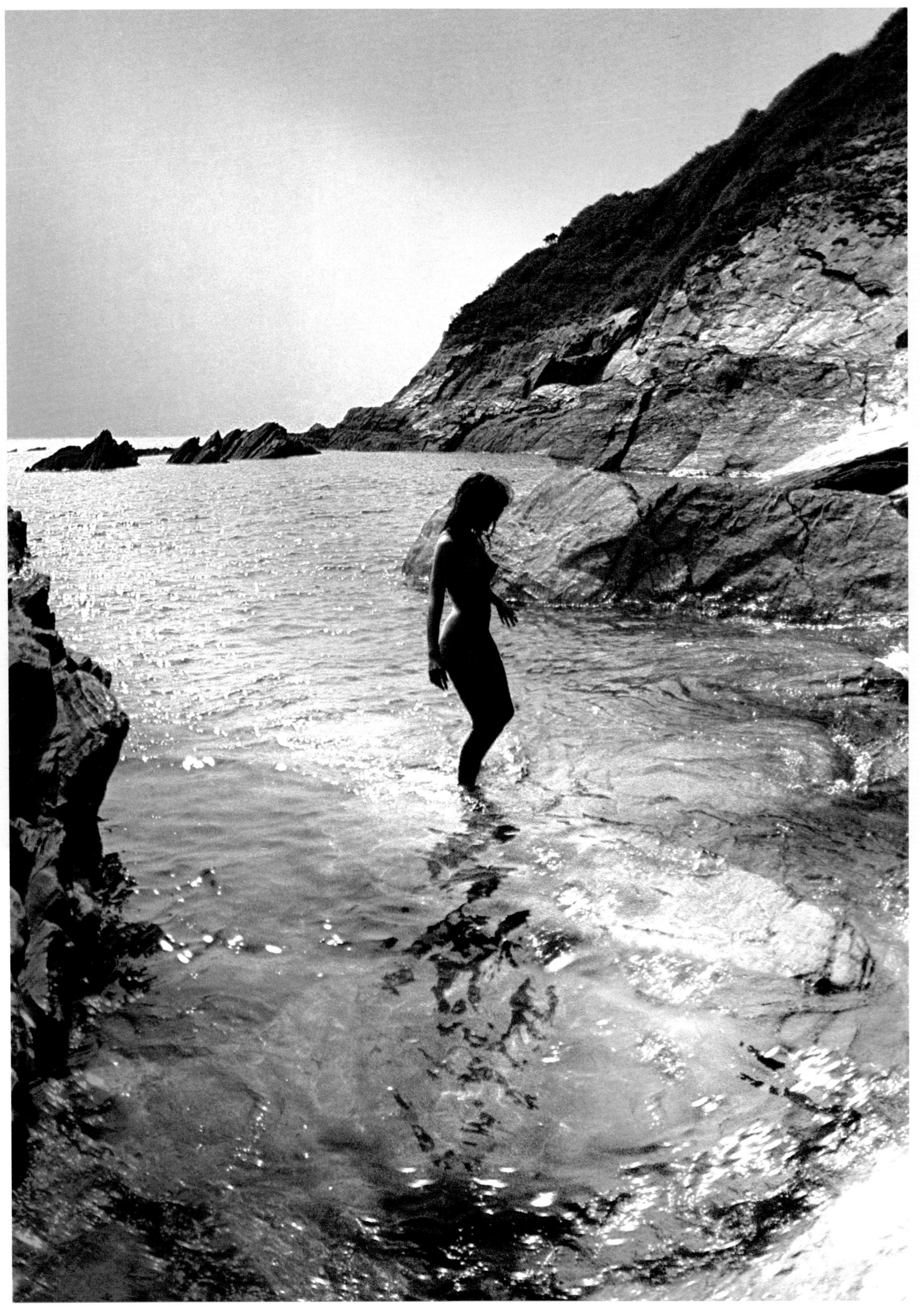

Fact file

Photographer:	Jonathan Charles
Model:	Marie
Location:	Dorset coast, UK
Time of day:	Mid-afternoon, July

Technical details

Camera:	Olympus OM-2
Lens:	24mm
Film:	Ilford HP5
Exposure:	Not recorded

The concept

'This was a grab shot, taken as Marie was carefully walking out of the sea over large flat and slippery stones,' recalls Jonathan. 'The lighting, the outlined shape of Marie and the setting just appealed to me.'

The location

The beach is on the Dorset coastline, east of Wembury, near Plymouth. Jonathan and Marie went there because it was totally deserted, even in the middle of summer and they could enjoy a peaceful afternoon swimming and sunbathing. Photography wasn't particularly part of the plan, but Jonathan always carries his camera with him for occasions like this.

Composition

Placed centrally in the frame, Marie is the focal point of this picture but Jonathan kept her relatively small to make her part of the scenery around her. It also allowed him to include the shadows and reflections in the water, which caught his eye as he took the shot. 'The swirling water around her looked, in that light, almost like mercury, forming a nice S-shaped line to reflect her shape.'

Lighting and technique

'The bright mid-afternoon sun was reflecting off the water and shining down on Marie from behind, making her almost in shadow,' describes Jonathan. 'The direct reflections highlight the textures of the skin, sea and slate rocks, and the dark shadows reproduce the dazzling effect of looking towards the glare of the sun.'

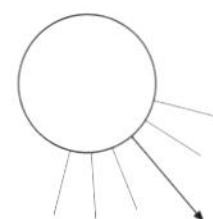

Bright sun on model's back

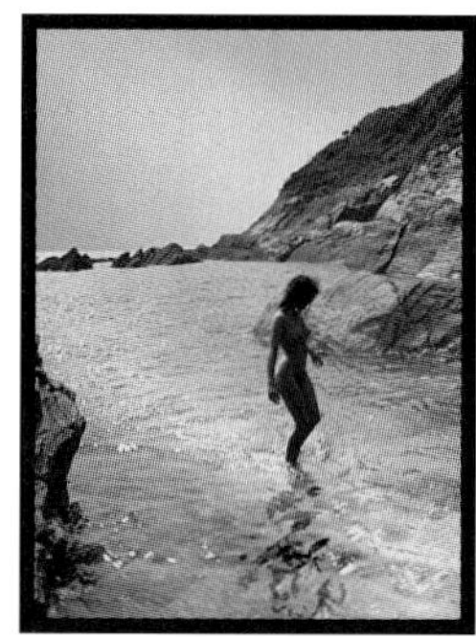

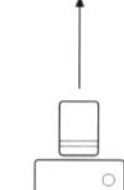

35mm camera

' This lighting, combined with high-contrast printing, is perfect if the aim is to include the subject as a natural part of the scene without emphasising her nudity.'

Jonathan Charles

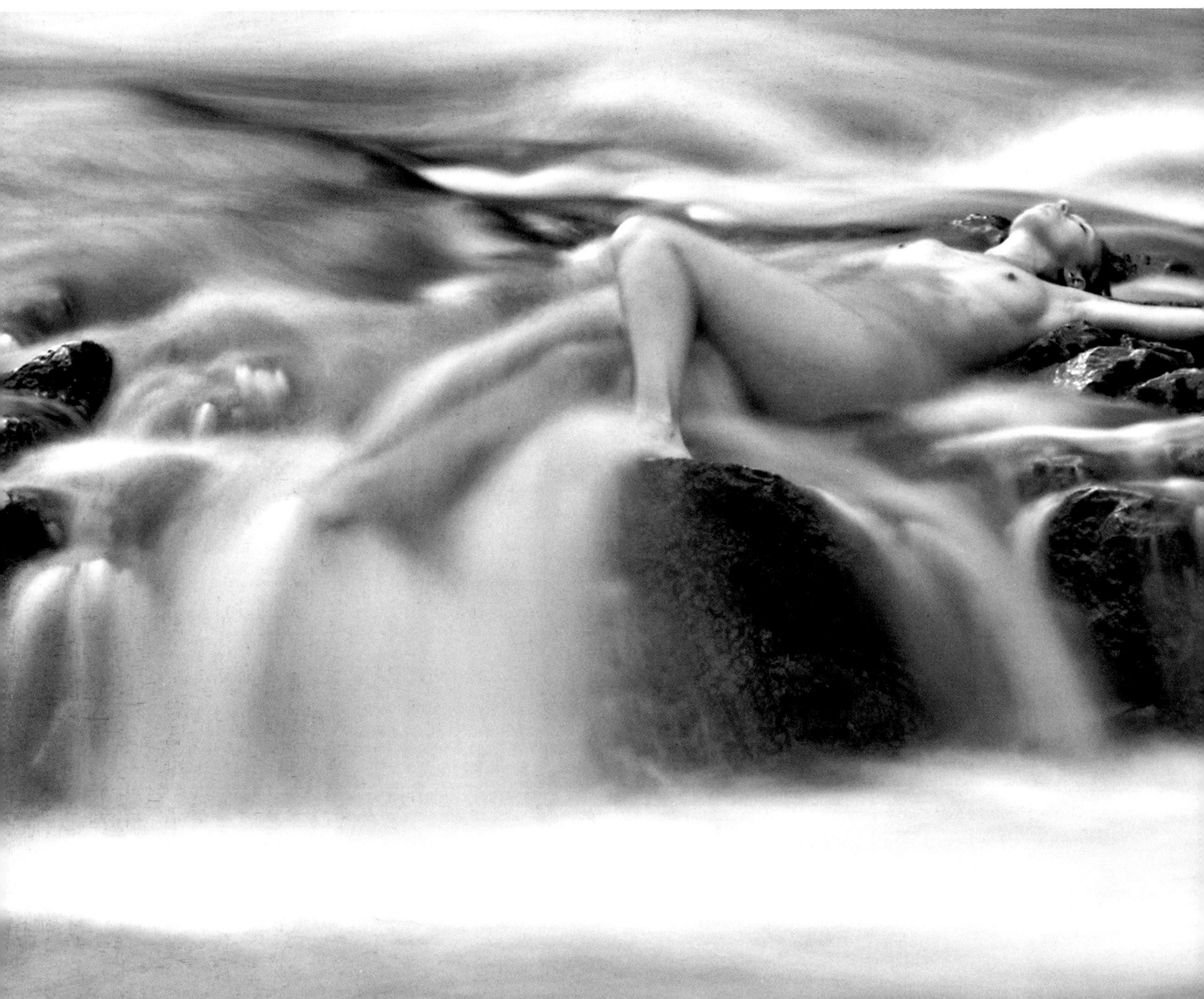

Fact file

Photographer: Eric Boutilier-Brown
Model: Trisha
Location: Gold River, Nova Scotia, Canada
Time of day: 3pm, May

Technical details

Camera: Wisner 4x5 Traditional with Calumet 6x12 film holder
Lens: 210mm
Film: Kodak T-Max 100
Exposure: 6secs at f/45

'The dark rocks set against the foam of the river guaranteed enough contrast to make the image vivid to the viewer.'

Eric Boutilier-Brown

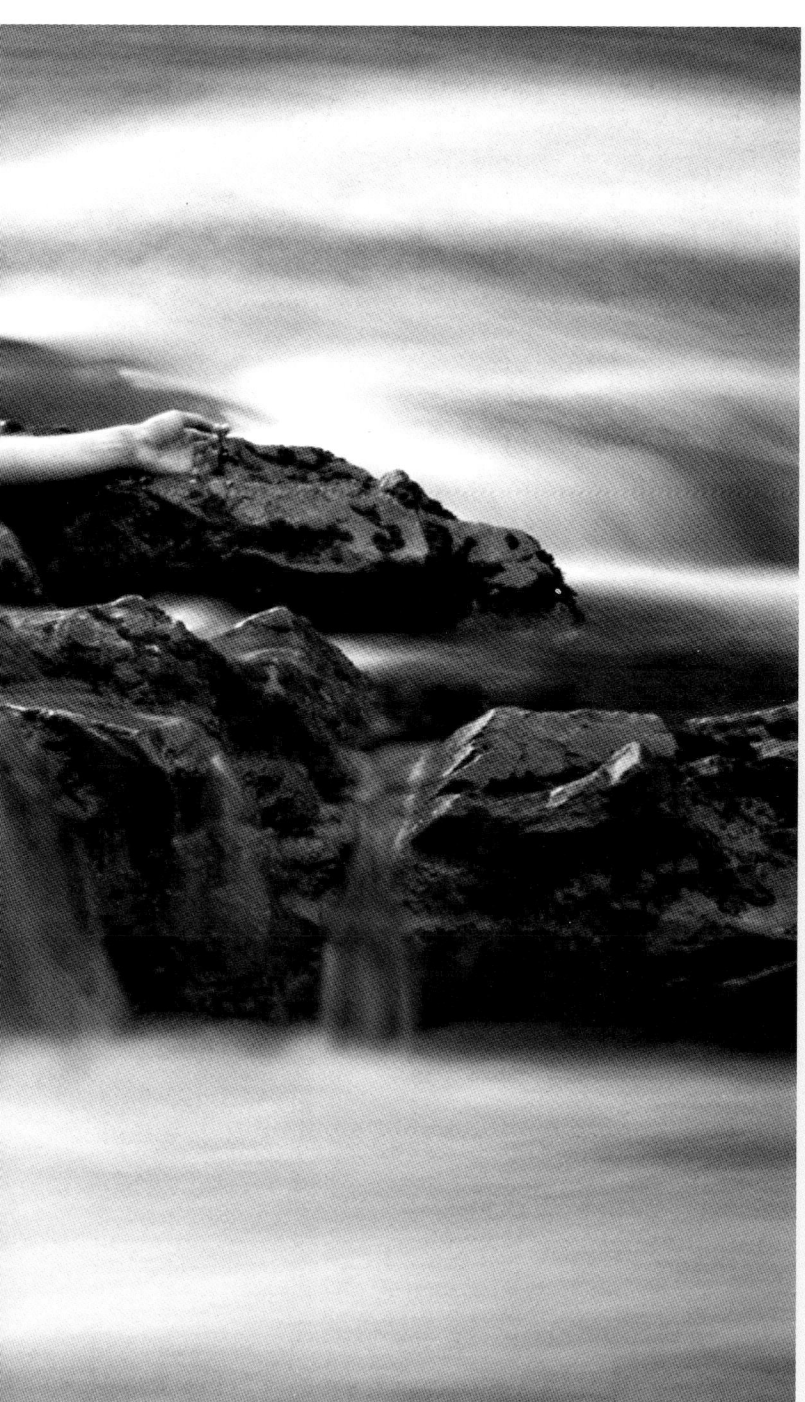

The concept

The idea for this image came from the location, which Eric felt leant itself to this kind of treatment. The flow of the water was just the right level and speed for him to be able to turn it into a completely soft mist.

The location

'Gold River is a fabulous place to work, with broad rapids and a rich variety of terrain alongside the river,' says Eric.

Composition

The 1:2 aspect ratio of the 6x12 roll-film back was ideal for this subject. It eliminated the upper and lower portions of the image, which were unnecessary and distracting. This panoramic view draws the eye along the image laterally. The tones of the model and the river are so similar that they subtly blend into each other.

Lighting and technique

An overcast sky, threatening rain, ensured soft, even lighting but did not allow a slow enough exposure to blur the water sufficiently. Eric had to use a 4x neutral density filter to cut down the light reaching the lens and give him a shutter speed of six seconds. 'If the rapids had been bigger and faster, an even longer exposure would be necessary, making it hard for Trisha to hold the pose. Too little water would have meant too little blur. Fortunately this was just right,' says Eric.

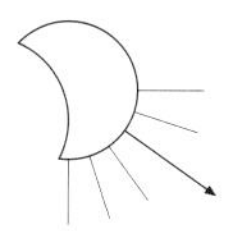

Sun behind clouds

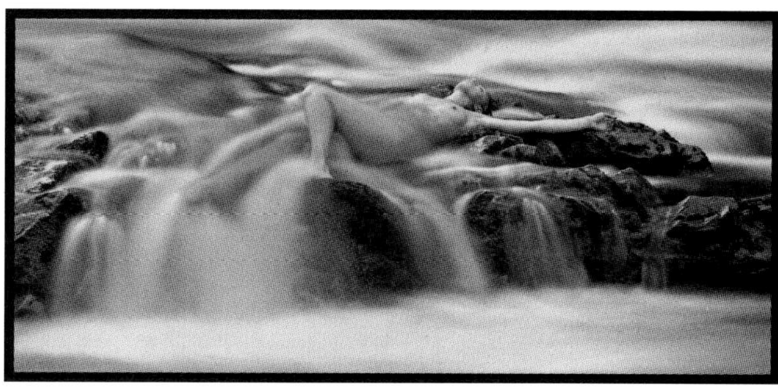

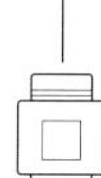

large format camera

'There were no special techniques used to capture this image. The real technique of photographing the nude in nature is finding the right spot with the right light, at the right time of day. That requires a lot of research ahead of time.'

Dale Lehmer

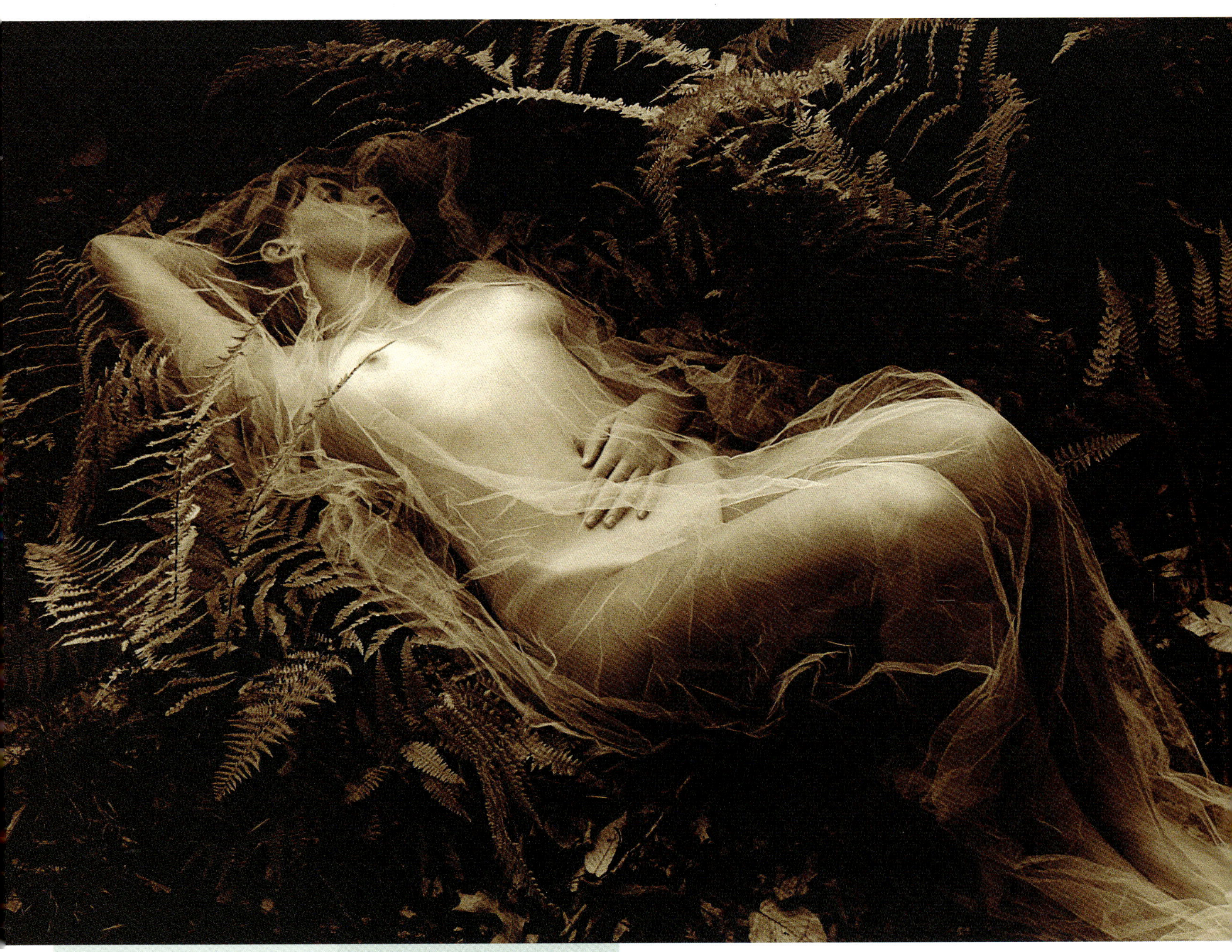

Fact file

Photographer: Dale Lehmer
Model: Nickie
Location: Photographer's property, New York, USA
Time of day: 2pm, October

Technical details

Camera: Olympus E20n digital
Lens: 35mm
Film: n/a
Exposure: 1/50sec at f/2.8

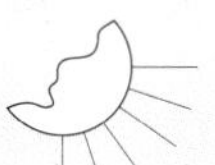

Sun behind clouds

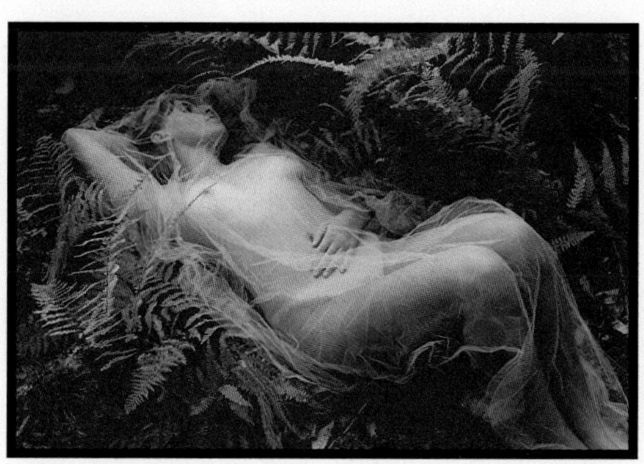

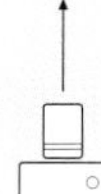

Digital SLR camera

The concept

Dale was trying to create an image that had a Pre-Raphaelite painting feeling to it, as well as convey the idea of unity between a woman and nature. 'The fabric adds an elegant and artistic feel to the image which I really like,' he says.

The location

Dale has an area of forest within his own property, 100 miles north of New York City. For this picture, he tried to find a place where there were some open areas of leaves and some ferns to create different textures.

Composition

'I wanted a close up for this image and so chose a diagonal angle, filling the frame with the model's figure,' explains Dale. 'I was aiming for an interesting perspective, shooting from the feet side, with her legs up, her head turned and a gesture that was somewhat shy and reserved, yet comfortable.'

Lighting and technique

'It was a drizzly, cold day and the sun was completely filtered through clouds and very diffused, which I feel adds greatly to this image. There were no heavy shadows and her body was uniformly lit by the natural light. She has very white skin which I think is perfect for the look of the picture.'

Fact file

Photographer: Trevor Yerbury
Models: Angela and Fiona
Location: Scotland, UK
Time of day: Mid-morning, summer

Technical details

Camera: Hasselblad
Lens: 150mm
Film: Kodak T-Max
Exposure: 1/60sec at f/4

The concept

As well as being one of the UK's top wedding and portrait photographers, Trevor Yerbury also takes fine art nude images for exhibition purposes. These two models had worked with him for two years and this was one of the last images he took of them. The inspiration for the picture came initially from the location.

The location

This was taken in a ruined gazebo in the grounds of an hotel on the Scottish borders. The previous year, one of Trevor's top models had held her wedding there and he loved the way the structure resembled a temple. He returned with this image very much in mind.

Composition

Because of the surroundings, the gazebo could only be photographed from this angle and, in any case, Trevor found that the symmetry of the pillars worked best for the composition. He placed the models centrally to emphasise this, with their upright pose and the tone of their bodies echoing the two structures but in a softer, sensual form.

Lighting and technique

On an overcast day, the lighting was generally diffused but there was just enough of a break in the clouds to allow the sun to provide some top light on the models. No artificial lighting, filters or any other accessories were used; the sun and the sky proved more than adequate for the job.

> ' I prefer not to use meters or reflectors to photograph nudes. I like to keep the lighting simple – just God's own.'

Trevor Yerbury

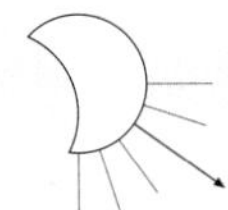

Sun through clouds providing top light

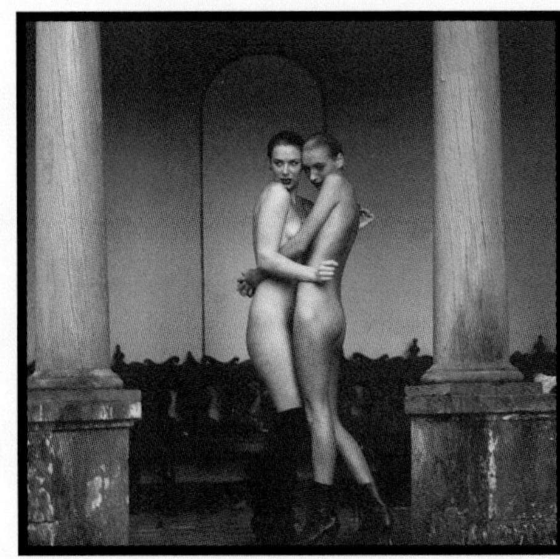

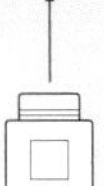

Medium format camera

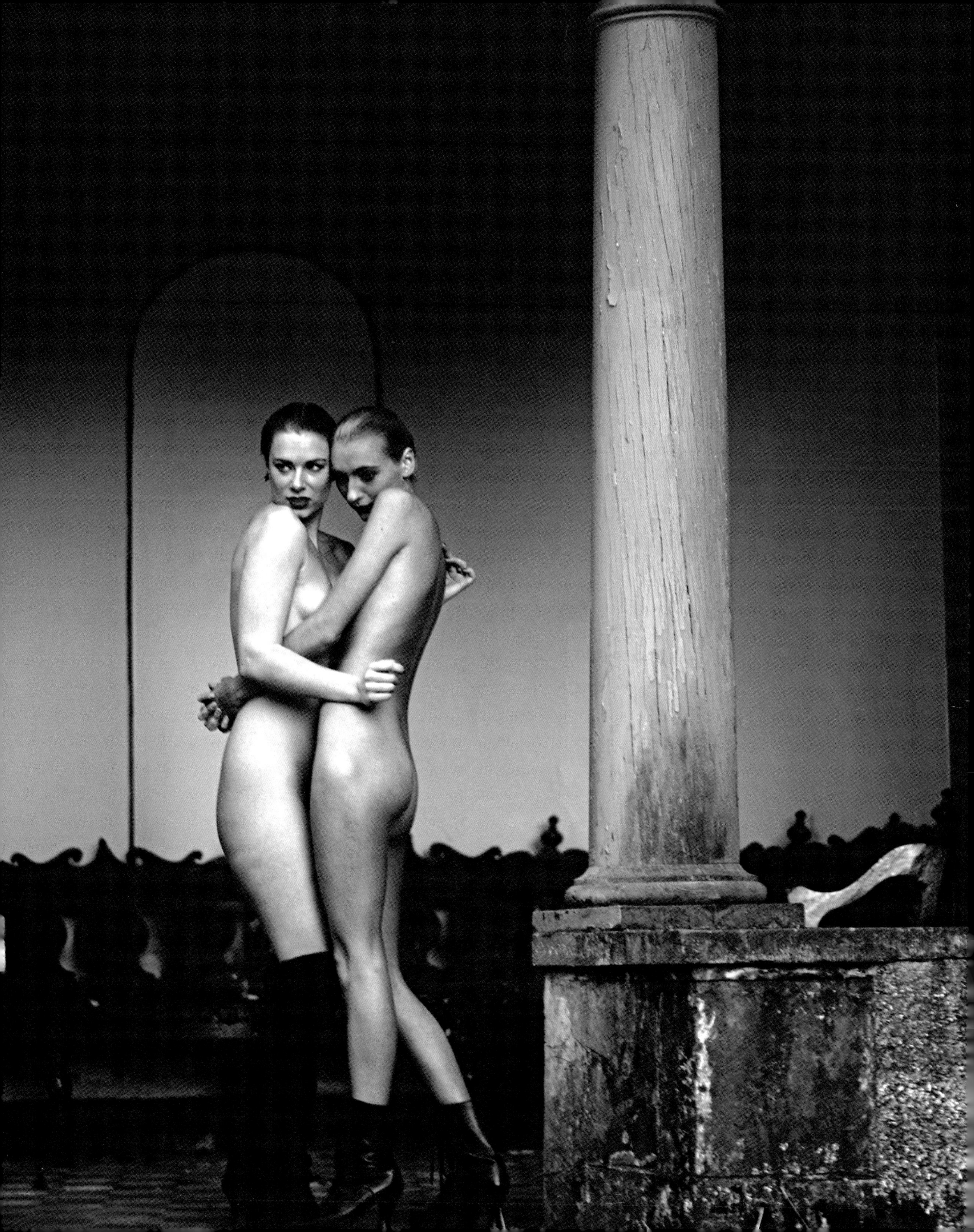

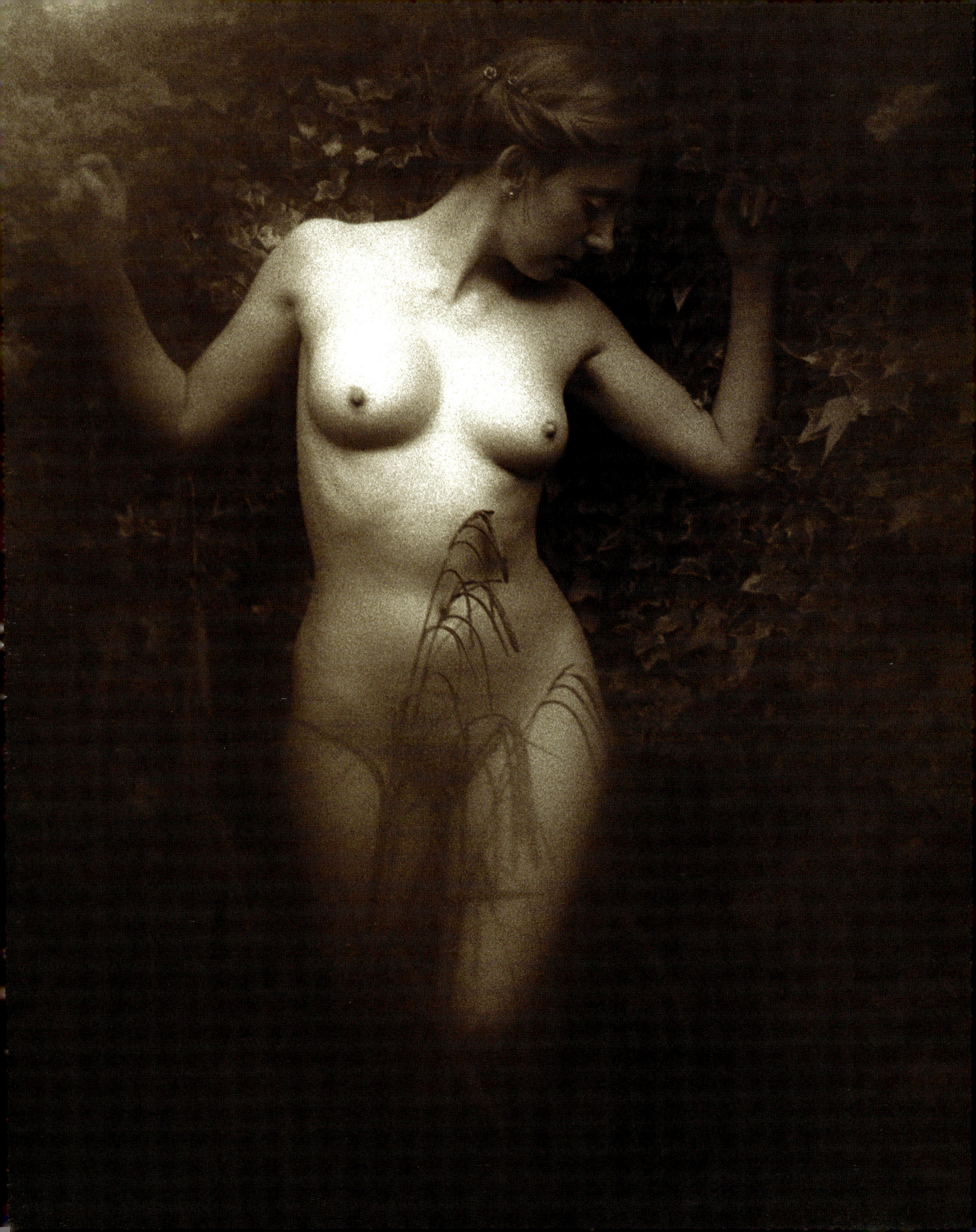

The concept

'I wanted to create a "statue" of Annabella so I gave her a Grecian hairstyle and pale facial and body make-up to suite the feeling of the shot,' explains Faye Yerbury, who along with her husband, Trevor, photographs nudes for exhibitions. 'Annabella has worked with us for over three years and is great at helping to interpret our thoughts and ideas.'

The location

Sometimes the best inspiration comes closest to home and this was taken in a corner of the Yerbury's Japanese-themed back garden. The dense foliage and particularly the ivy make it look like a forgotten place with a statue almost buried within it.

Composition

The likeness to a classical statue is very convincing, due to the pale skin, the background and the moody lighting. Faye has also been clever to partly obscure the face, hands and legs which, if included, would have made the figure look too life-like and modern.

Lighting and technique

This was a very shaded area and Faye wanted most of the foliage to remain dark but she needed some light on the model's body. Achieving the right effect was a matter of waiting and observing how the light would fall during the day. At 8pm on a summer evening, the sun had passed over the trees and was providing top lighting on the models shoulders and breasts – exactly what was required. To add a little extra warmth, Faye placed a Cokin P.695 champagne filter over the lens. Although intended for use with colour film, it still has a noticeable effect on the tone of the image after it has been made into a black-and-white image.

<table>
<tr><td colspan="2">Fact file</td><td colspan="2">Technical details</td></tr>
<tr><td>Photographer:</td><td>Faye Yerbury</td><td>Camera:</td><td>Nikon F70</td></tr>
<tr><td>Model:</td><td>Annabella</td><td>Lens:</td><td>528–300mm</td></tr>
<tr><td>Location:</td><td>Garden, Scotland, UK</td><td>Film:</td><td>Kodak 5037 EPT</td></tr>
<tr><td>Time of day:</td><td>8pm, July</td><td>Exposure:</td><td>Automatic</td></tr>
</table>

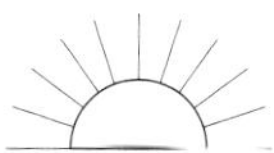

Low sun

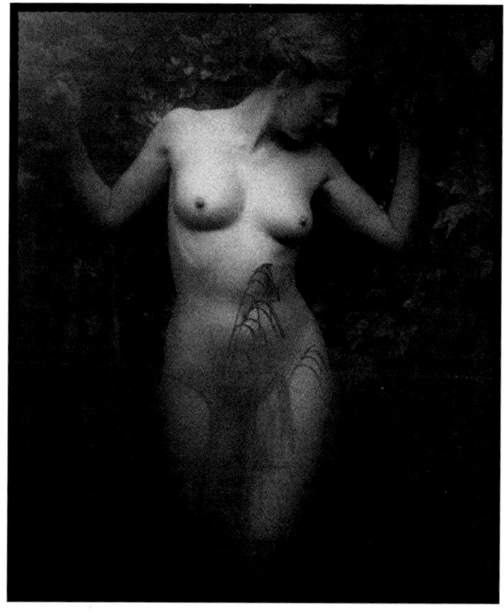

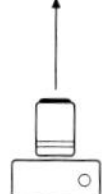

35mm camera

'I took the shot with colour film but when I saw it on the computer screen, black and white was clearly more the effect I was looking for.'

Faye Yerbury

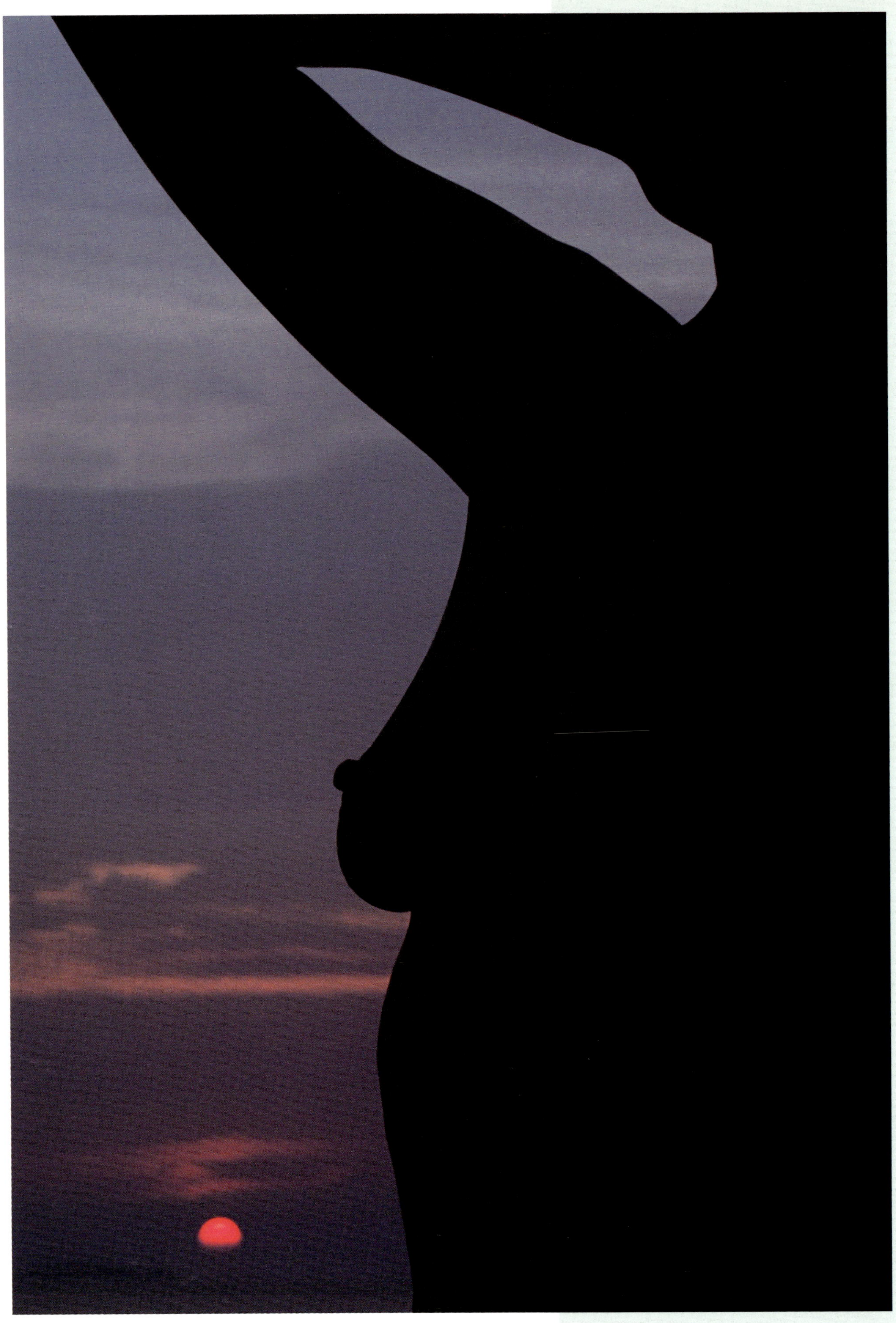

The concept

'I was attempting to capture the silhouette of Sonya with the evening sunset over the sea in the background,' explains Dale.

The location

'The landscape or location is always the starting point to my pictures,' says Dale. 'I like to find places that are romantic, secluded and perhaps exotic, with wonderful textures and warm colours. Thailand is a beautifully warm and sensuous country.'

Composition

Dale and the model stood on a high balcony to fill the background entirely with the stunning sky, including the small glow of the setting sun right at the bottom of the frame. Using a 35mm lens, he cropped the image afterwards to achieve the right balance of the silhouette and the sky – they are roughly equal in the composition. The model's pose emphasises her soft round curves and flowing lines.

Lighting and technique

Dale didn't use a tripod here and was quite surprised at how sharp the image came out in such low light. By metering for the brighter sky, the darker foreground subject was reduced to a silhouette. The trick with silhouettes is to keep the composition simple and make sure the outline of the figure is interesting and easily recognisable.

Fact file

Photographer:	Dale Lehmer
Model:	Sonya
Location:	Phuket Island, Thailand
Time of day:	8pm, May

Technical details

Camera:	Olympus E20n digital
Lens:	35mm
Film:	n/a
Exposure:	1/400sec at f/4

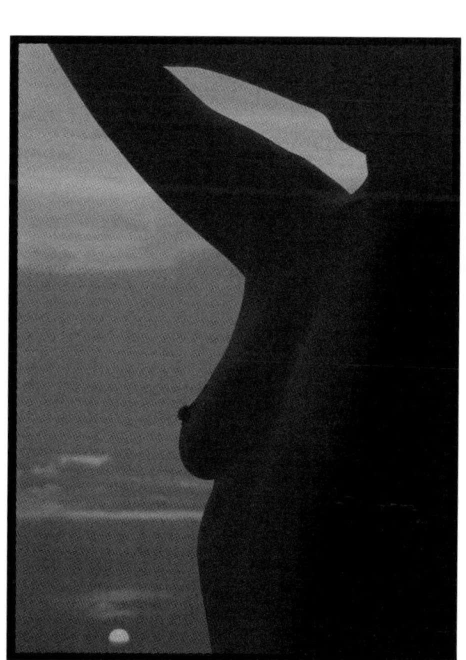

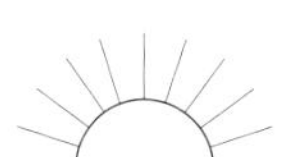

Low sun (in picture)

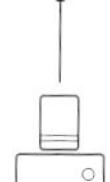

Digital SLR camera

'I think silhouettes are extremely interesting because you can look at them in two ways – the figure or the space around her.'

Dale Lehmer

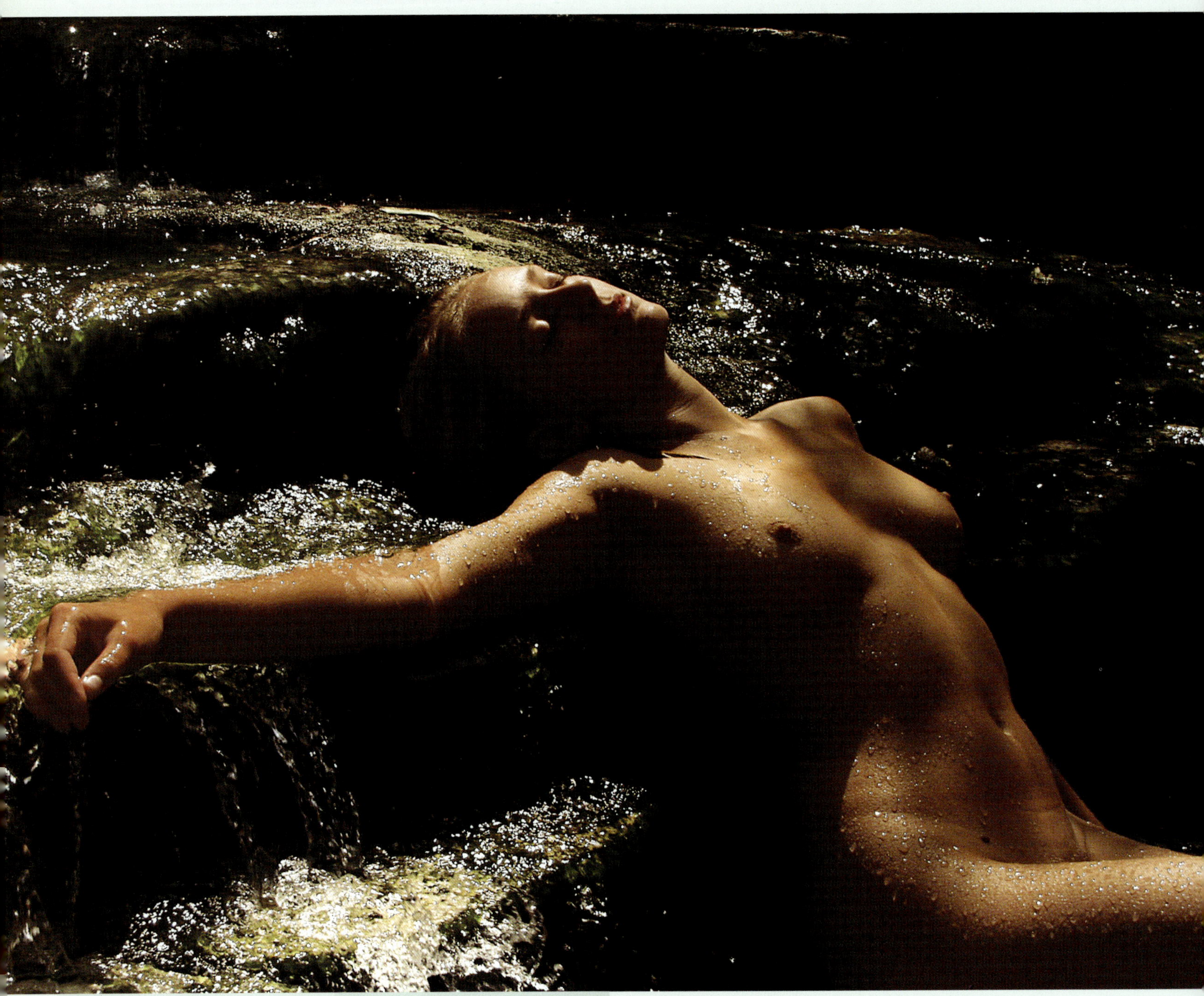

Fact file

Photographer: Dale Lehmer
Model: Claire
Location: Minnawaska State Park, New York, USA
Time of day: 4pm, June

Technical details

Camera: Olympus E10 (digital)
Lens: 35mm
Film: n/a
Exposure: 1/640sec at f/8

'The direction and strength of the sun is most important in creating negative space, as this will simply be created from shadows.'

Dale Lehmer

The concept

'As with most of my nudes in nature, my vision is to convey the feeling of an organic beauty and unity of my models in the landscape – to make them part of it, relaxed, natural and not posed,' explains Dale. 'I want the eroticism and sensuousness of the image to be generated from the beauty of the entire scene, and not just from graphic focus on the naked model.'

The location

'It took a two mile hike to get to this waterfall in Minnawaska State Park. It's almost on top of a mountain, in a gorge, and is a series of ledges almost 50 feet high. As with my other locations, I studied this place beforehand, visiting several times to study the light patterns during the day, and find exact spots to place the model. Sometimes I even do mock shoots with a dummy model to prepare for the real thing.'

Composition

Dale found a place in the waterfalls with shelves and ledges that would create shadow lines across the image. He placed Claire on a diagonal, including a little negative space to the right of her and at the top of the image. Her pose is totally relaxed, as if she is sleeping.

Lighting and technique

'The sun only gets down in this section of the gorge at about 2pm, so it is rather bright, but filtered through leaves to some extent. I underexposed the image enough to still see Claire and the glistening water, but to create the tone and mood I was looking for – almost as if it were shot under moonlight.'

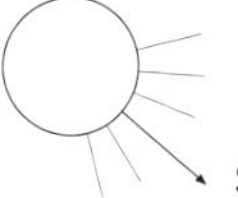

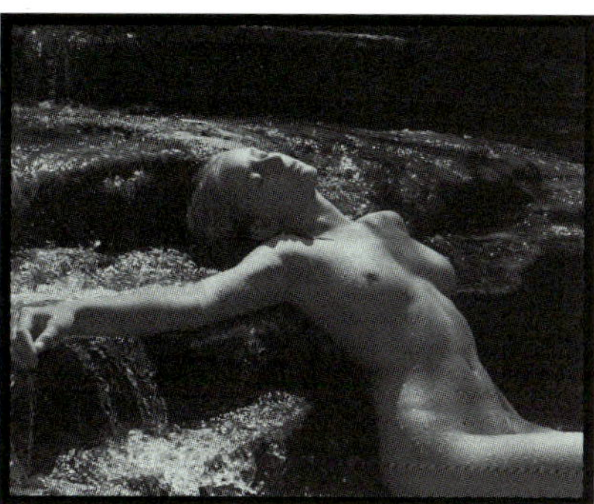

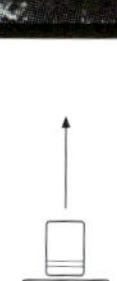

This was taken during the same shoot as the main picture, but earlier in the afternoon. The sun was to the left and slightly behind the model so the sides of the ledges were in shadow. Again, Dale underexposed, which makes the image look as though it was taken much later in the day.

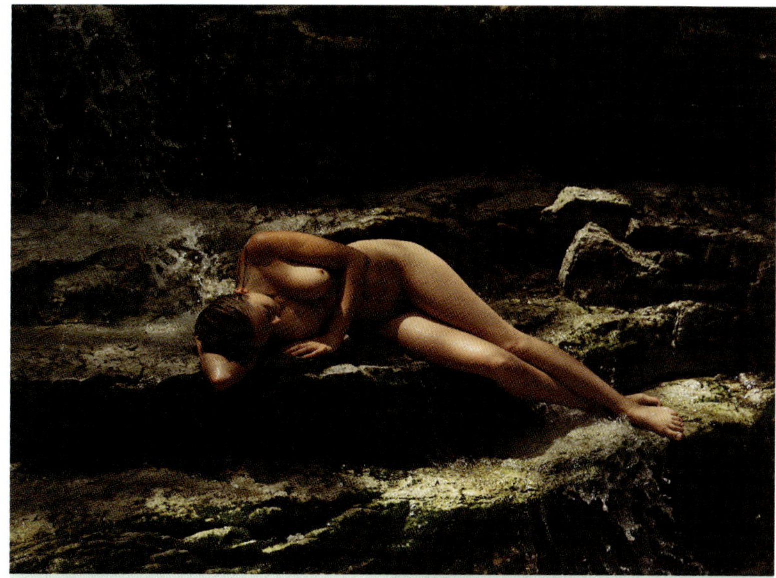

Fact file		Technical details	
Photographer:	Dale Lehmer	**Camera:**	Olympus E10 (digital)
Model:	Claire	**Lens:**	35mm
Location:	Minnawaska State Park, New York, USA	**Film:**	n/a
		Exposure:	1/640sec at f/5
Time of day:	2pm, June		

Fact file

Photographer: Trevor Yerbury
Model: Karen
Location: Beach near Edinburgh, Scotland, UK
Time of day: Evening, August

Technical details

Camera: Hasselblad 500c
Lens: 250mm
Film: Kodak T-Max 100
Exposure: 1/60sec at f/8

Standing, rather treacherously, high up on the rocks, the model's pose was planned to look as though she was in flight. She was facing directly into the early evening sun, which has given her body an intense glow with a rim of shadow to accentuate her form. ▶▶

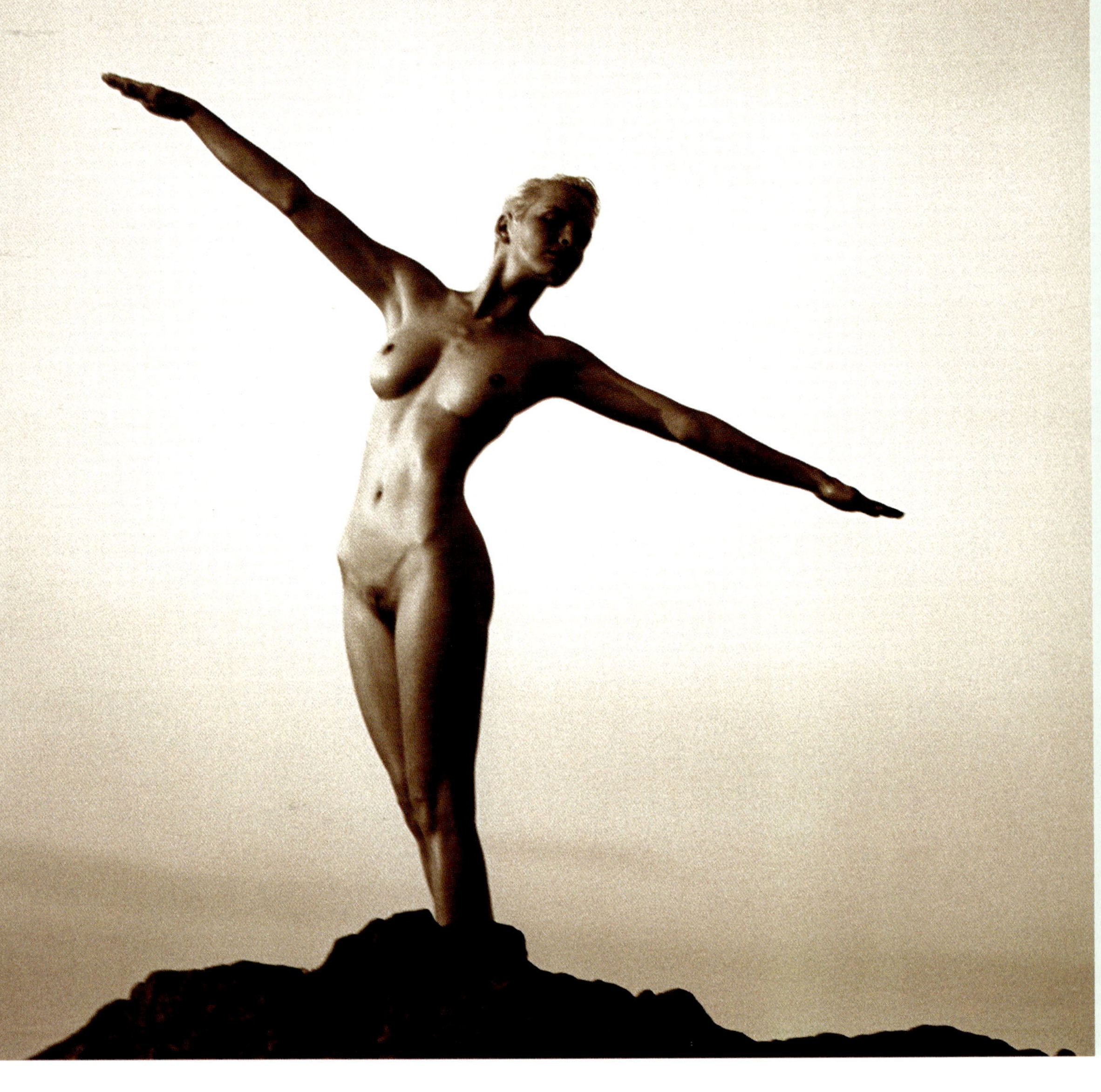

'The model was standing on a very high – and uncomfortable – outcrop of rocks and found it extremely difficult to hold this pose.'

Trevor Yerbury

The concept

Part of Trevor's personal and exhibition work, this image draws part of its inspiration from classical mythology. 'The idea was to create a simple image, with perhaps some acknowledgement to the sirens, luring sailors to their doom,' he explains.

The location

Less than 20 miles from his base in Edinburgh, this beach is a favourite location for Trevor, who finds the combination of sand, rocks and a broad expanse of sky and sea lends itself to many different possibilities for nude photography.

Composition

Standing on rocks to give her height above the camera, the model was draped in a simple Grecian manner with some silk voile and her statuesque pose reflects this classical theme. Trevor placed her to one side of the frame, allowing plenty of space on the left side for her to 'look out' over the sea.

Lighting and technique

Trevor never uses any additional light source, or even reflectors, for his outdoor work. He prefers, where possible, to time his shoots to make the best possible use of the existing light. This was taken at one of his favourite times of day – late on a summer's evening. The light was coming from the left of the image and the clouds, lit by the setting sun, add to the atmosphere. 'The print was printed down by at least one stop to bring the clouds more into play and add a more dramatic effect,' he explains.

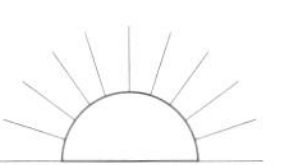

Low sun

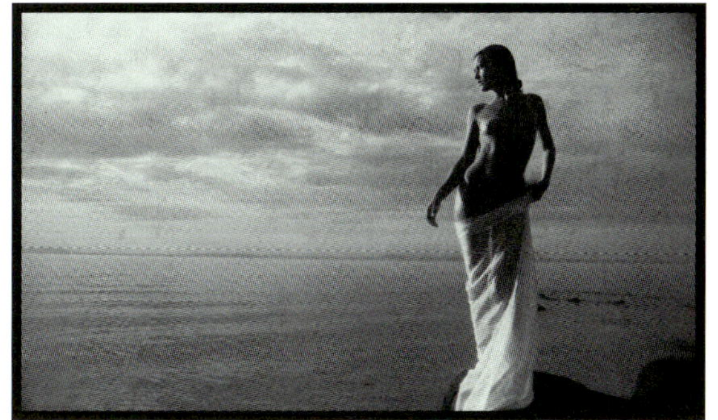

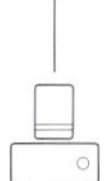

35mm camera

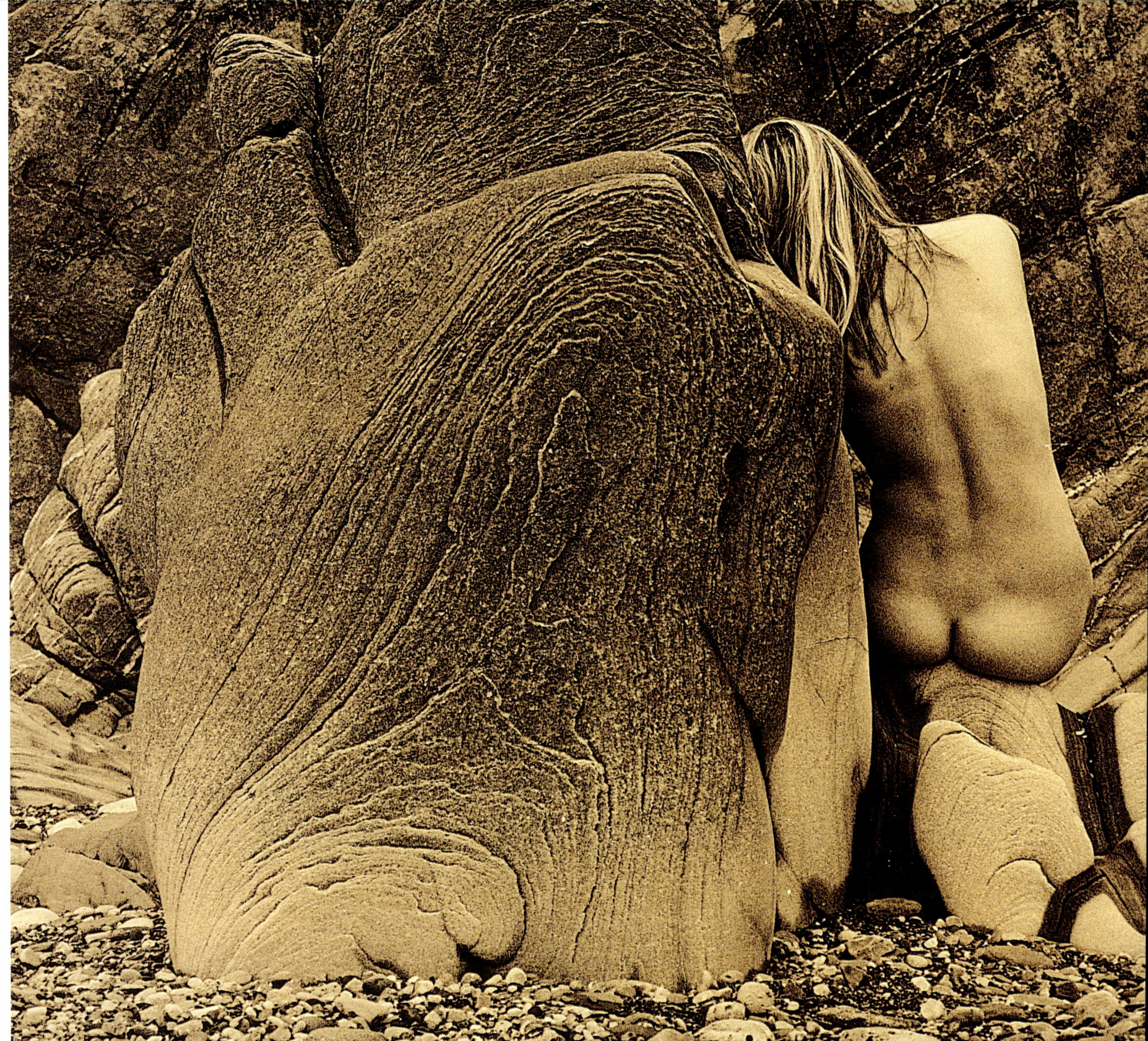

Fact file

Photographer: Bob Carlos Clarke
Model: Sue
Location: Ballyquin beach, County Waterford, Ireland
Time of day: Early afternoon

Technical details

Camera: Pentax 6x7
Lens: 105mm
Film: Kodak Tri-X pan
Exposure: Not recorded

'When you photograph a model it's a duet – a tango. When it goes well it's better than sex, and lasts forever.'

Bob Carlos Clarke

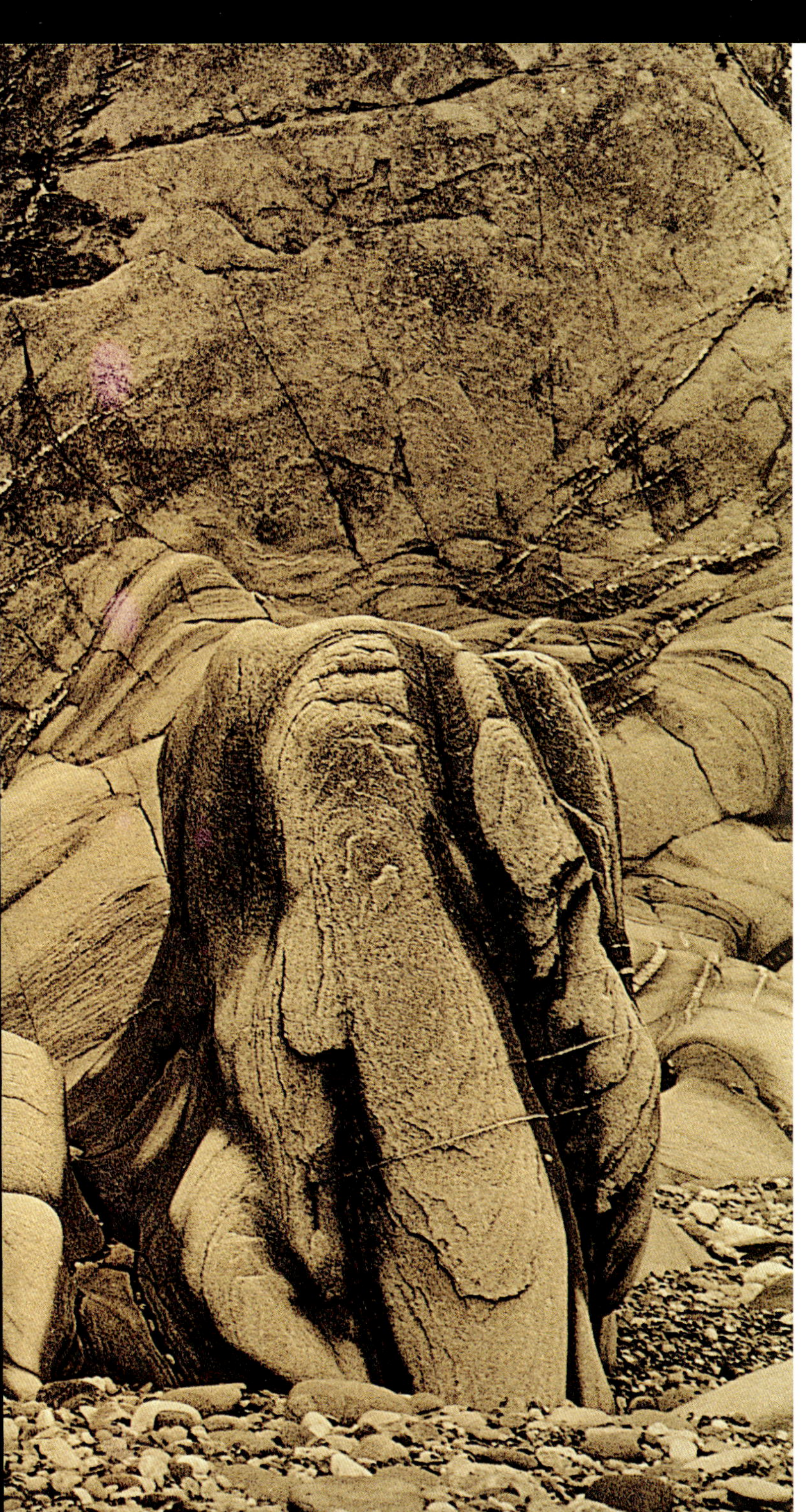

The concept

This was a personal, and previously unpublished, picture taken during an early afternoon shoot on a beach in Ireland. Bob was inspired by the amazing lines and curves of these rock formations; he wanted to capture their form and texture.

The location

The beach and the rock location could be almost anywhere in the world but Bob was lucky enough to have lived in a small wooden house on the cliff above this beach in County Waterford and have this ideal setting on his doorstep.

Composition

He placed the model so that the shape of her limbless back almost looks like another boulder, with the strands of her hair echoing the lines on the adjacent rocks, using his instinct and intuition as to what would perfectly compliment the rocks.

Lighting and technique

The early afternoon light, to the left of the model, has created soft shadows that provide modelling on her figure. Bob felt that the setting and the texture of the rock created atmosphere enough for this picture so all he did was point and shoot. The black-and-white print was selenium-toned to add warmth and richness. It also makes the model appear to blend in with her environment even more.

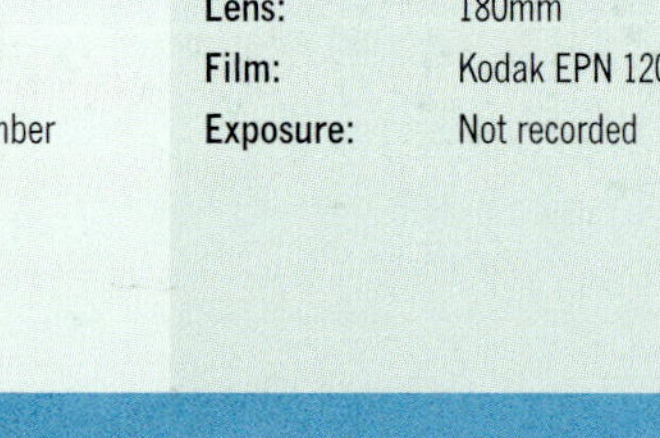

Fact file

Photographer: Arnold Henri
Model: Jacqueline
Location: North coast of France
Time of day: Late afternoon, November

Technical details

Camera: Mamiya RZ67
Lens: 180mm
Film: Kodak EPN 120
Exposure: Not recorded

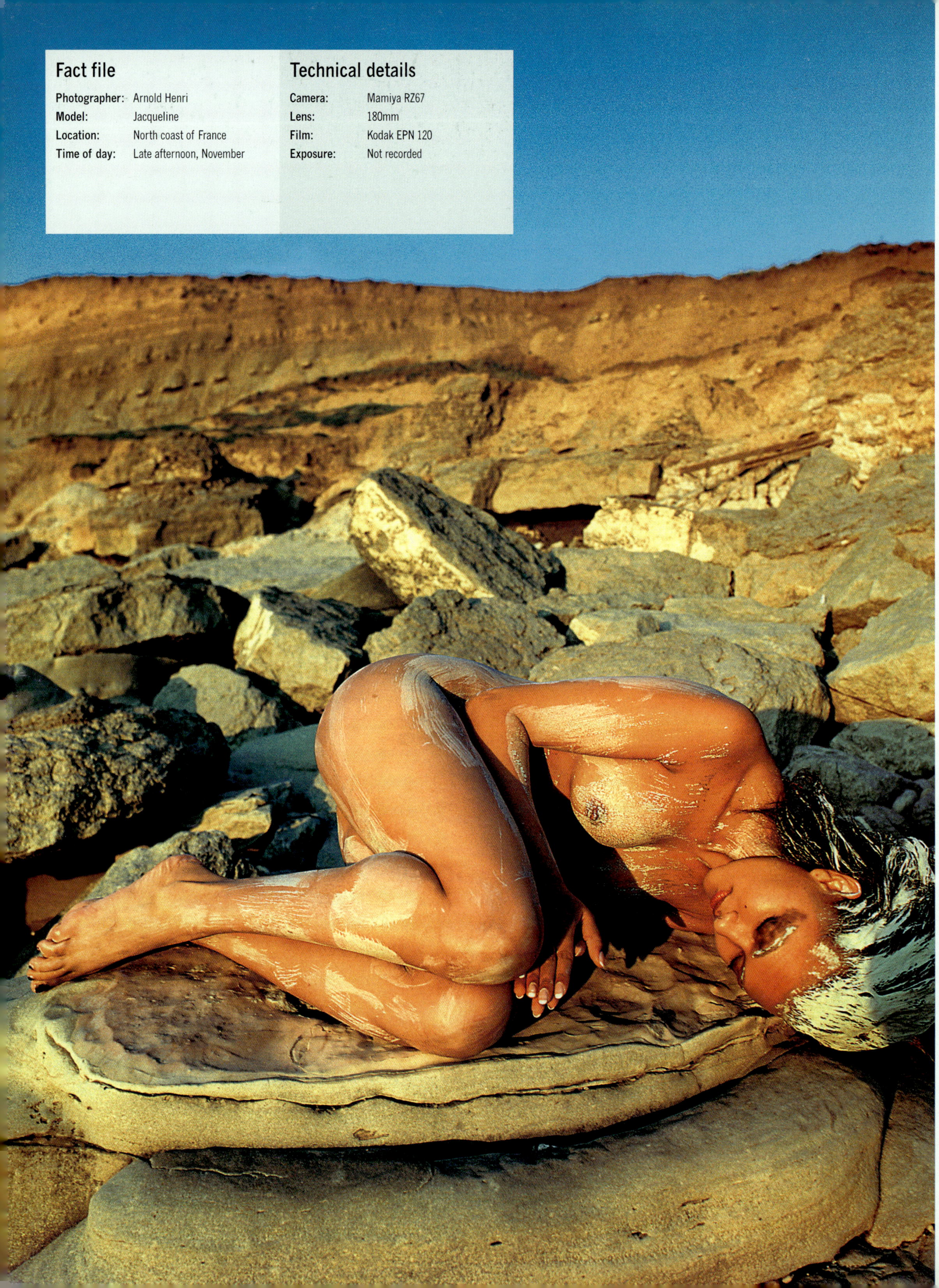

The concept

This was part of a calendar shoot that Arnold undertakes every year. In each shot, the model was given a kind of primitive look, with dry clay in her hair and sand on her body, to make her seem to blend in with her coastal surroundings.

The location

Based in Belgium, Arnold Henri knew this location in northern France from previous fashion shoots he had done there. 'There were several reasons why we used it here,' he says. 'It's only a couple of hours' drive away and has good access to the beach by car. That was essential for keeping the model warm in between shooting and handy for the lighting equipment. There were also few tourists around at that time of year.'

Composition

This image was inspired by the large flat rock, which was perfect to fit the curled-up figure of the model and especially attractive in the warm light. Arnold balanced the composition by placing the model in the bottom third of the frame, rocks in the middle and a contrasting band of blue sky in the top third.

Lighting and technique

A winter shoot in northern Europe is an unpredictable business and when there is a team of people involved, as there was for this calendar shoot, re-scheduling may not be practical so you're completely at the mercy of the weather. It also means much shorter days, of course, so faster work is often required. Arnold had no option but to shoot in November but he was extremely lucky with the light. As the sun dropped down to the horizon in the afternoon, it produced this wonderful golden glow on the model and the same tone on the surrounding rocks. No reflectors or filtration was necessary.

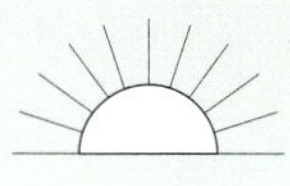

Low sun

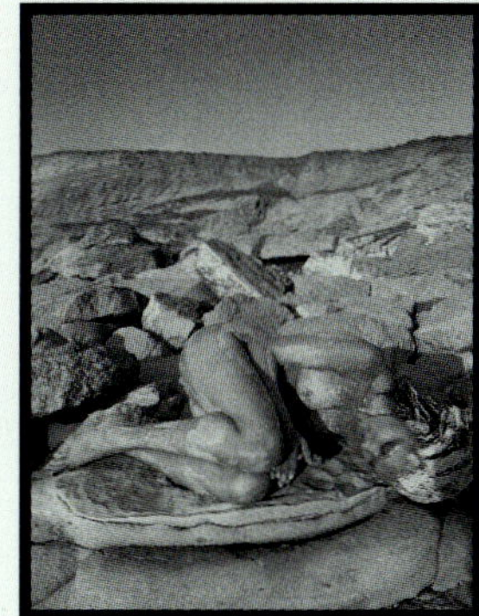

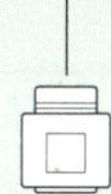

Medium format camera

Taken just a couple of hours earlier than the main picture (left), the difference in the colour of the light is very obvious. The model was in the shadow of the cliffs above her, so all the light on the scene is cold and harsh from the steel blue sky, reflected off the rocks around her. ❯

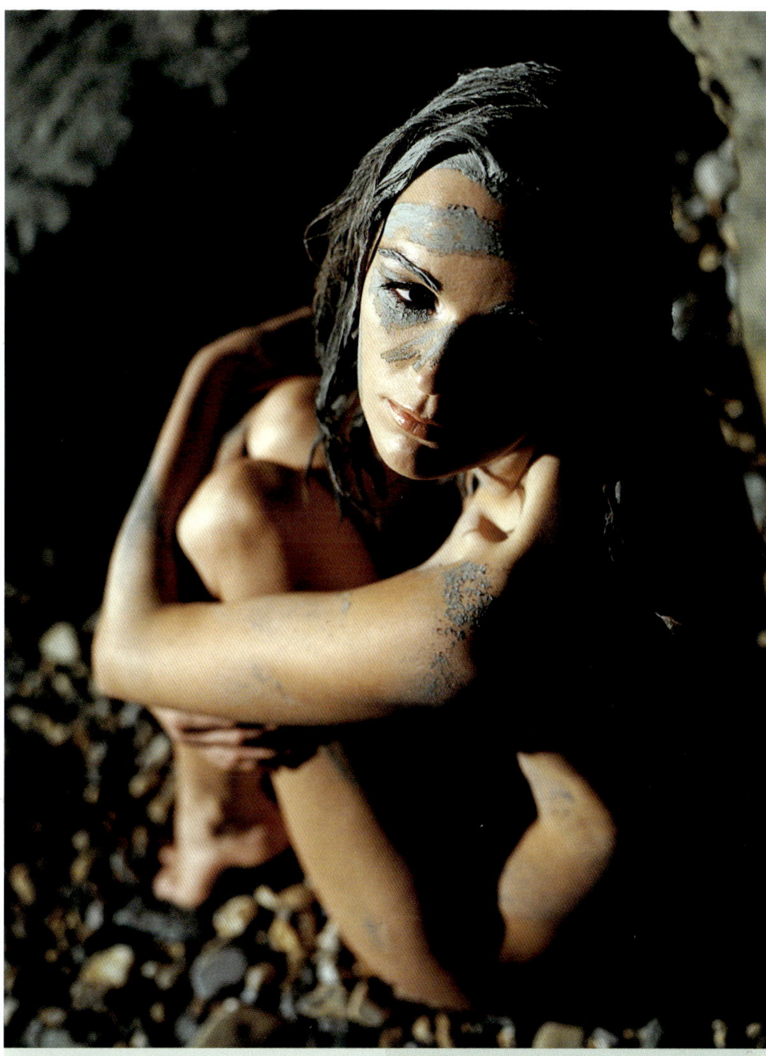

Fact file

Photographer: Arnold Henri
Model: Jacqueline
Location: North coast of France
Time of day: Early afternoon

Technical details

Camera: Mamiya RZ67
Lens: 110mm
Film: Kodak EPN 120
Exposure: Not recorded

' I don't always photograph the nude outside, but I like to use the contrast between a fragile human figure and harsh surroundings.'

Arnold Henri

Fact file

Photographer: Sylvie Blum
Model: Natalie
Location: Mallorca, Spain
Time of day: Early morning, August

Technical details

Camera: Hasselblad 500CM
Lens: 80mm
Film: Ilford FP4
Exposure: Not recorded

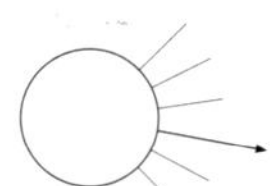

Low sun

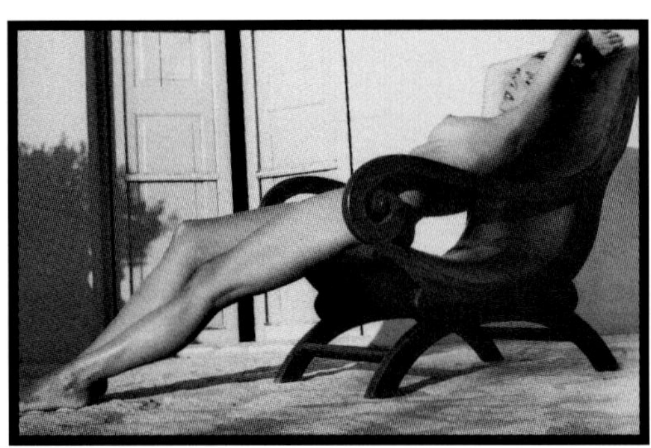

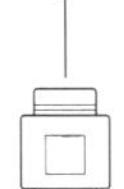

Medium format camera

The concept

'I was staying at a finca on the island of Mallorca and when I first saw this chair, I liked it so much I wanted to use it in a picture,' recalls Sylvie. 'The most important thing for me was to show the chair, but also not to hide the model's figure.'

The location

Sylvie has a skill in finding simple, accessible settings to make striking pictures. The all-important chair was inside the house she was staying in, but she moved it outside on to the terrace to make the warmth of the sunshine integral to the atmosphere of the shot.

Composition

'It wasn't easy finding a perfect position for both the model and the chair,' recalls Sylvie. 'I finally posed her stretched out to show the full length of her body, instead of following the lines of the chair. I wanted her expression to give the feeling that she was in a private, relaxed situation.' The shuttered doors in the background are also an important detail in the composition. Slightly ajar, they make the viewer wonder what is inside.

Lighting and technique

Because she was staying at the location, Sylvie was able to observe the lighting at different times of day to establish when she would get her desired effect. They began shooting just after sunrise so the light was very soft on the model, who was facing directly into it. Sylvie always takes several Polaroids to check the light and composition and then keeps the shoot with the real film as short as possible to keep the model's discomfort to a minimum.

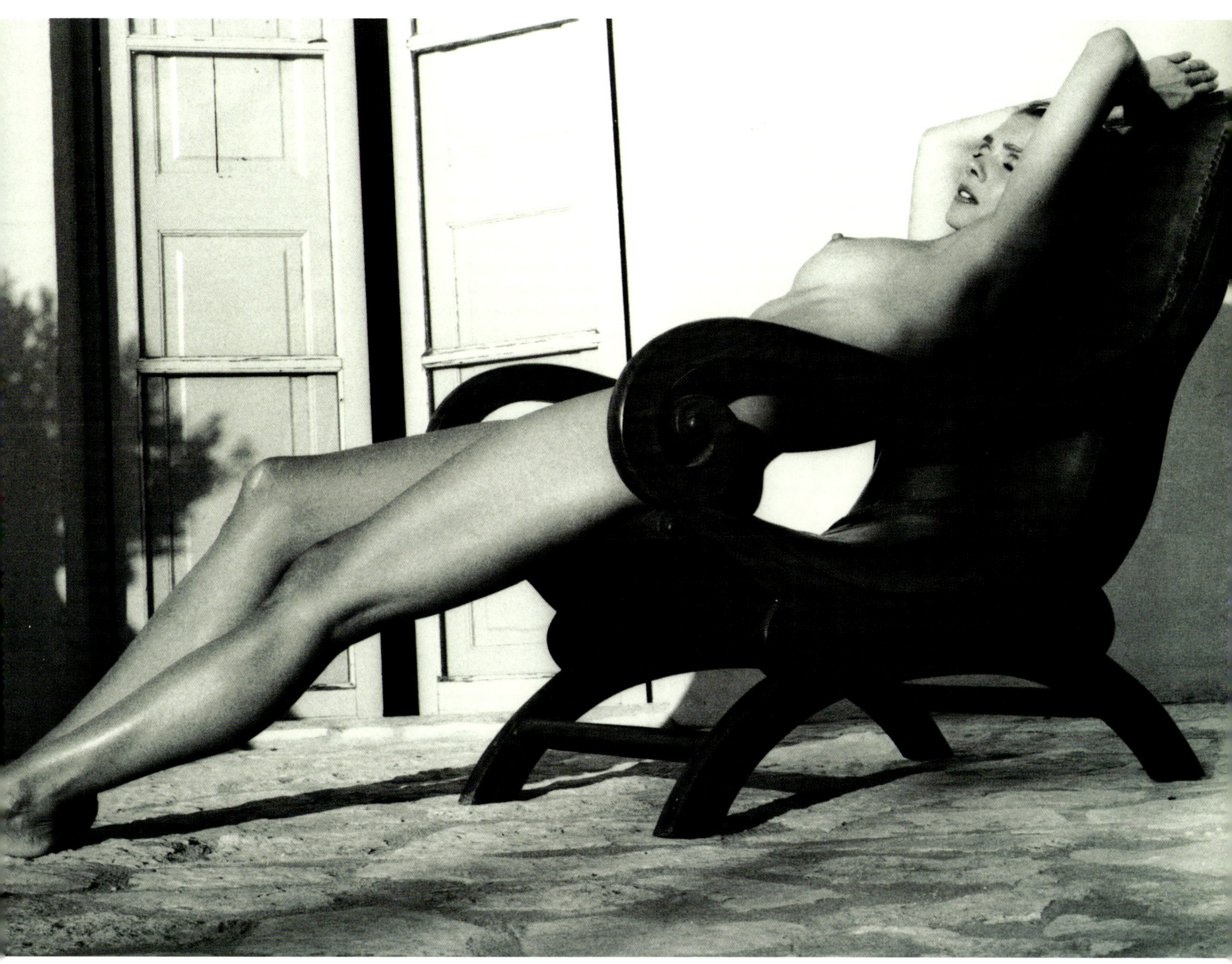

'I spend a lot of time in the darkroom, figuring out what I had in mind when I took the shot. I want my pictures to be timeless and I think the printing is as important as the shooting.'

Sylvie Blum

Chapter 3: **Close ups**

Nude photography can have a sense of identity, time and location, or it can abandon all those to concentrate on the form of the model with the environment taking second place. This section looks at the latter style, where the photographer has focused on the body in detail, in careful lighting, against a complimentary background.

Water and sand are effective choices for this; water enhances the fluidity of the body while the texture of sand contrasts with that of the skin. They also both possess reflective qualities and, perhaps most importantly, sensual connotations.

Close ups can also have a surprising subtlety to them, achieved in this section by images where selective focus has produced a dream-like and impressionistic feeling.

The concept

'I've been working on a series of personal creative pictures featuring women in close up with the sea in the background,' explains Manolis. 'I am based on the island of Crete and I find some of the lesser-known bays and beaches here a constant source of inspiration.'

The location

'This was taken on one of the beaches in Crete that remains completely unspoilt. I chose it for its beauty and tranquility,' he says.

Composition

The success of this image lies in its naturalness and simplicity and it works particularly well in black and white because of the subtle range of tones. Shooting close up and from a low angle, Manolis included only what was necessary in the frame, allowing space for the model's hair, spread out on the sand to echo the movement of the waves.

Lighting and technique

Manolis always photographs the nude using only natural light, either early in the morning or during the late afternoon when the effect of the sun is warmer and softer. The low sun was behind the model here, catching the top edge of her body and creating shadows on the camera side, which help define the contours of her torso and show the texture of the sand and water.

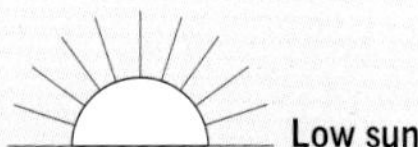

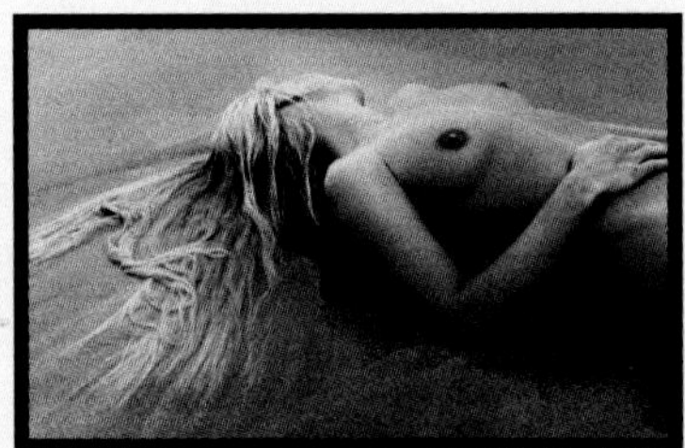

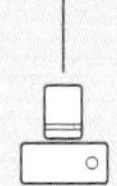

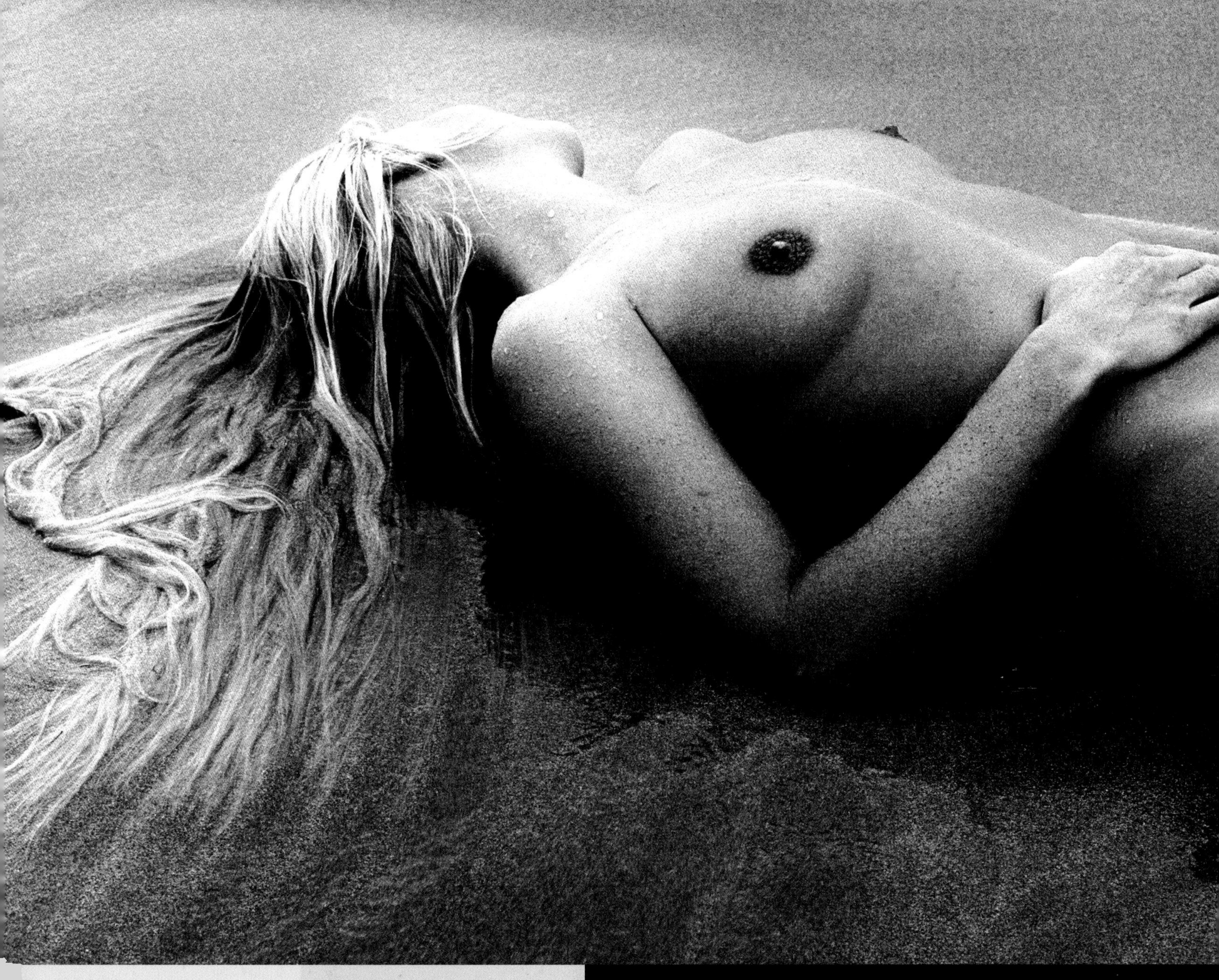

Fact file

Photographer: Manolis Tsantakis
Model: Anonymous
Location: Crete, Greece
Time of day: 5pm, September

Technical details

Camera: Nikon F3
Lens: 50mm
Film: Ilford HP5
Exposure: 1/60sec at f/16

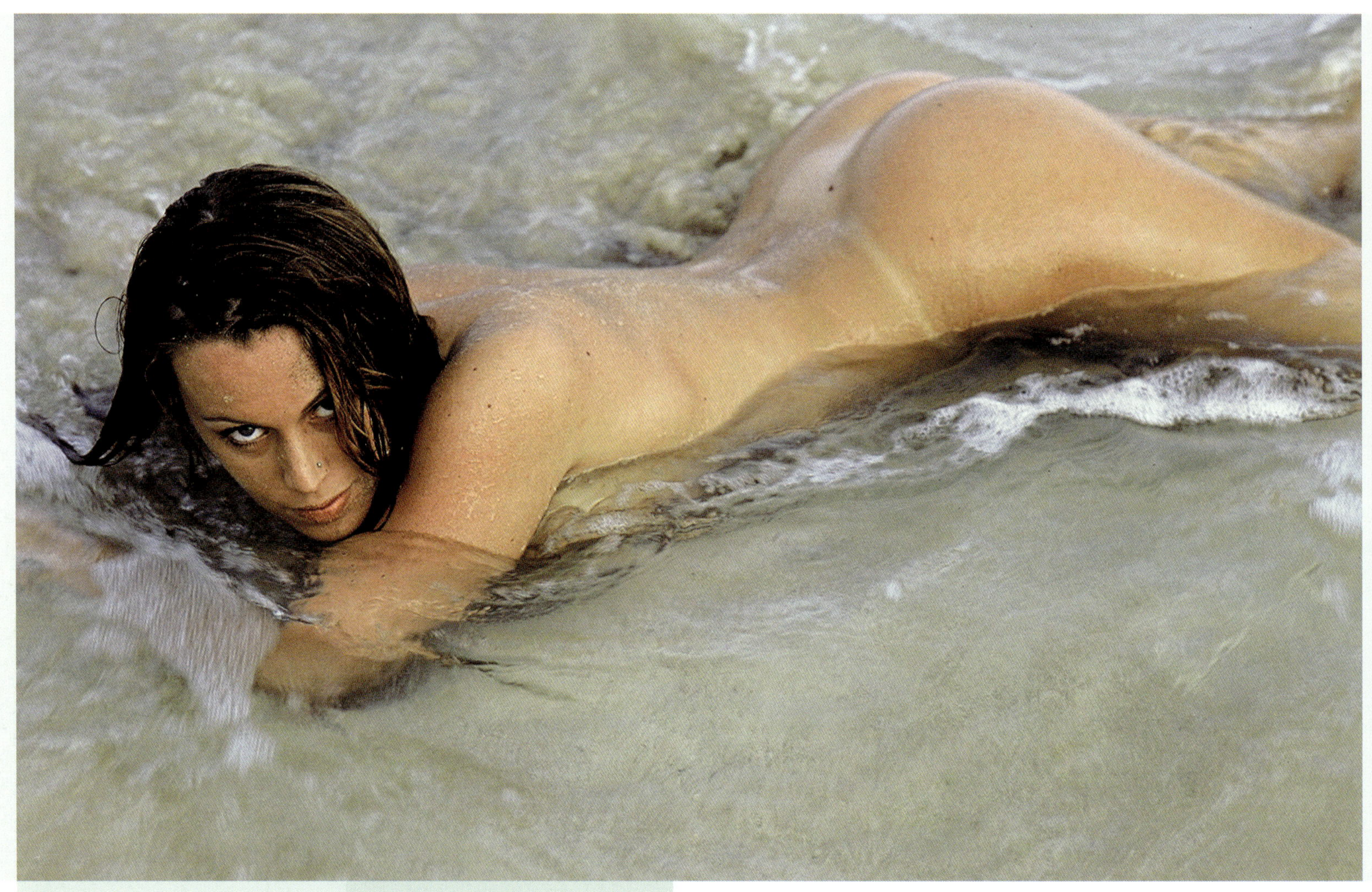

'I find it best to let the model take up positions she feels comfortable with and seem natural to her and then, if possible, I change only minor details.'

Rene de Haan

The concept

'I didn't have any particular ideas behind this picture,' says Rene. I went to the beach with the model and we tried out lots of different poses until we hit on something that worked. I liked the movement of the water here and the way that her eyes came out so strongly.'

The location

The beach has long been a favoured location for nude photography. It's a natural place to see the human body and the combination with sea and sand can be very sensual. Rene knows the island of Fuerteventura very well and has no problem finding quiet beaches and consistently good weather, even at the end of October.

Composition

As Rene says, the eye contact between the model and the viewer is very strong here, and quite unusual in nude photography where the model's face is often obscured, either for artistic reasons, or because he or she prefers to remain anonymous. The composition is nicely balanced, with sufficient water around her to provide negative space. Placing the model at a slight angle in the frame is also more interesting than if she had been completely horizontal.

Lighting and technique

It had been a warm and sunny day but by 7pm, when this was taken, the light was much softer, with no harsh shadows or unwanted reflections on the water. Rene didn't require any filters, flash or reflectors to take this image, just a 35mm camera, hand-held.

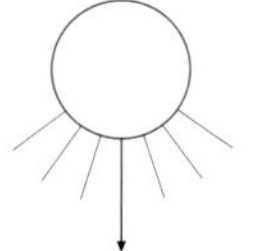

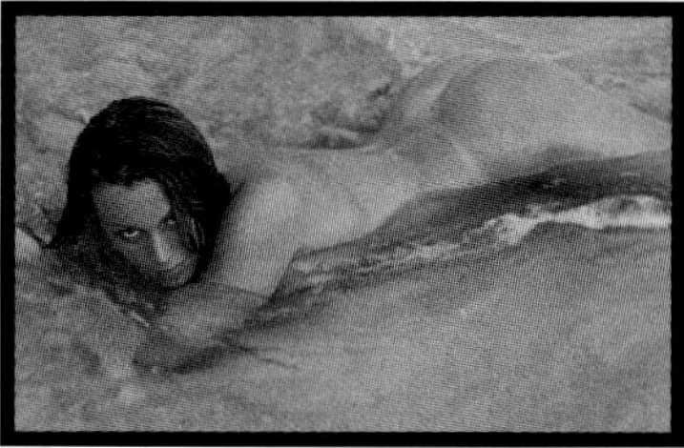

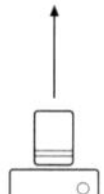

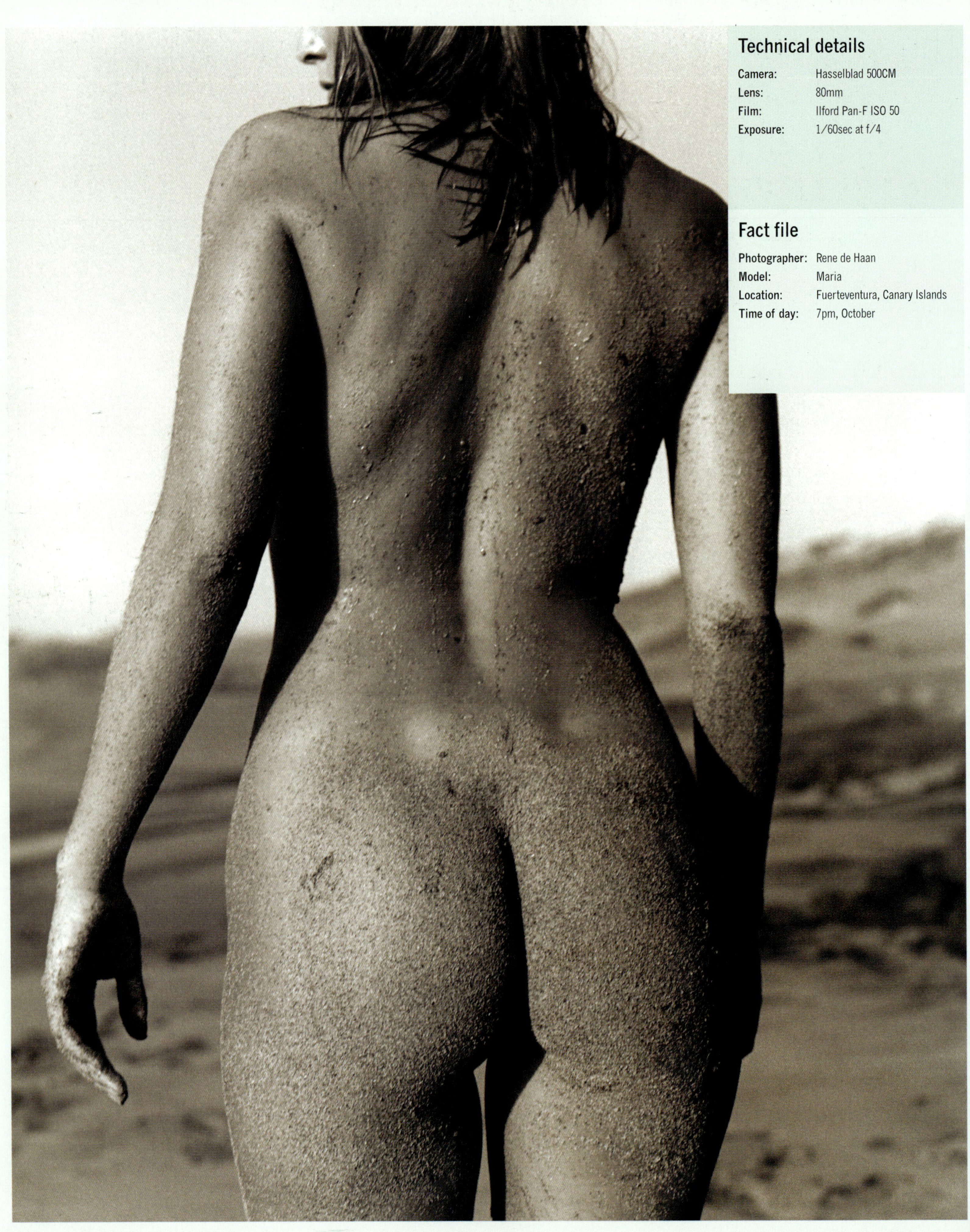
Technical details
Camera: Hasselblad 500CM
Lens: 80mm
Film: Ilford Pan-F ISO 50
Exposure: 1/60sec at f/4

Fact file
Photographer: Rene de Haan
Model: Maria
Location: Fuerteventura, Canary Islands
Time of day: 7pm, October

The concept

'I wanted a subtle eroticism and a natural feel,' says Rene. 'Sand, wet skin, a beautiful female body – it always works.'

The location

Rene made a special trip to the island of Fuerteventura for this shoot. The weather is still pretty reliable in October, when he went, and there are many quiet beaches where nude photography will not cause alarm or attract unwelcome spectators, particularly later in the day when the tourists have mostly disappeared.

Composition

Rene believes in keeping his images simple and this is a very classic pose. The close-up composition, cropped from the square 6x6cm format, concentrates entirely on the form, shape and texture of the model's body with just a little subtle information about the beach in the background. It demonstrates that strong, sensual images can be made with the minimum of artificiality.

Lighting and technique

Rene starts shooting in the late afternoon to benefit from the warm, soft light of the sun at that time. During summer, it leaves him with a few hours of usable, but changing light before sunset. Here the sun was behind and slightly to the right of the camera position, creating good modelling on the body and bringing out the texture of the sand on the skin.

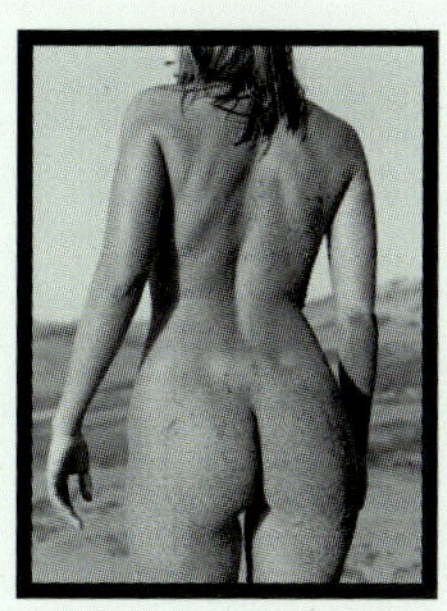

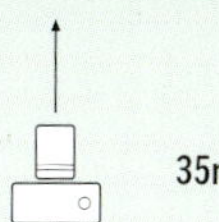

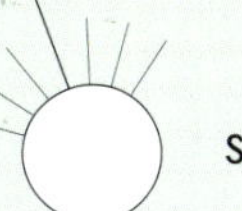

'Keep it simple. You don't always have to try to add a lot to a beautiful body.'

Rene de Haan

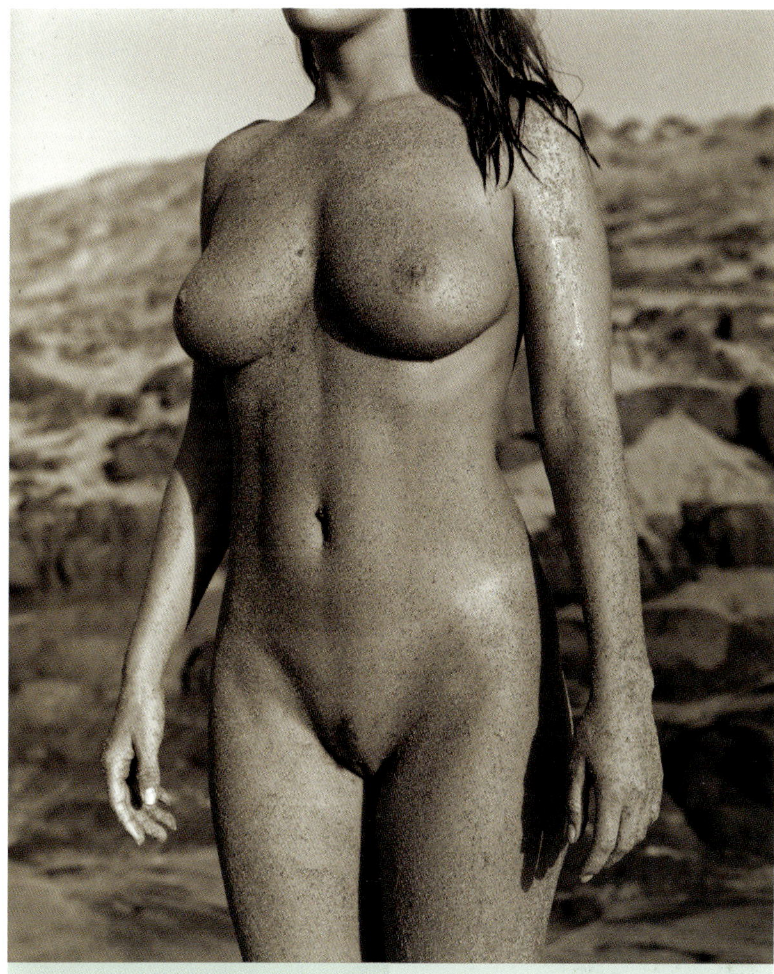

Technical details		Fact file	
Camera:	Hasselblad 500CM	Photographer:	Rene de Haan
Lens:	80mm	Model:	Maria
Film:	Ilford Pan-F ISO 50	Location:	Fuerteventura, Canary Islands
Exposure:	1/60sec at f/4	Time of day:	7pm, October

This is almost the exact reverse of Rene's other shot, taken shortly afterwards. Here, though, he has made more use of the rocks to add interest in the background, lining up the top of them with the model's shoulder height. Again, the warm evening light casts much softer shadows than the harder light earlier in the day.

Fact file

Photographer: Jonathan Charles
Model: Liz
Location: Near Chipstead, Kent, UK
Time of day: Early morning, July

Technical details

Camera: Olympus OM2
Lens: 100mm
Film: Kodachrome 25
Exposure: Not recorded

'Using the nearly horizontal morning sun as a side light creates very dramatic shadows and, unlike the midday down light – which is generally unflattering – the effect can enhance the smooth shapes of the body.'

Jonathan Charles

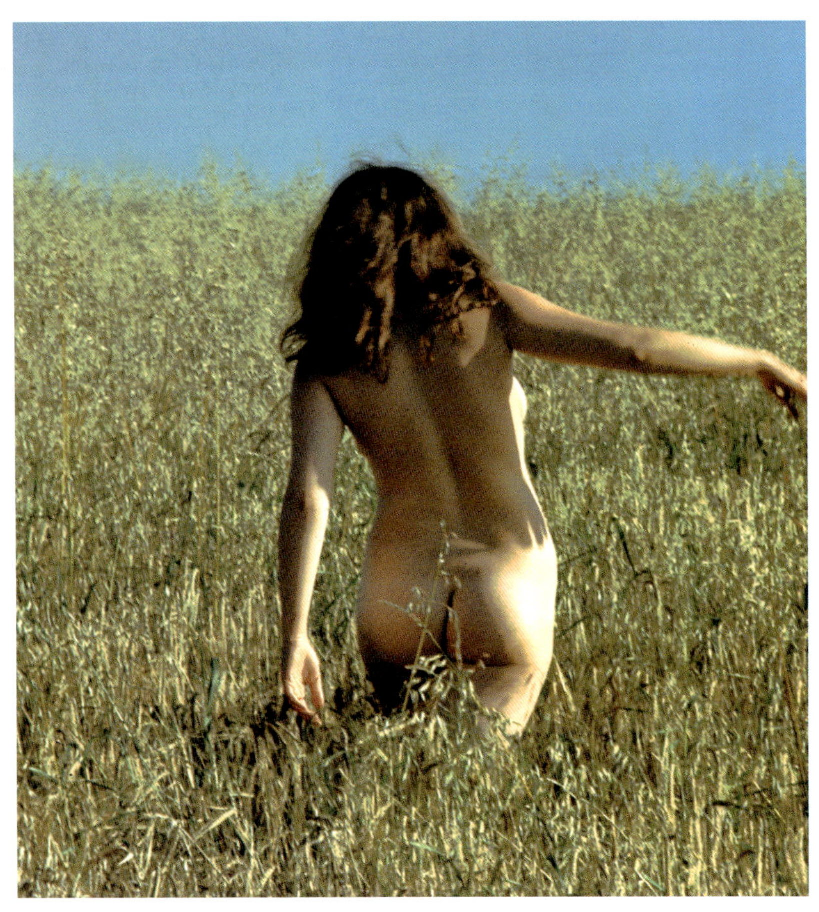

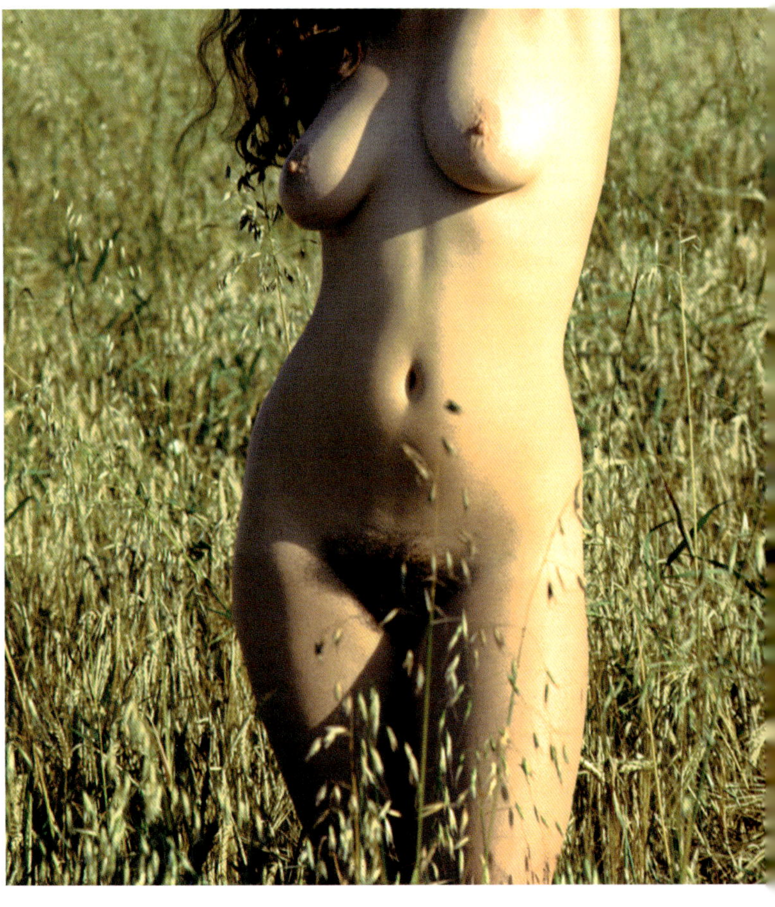

The concept

'I took this series of shots as Liz was dancing around in circles, to represent a feeling of freedom and enjoyment of the air and sunshine,' explains Jonathan.

The location

Jonathan and his model made an early morning trip to a hillside in Kent to take these pictures. He was attracted by the broad, uninterrupted sweep of the wheat field, which, with the blue sky, made a natural, textured background and provided the sense of space he was after.

Composition

'This is a simple, linear design, read from left to right,' says Jonathan. Each frame shows a different aspect of the model's body, getting progressively closer to the viewer, to make an unusual and arresting panel. There is symmetry in the way the middle two frames have purely the grass in the background, while those on the left and right each have a horizon line with a band of blue sky to add a touch of contrasting colour to the sequence.

Lighting and technique

Instead of using a zoom lens to frame each individual shot, Jonathan kept to a 100mm lens and stayed in roughly the same position while the model came closer. The idea was to capture the spontaneity of her spinning movements, although he didn't want her blurred and so used a fast shutter speed. The light was from the same direction in each frame – to the right of the camera at a low angle. This gives uniformity to the images and provides beautiful modelling on Liz's figure.

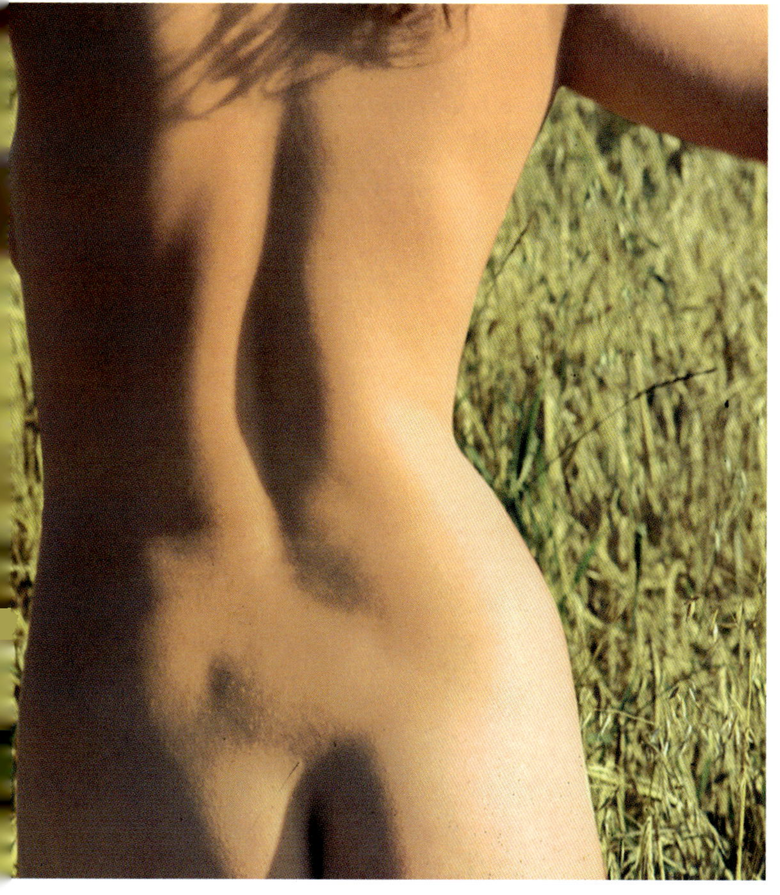
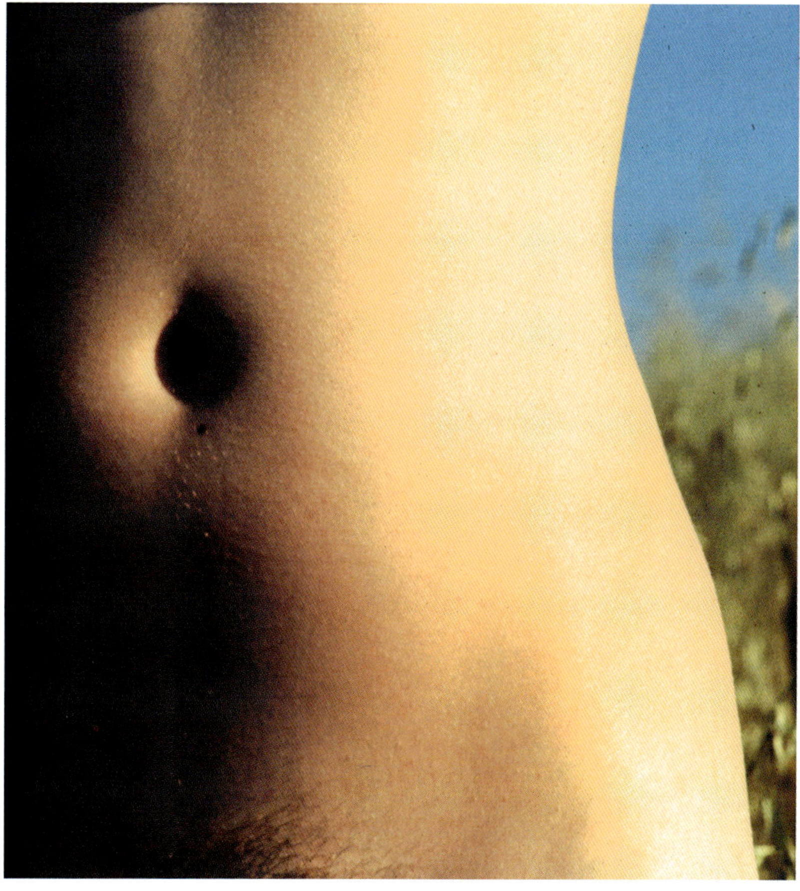

The concept

'I didn't have any great ideas behind this picture,' Rene admits. 'I don't think you can really go wrong if you keep it simple and work with a great model in beautiful natural light.'

The location

Because the sand is simply used as an undistracting background, this picture could have been taken on virtually any beach. Rene found it worthwhile to travel to Fuerteventura to undertake a whole series of shots because, while relatively quiet in October, the weather is pretty reliable and there are many beaches to choose from, offering a range of possibilities.

Composition

Rene's shot is without any kind of artifice and relies on its shapely subject matter for impact. It's helped a great deal, however, by the diagonal line of the figure across the frame, which gives the composition great strength and draws the eye along.

Lighting and technique

Rene began shooting at around 7pm when the sun was quite low, producing a soft light that was warm in tone. He positioned the model so the sun was behind her, which gives good modelling to the figure. Earlier in the day, when the light was harsher, the shadow areas would have been too deep and hard to produce this effect.

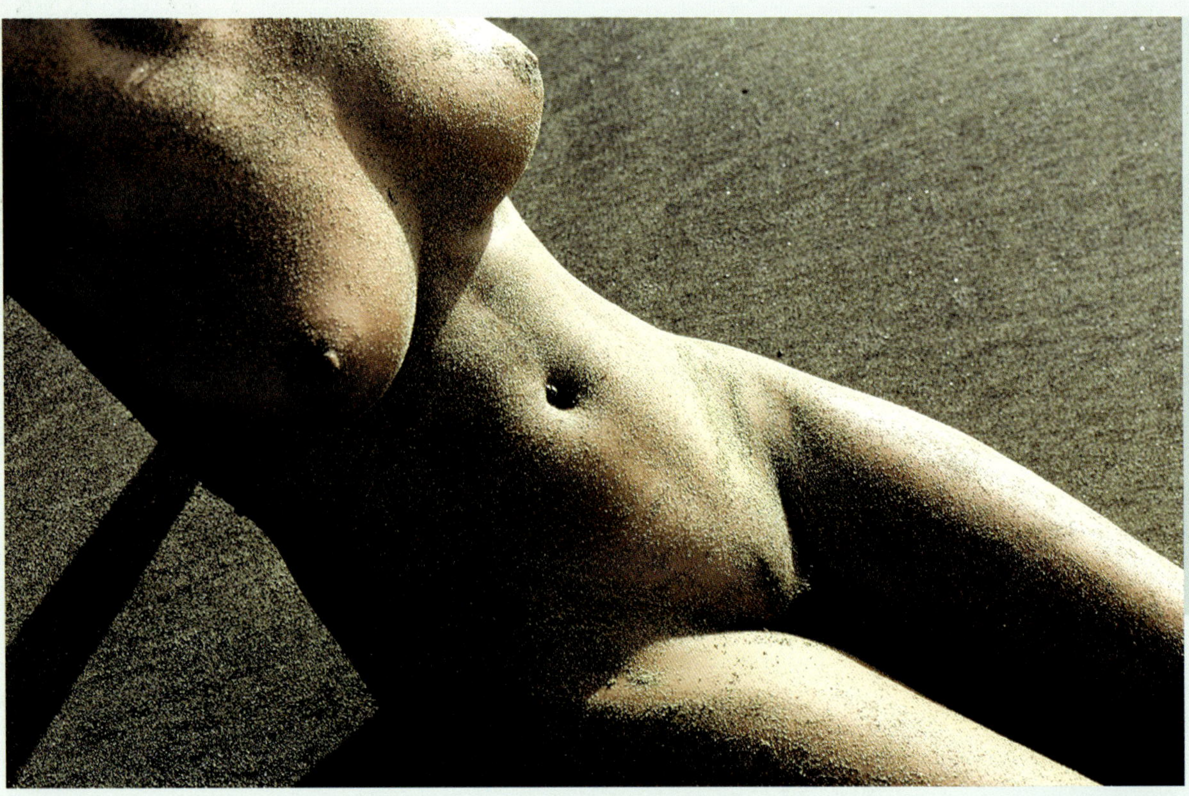

Fact file

Photographer: Rene de Haan
Model: Maria
Location: Fuerteventura, Canary Islands
Time of day: 7pm, October

Technical details

Camera: Canon A1
Lens: 85mm
Film: Fuji Velvia
Exposure: 1/60sec at f/5.6

'I like the texture of the skin and the sand in this picture. I think it makes the model look rather like a statue.'

Rene de Haan

Fact file

Photographer: Blake White
Model: Jasmine
Location: City park, Colorado Springs, USA
Time of day: Mid-morning, August

Technical details

Camera: Olympus 3020 (digital)
Lens: 32–96mm
Film: n/a
Exposure: 1/500sec at f/2.8

This intimate close up was taken in strong natural daylight, slightly diffused by light cloud cover. Blake used a three megapixel digital camera which he finds gives him good quality images if he prints them at 5x7 or 10x8 inches. He often uses Photoshop to make minor 'tweaks' but in this case he made no adjustments. ⤓

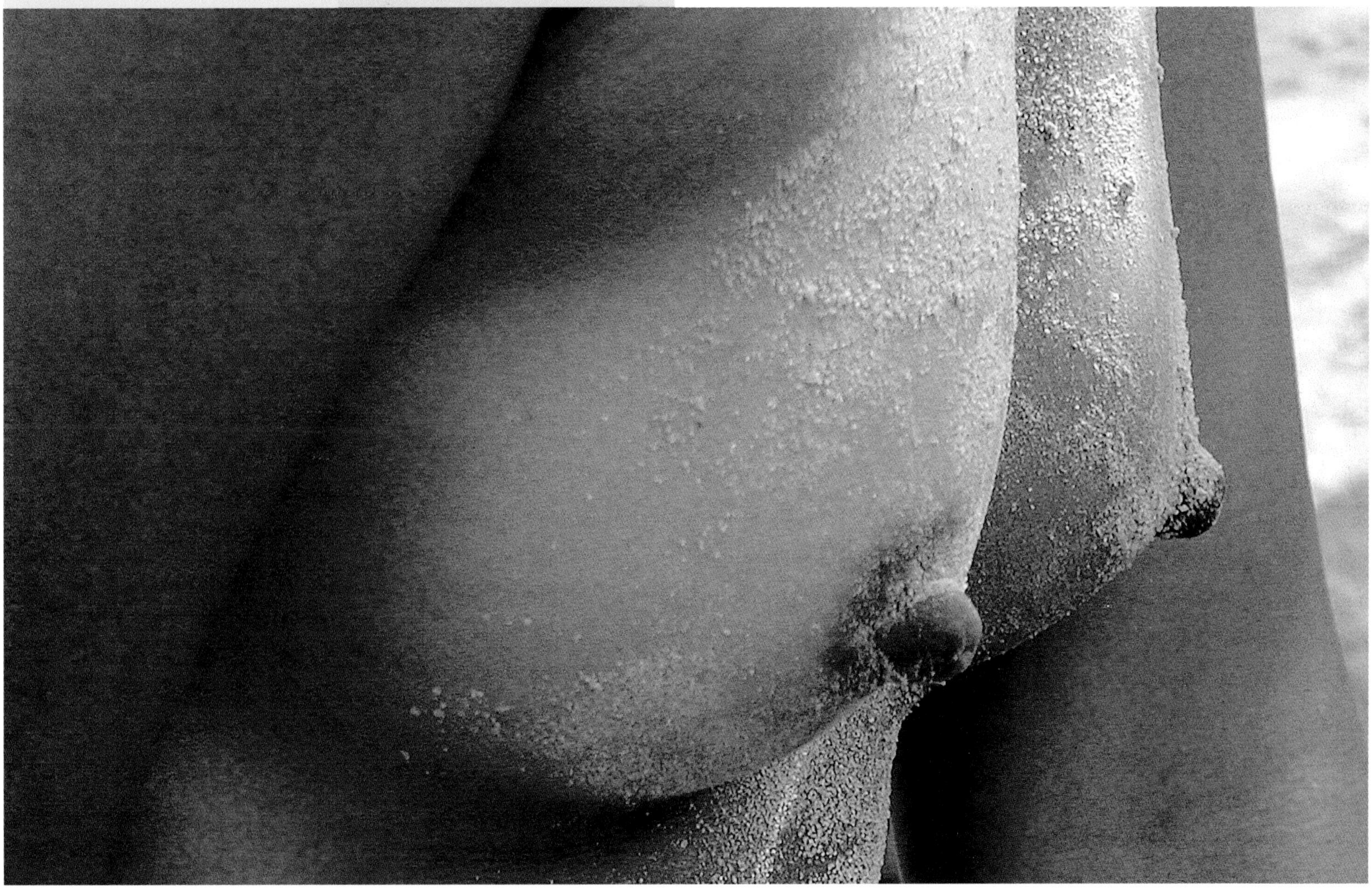

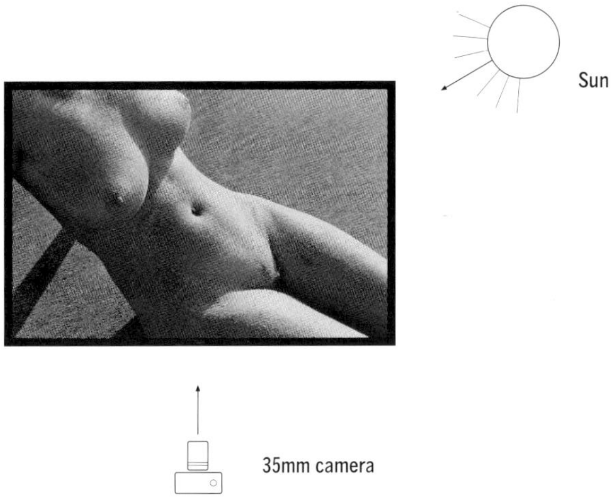

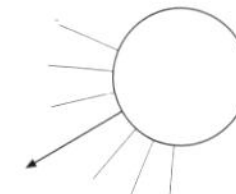

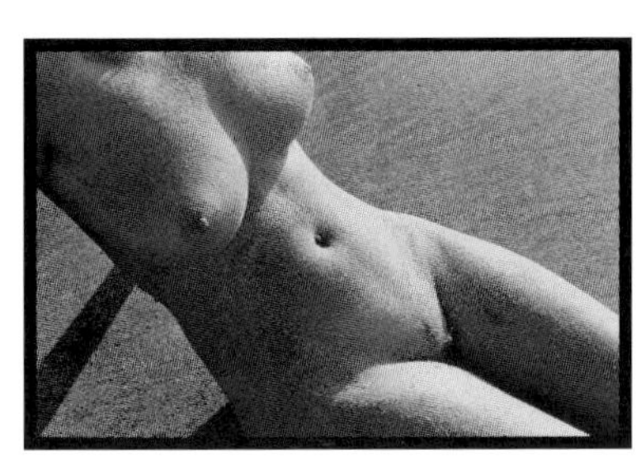

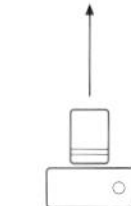

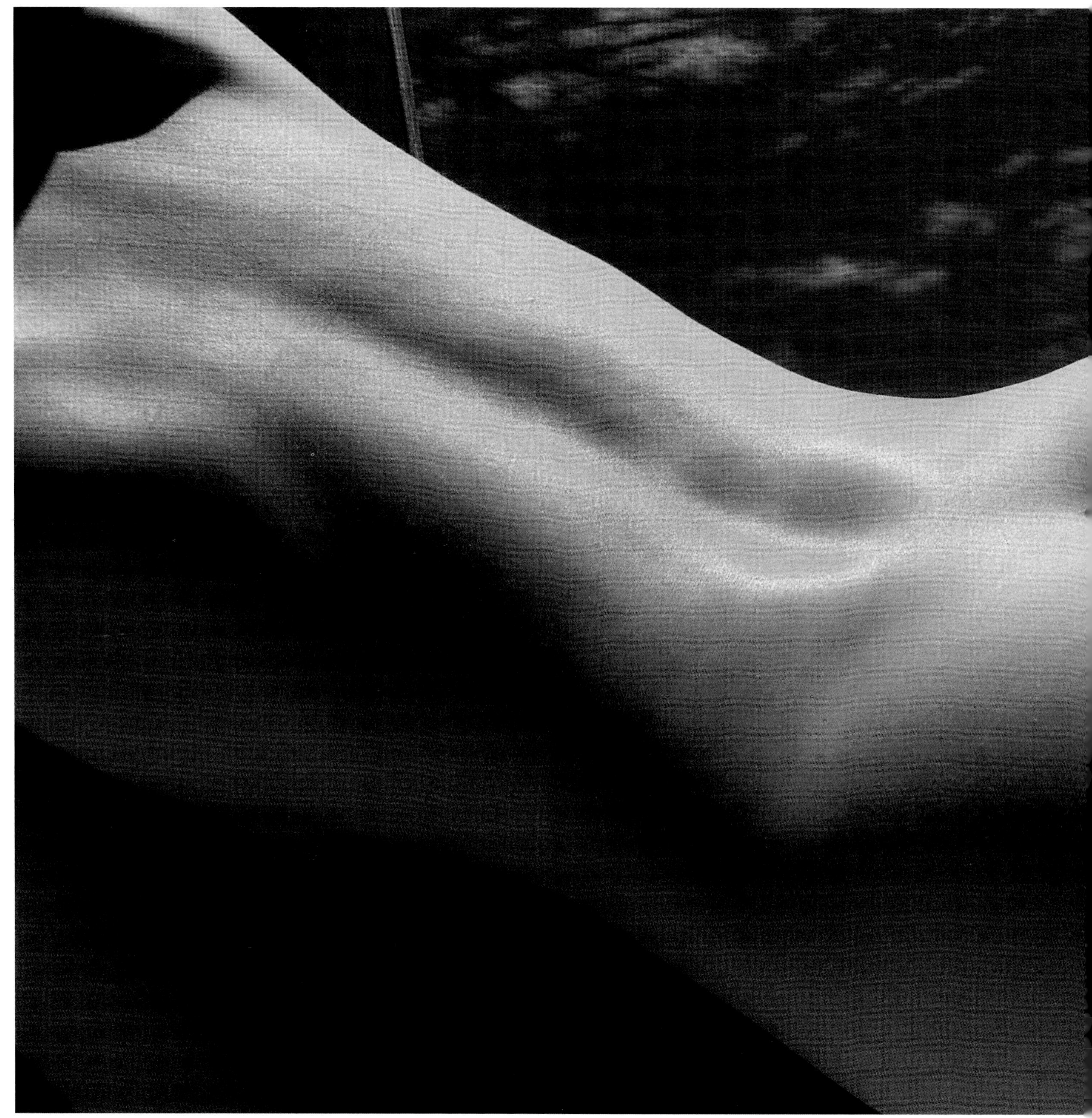

'The negative space is important here. The way the shadow line and area complements the background line and area is a strong design element.'

Joris van Daele

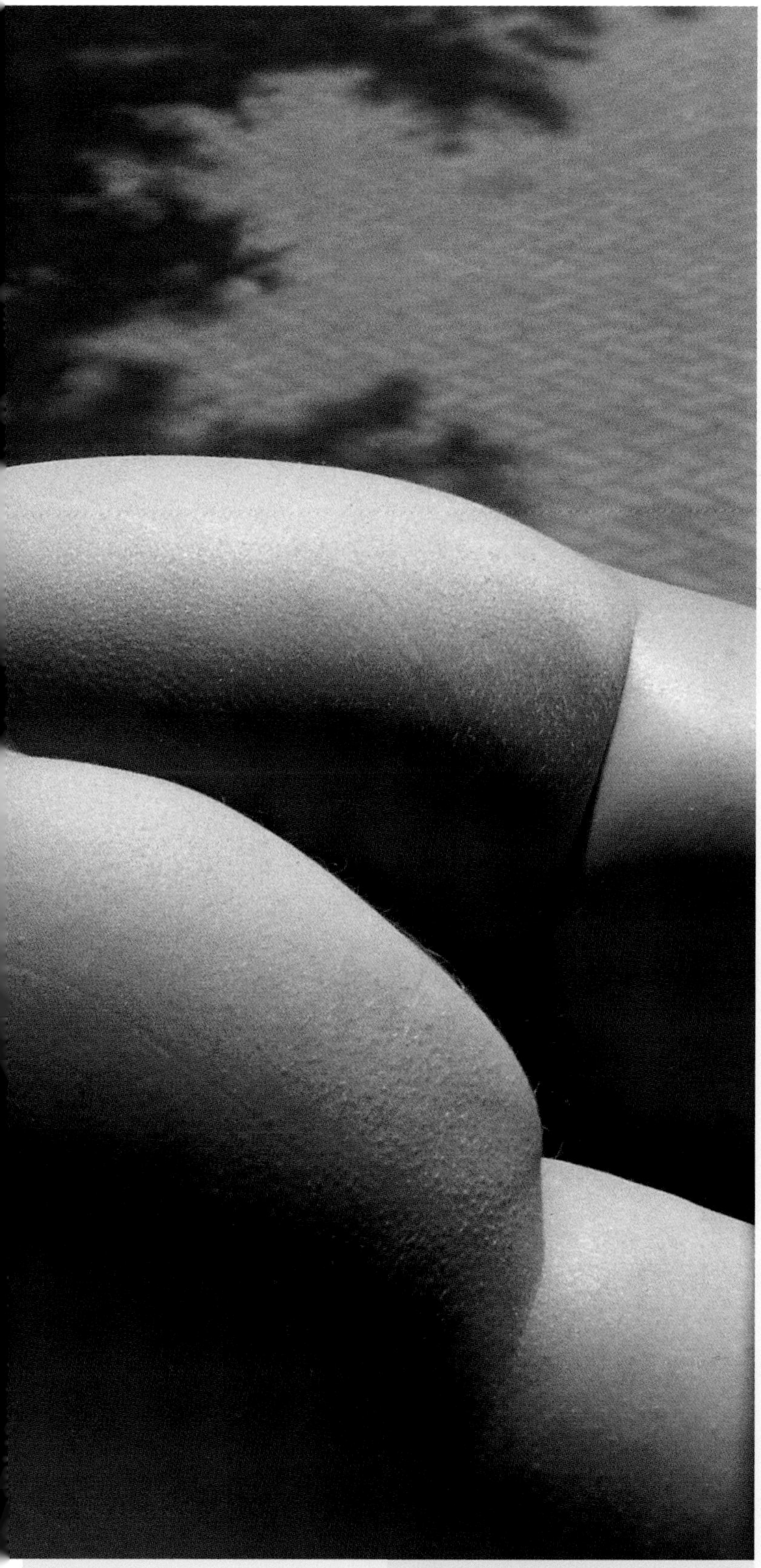

The concept

'I am collecting images for a book of nudes of professional dancers and athletes and Hope is a dancer from the USA who came to Ontario for this session with me,' explains Joris van Daele. 'She had done some lively dance gestures which I had photographed but I wanted an image in the figure-style which I often exhibit.'

The location

Joris chose an old mansion on an estate in London, Ontario for the shoot. 'I hardly ever use a studio lately as spaces like these add atmosphere and interest to my work,' he says. Here, Hope was lying on the outside ledge of a south-facing window, with Joris taking the picture from the other side of the open window, inside.

Composition

'The framing of this image was dictated by the overall light-dark balance, negative spaces and repetition of the 'C' and 'S' curves which are so strong. The dividing shadow line was the most important to me and I framed carefully so that the weight of this darker area would not overwhelm this otherwise high-key moment,' Joris explains.

Lighting and technique

Joris balanced the indoor and outdoor light with a large, flexible reflector, placed inside the window, from the floor up to the height of the ledge at a slight angle. This lowered the extreme lighting range and softened the shadow on the lower side of the model's body. He asked her to adjust her position until her entire back was directly lit by the hard sunlight. The print was made with a little burning-in of the background as much of this was in sunlight, and too bright on the test print.

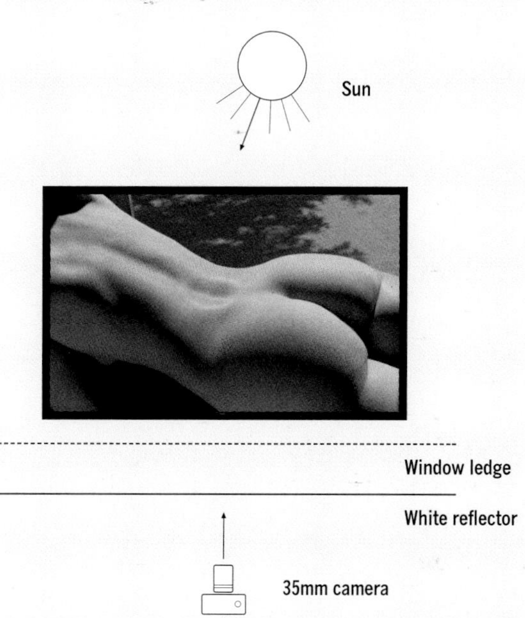

Fact file

Photographer:	Joris van Daele
Model:	Hope
Location:	Estate, Ontario, Canada
Time of day:	1pm, September

Technical details

Camera:	Canon AE2
Lens:	38–135mm
Film:	Kodak T-Max 400
Exposure:	1/250sec at f/11

The concept

Walo Thönen was teaching a group of photographers at a workshop during a photographic holiday and he took this picture as a demonstration of the impact of going in close on the subject.

The location

The group were staying at a finca in Ibiza and taking pictures in the grounds of the property, as well as elsewhere on the island. This image was taken during a shoot at the finca's swimming pool, which was ideal for close ups using water.

Composition

The water was still pretty cold at 10am and so Walo had to work quickly. He had the idea for the composition before the model entered the pool so he could direct her into this pose, rather than look for the right shot once she was in there. The strong diagonal line of her body has much greater impact than if she had been horizontal to the camera.

Lighting and technique

The lighting came purely from the bright sunshine reflecting off the surface of the swimming pool. Walo shoots with slide film and then uses Photoshop on the computer to make small adjustments and he has these in mind as he takes the picture. The shadow area in the top left-hand corner of the image was the wall of the swimming pool, which he darkened further in Photoshop. He also doubled the layer of the image, added blur to one layer and then sandwiched the layers together to give a slight softness to the model's body and the water.

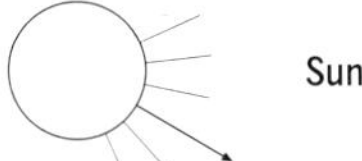

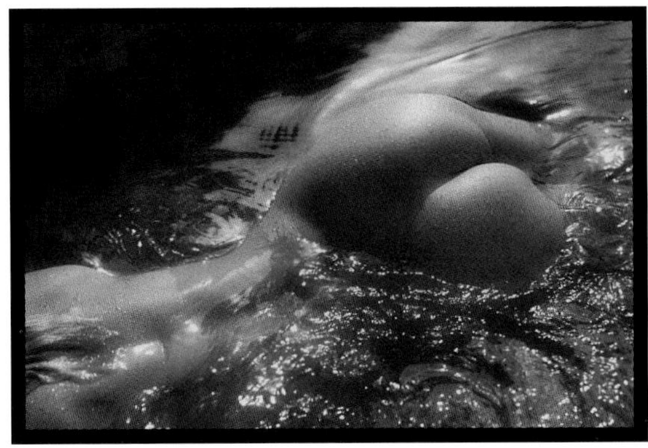

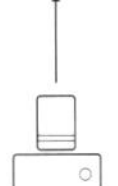

Fact file

Photographer: Walo Thönen
Model: Carina
Location: Ibiza, Spain
Time of day: Mid-morning, May

Technical details

Camera: Nikon F100
Lens: 50mm
Film: Fuji Sensia 100
Exposure: Aperture priority at f/8

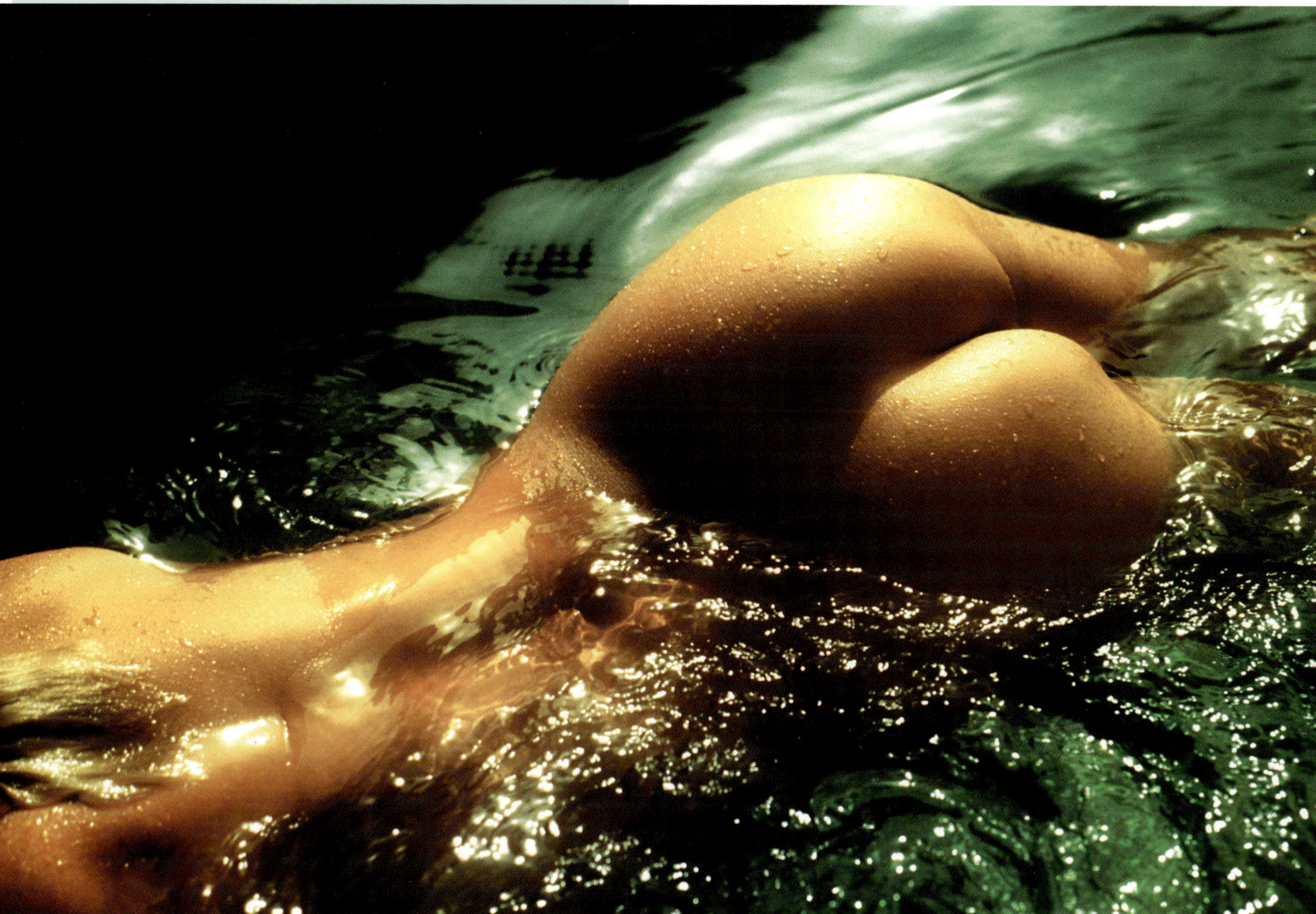

'There are so many ugly pictures to see every day, I like to show the good things about people.'

Walo Thönen

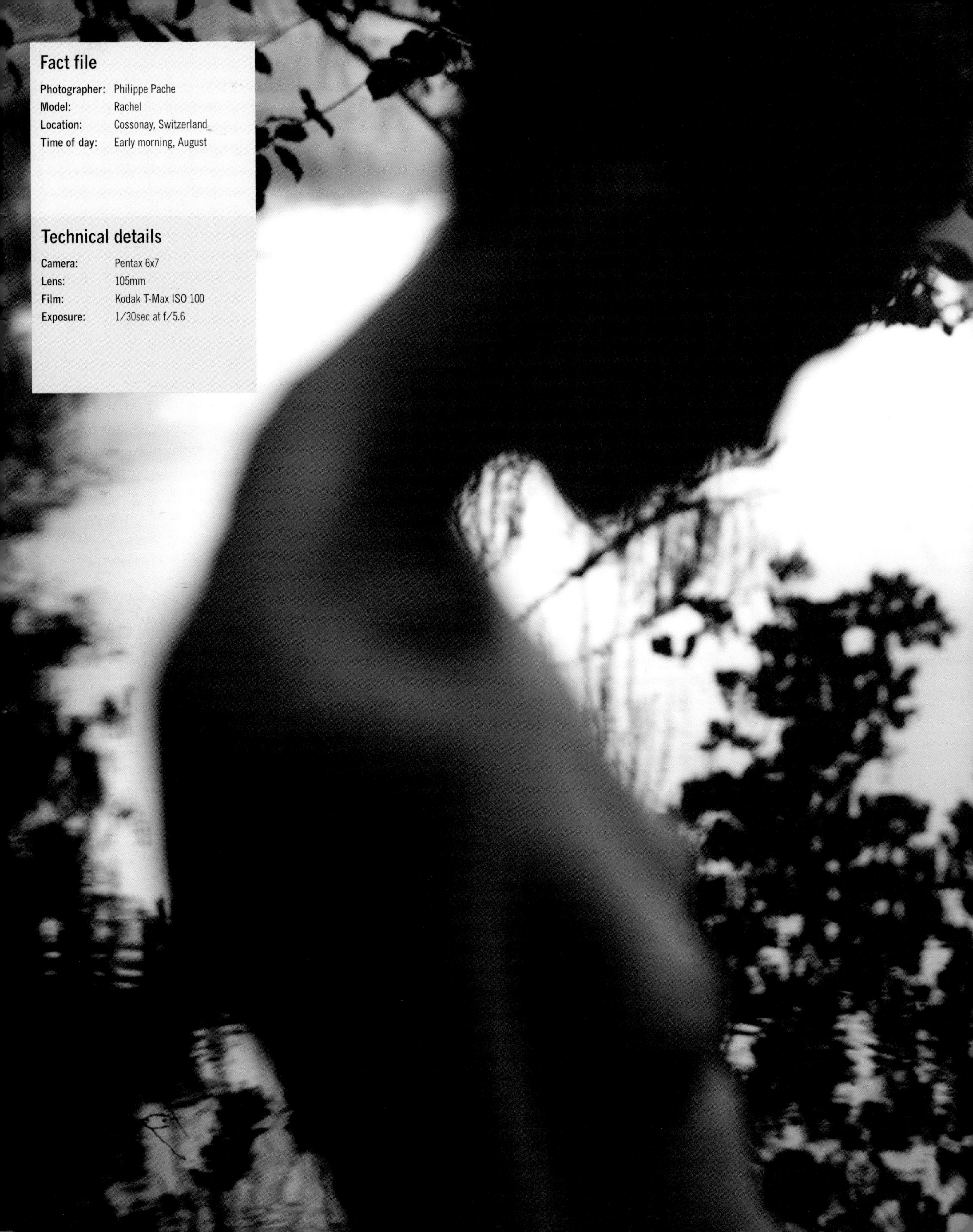

Fact file

Photographer: Philippe Pache
Model: Rachel
Location: Cossonay, Switzerland
Time of day: Early morning, August

Technical details

Camera: Pentax 6x7
Lens: 105mm
Film: Kodak T-Max ISO 100
Exposure: 1/30sec at f/5.6

The concept

Philippe didn't have a set idea of the precise image he wanted to take away from this shoot but he did want to convey a poetic feeling of a human being as part of the surrounding nature, rather than an image of a beautiful woman. It was taken purely as a personal picture, although later bought by Dior Parfums for use in a catalogue.

The location

'I love this wonderful little lake, l'étang du Sépey, and I came with this model, with whom I work quite often,' says Philippe. The still water, surrounded by plants and foliage provided the calm, natural atmosphere he wanted for the image.

Composition

While placing the model close up and centrally in the frame, Philippe has created an impression of a woman rather than a portrait of her, through the lighting and soft focus. This is counterbalanced by the relative sharpness of the delicately-shaped foliage at the top of the image and the reflections on the water which place her in a real context and prevent the whole image from appearing blurred and smudgy.

Lighting and technique

This was taken early on a rainy morning using only natural light. The weak, overcast sun was behind the model, leaving her face in shadow to add to the sense of mystery. Using a 105mm lens close up, Philippe focused on the leaves behind the model, and the shallow depth of field rendered her out of focus. The final print was selenium toned to improve its archival qualities.

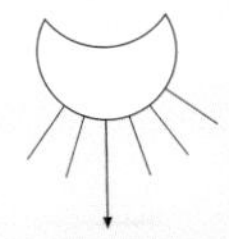

Sun behind clouds

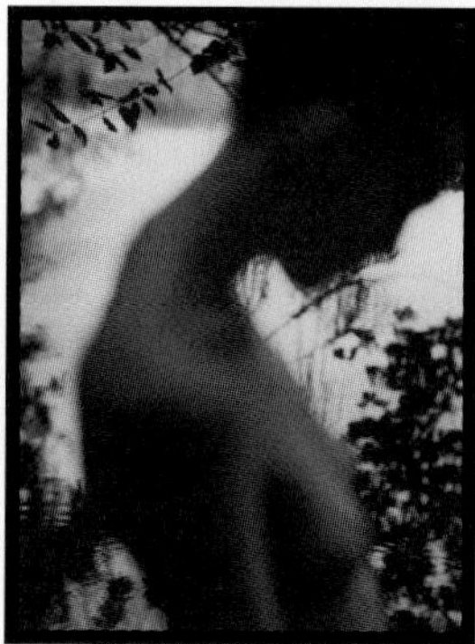

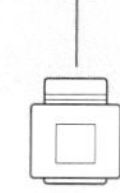

Medium format camera

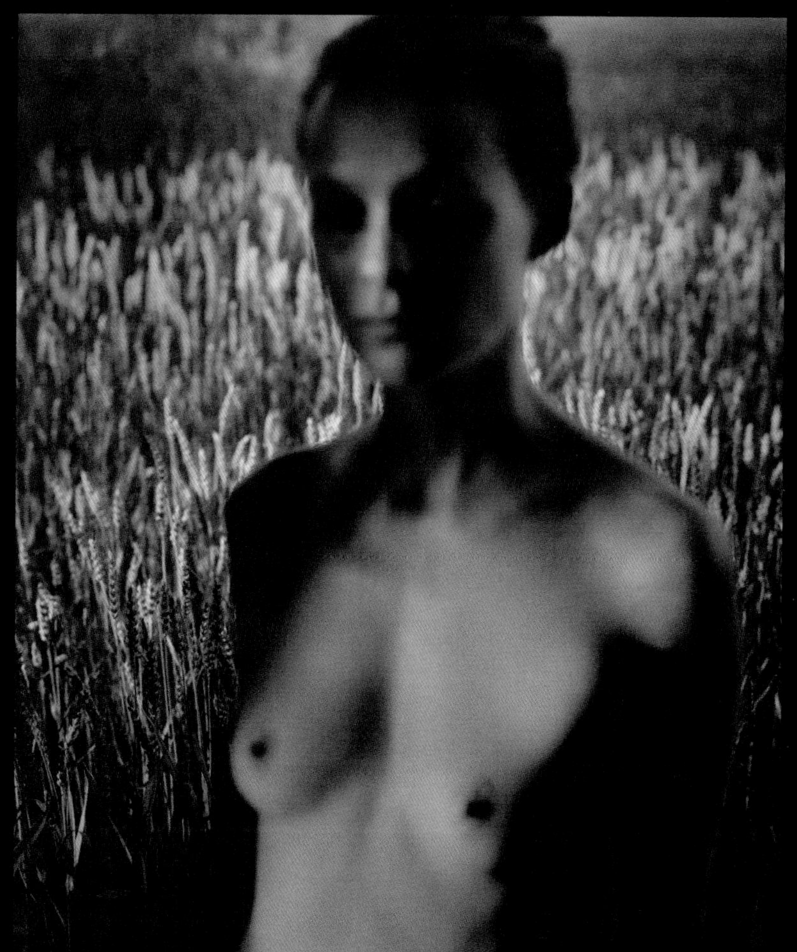

Fact file		Technical details	
Photographer:	Philippe Pache	**Camera:**	Pentax 6x7
Model:	Rachel	**Lens:**	105mm
Location:	Vevey, Switzerland	**Film:**	Kodak T-Max 100
Time of day:	Late afternoon, July	**Exposure:**	1/60sec at f/5.6

Just before sunset, the last rays of light were filtering on to the model through a tree behind the camera. Again Philippe focused on the background rather than the model to convey the sense that she is an apparition.

'I never have an exact idea of the image I would like to do, it just comes from the emotion of the moment. I like mystery, and that is what I look for in all my photographs.'

Philippe Pache

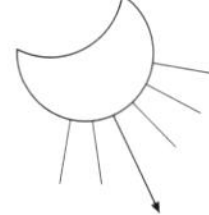

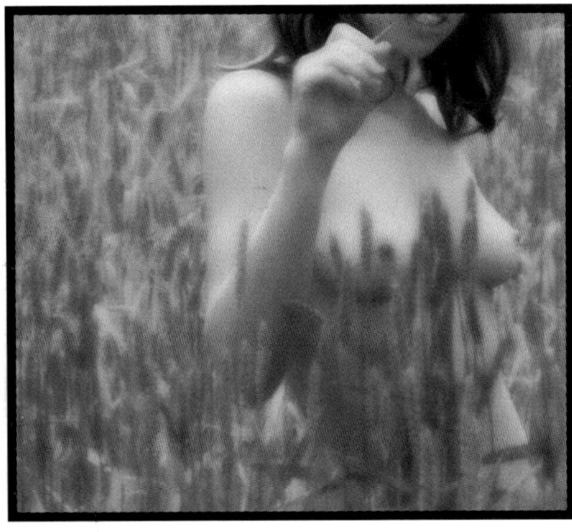

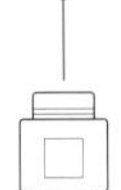

The concept

'This wasn't a planned shot at all,' says Jonathan. 'It was taken during a spontaneous moment and it was just lucky that I had my camera with me.'

The location

Jonathan was spending a day in the country with his girlfriend and this field of barley wasn't chosen for its photographic potential but as a pleasant place to relax in the sun.

Composition

The original image was taken with a 28mm lens and included all of the model as well as the surrounding landscape. Jonathan cropped it quite dramatically with Photoshop to make the picture more abstract and timeless in its appeal. He also added the appearance of selective focus – as though he had used a narrow depth of field to keep the model in focus, but blur the foreground. This was done by using a softening filter in Photoshop on the barley. 'The grasses were moving slightly in the breeze when I took the picture, but I couldn't get a long enough exposure to show this and so they looked a little sharp and obtrusive on the original image,' he explains.

Lighting and technique

'The light was from a slightly overcast sky, giving a very soft, even illumination which is particularly good for showing the delicate tones of fair skin,' says Jonathan. 'The colour cast tends to be slightly blue, but this can be compensated for by using a warm-up filter or, as in this case, by shifting the colour balance slightly with Photoshop.'

'With Photoshop you can re-create the effect that you saw and the feeling you had when you took the picture, rather than being limited to the way the camera captured it. If you haven't got the right light originally, though, you can't invent it on a computer.'

Jonathan Charles

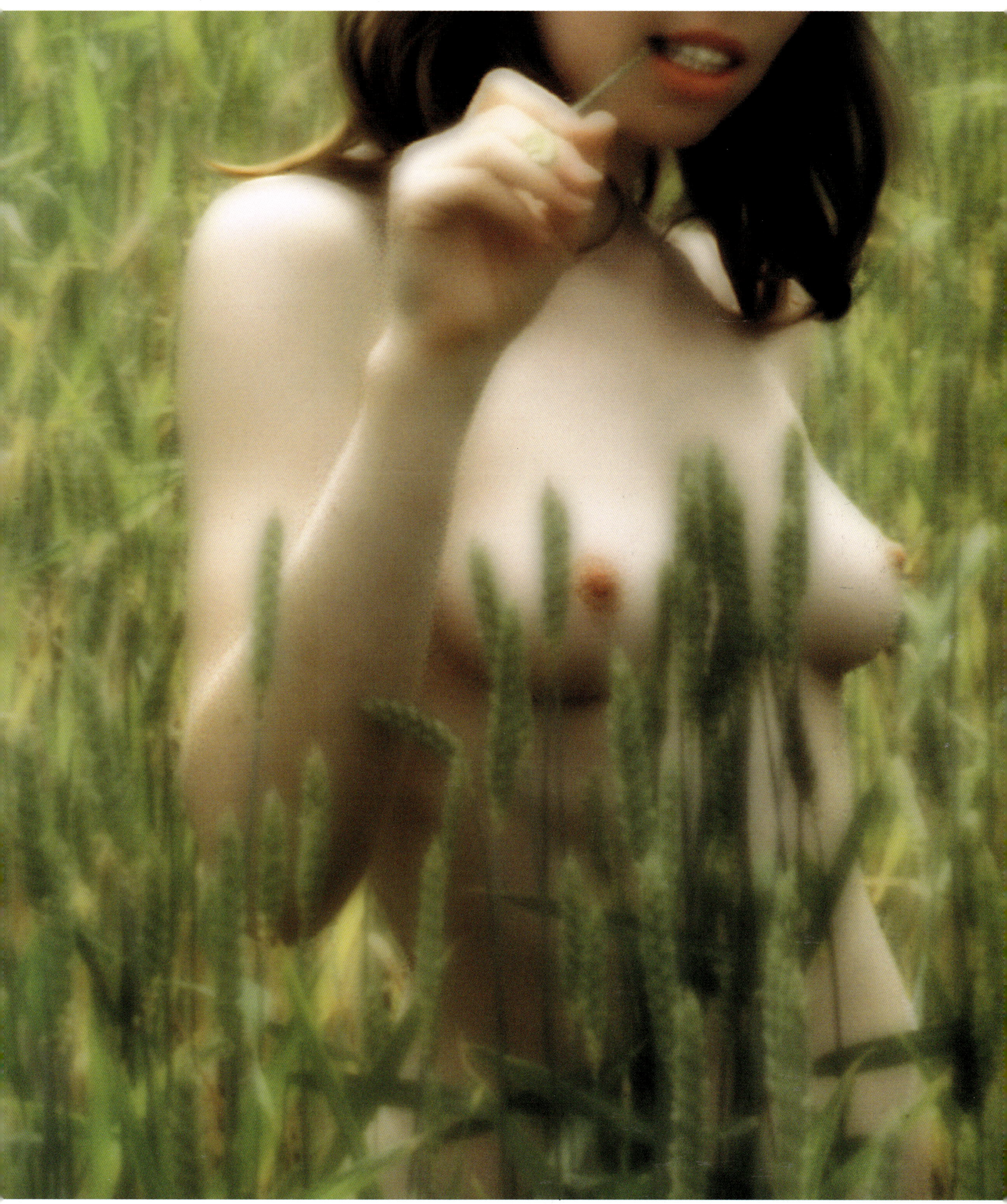

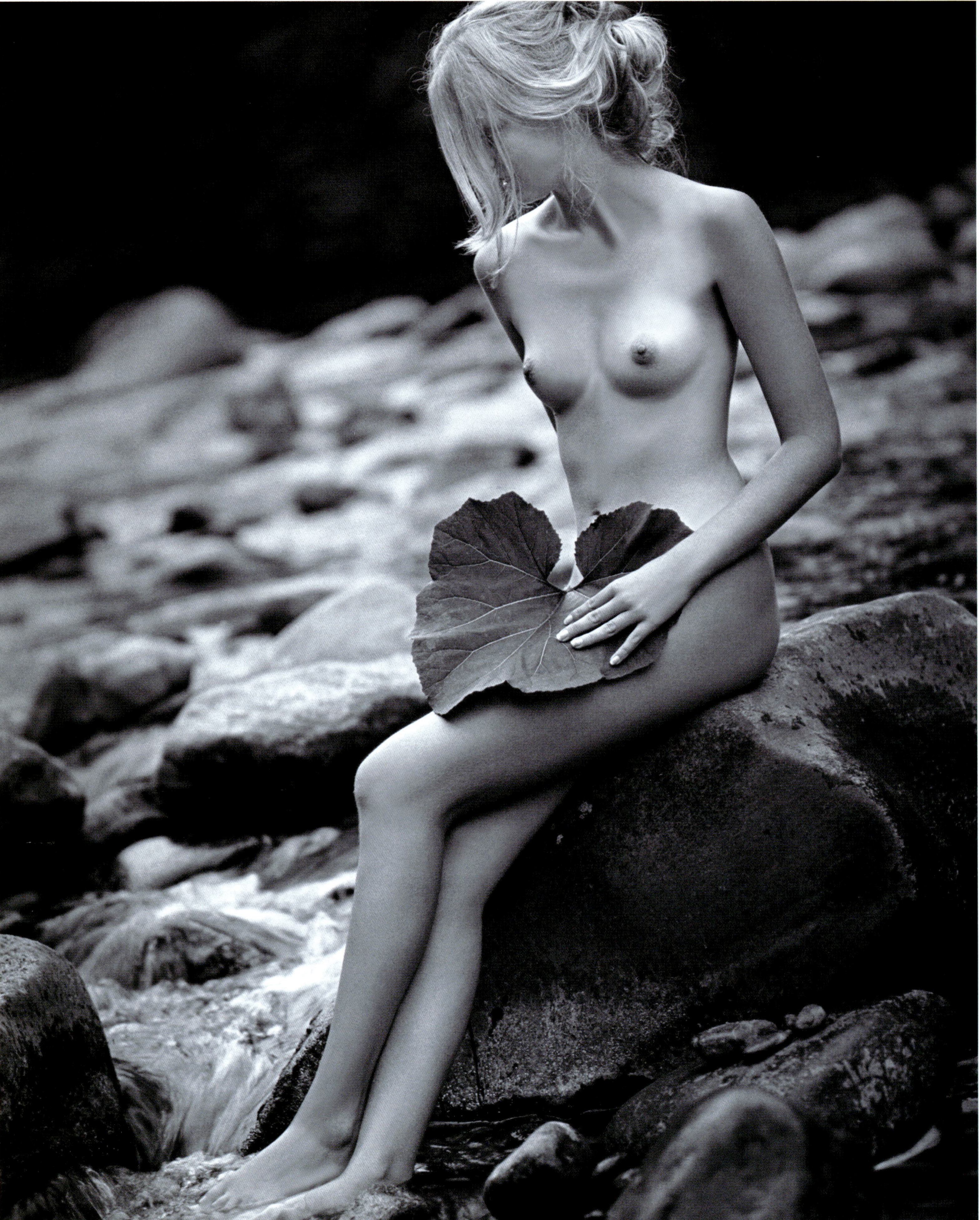

Chapter 4: **Light & tone**

It isn't only the direction and intensity of sunlight that will have an impact on your pictures, but also the colour of it. The time of day again has a major influence here. Stark midday light turns golden as the afternoon progresses, then gradually more orange in the approach to sunset.

The weather has an influence, too, as overcast skies tend to give everything below them a cool tinge ranging from fairly subtle to very pronounced under stormy clouds. Then there are the surroundings. If the frame is largely filled with brown and green shades of trees and foliage, the picture will have more of an earthy warmth than clear blue sky over water, or light reflected off nearby grey rocks.

The prevailing colour of the light will affect the skin tones of the model. Many photographers find the warm glow of the so-called 'golden hour' before sunset preferable for the tanned look it gives to the skin. But there is no 'right' way and you can see from the following cool-toned images that these too can be effective in creating atmosphere.

This section also looks at ways of boosting contrast to clearly define areas of light and dark, and how the use of colour in the surroundings can add impact to an image.

Fact file

Photographer: Emil Schildt
Model: Kala
Location: Aarhus, Denmark
Time of day: Early morning, June

Technical details

Camera: Diana
Lens: Fixed
Film: Kodak Tri-X pan
Exposure: 1/45sec at f/11

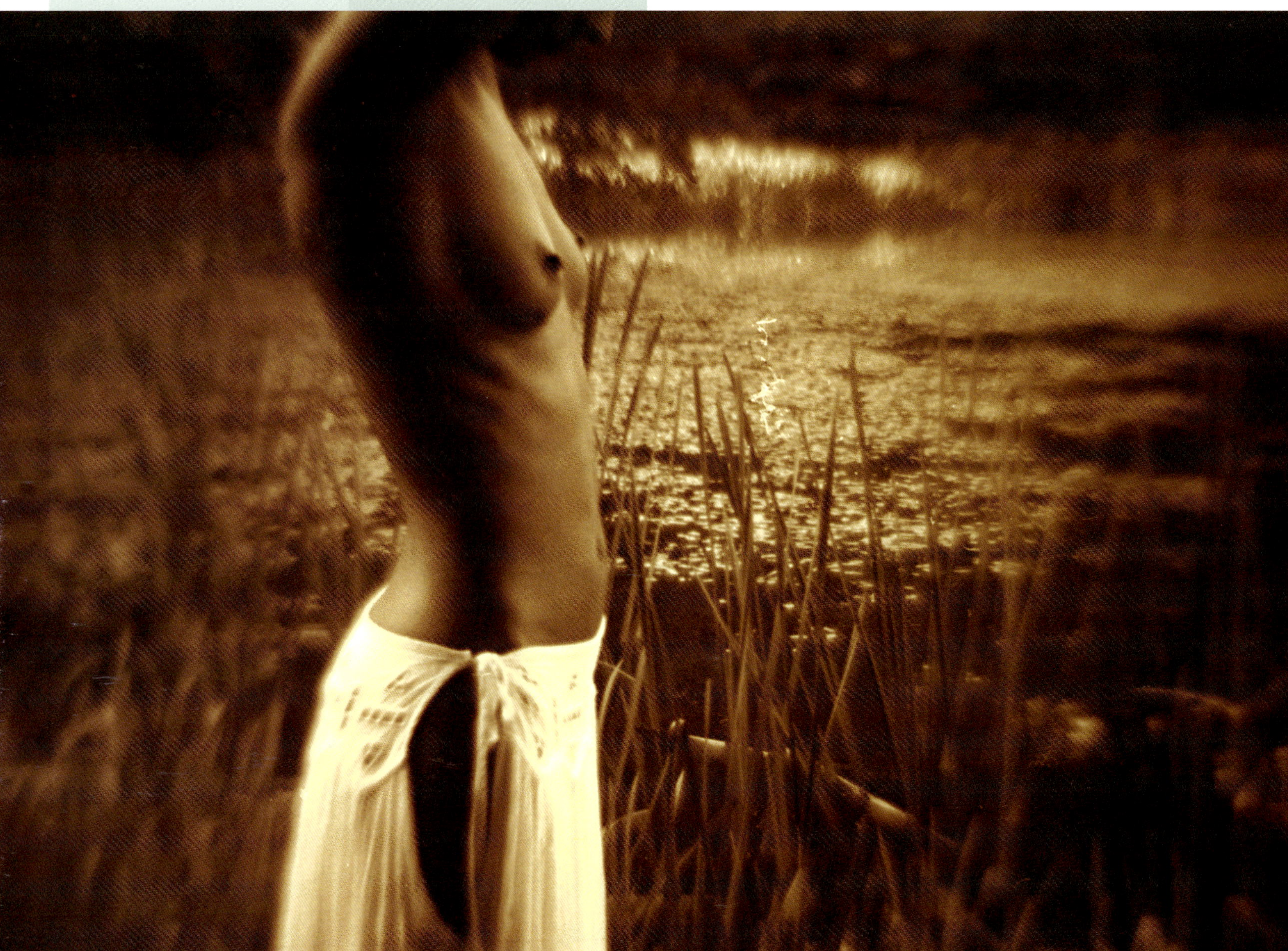

'When I'm using this camera, I don't actually feel like a photographer. Having this toy, plastic thing in my hand makes me think "let's have a go, it doesn't matter that much".'

Emil Schildt

The concept

A teacher in photography, Emil uses his unusual 'Diana' camera for fun and interest – and also manages to take beautiful pictures with it. His model, Kala, is also a photographer and the two of them set out that day to experiment.

The location

'We went out very early in the morning, first to the sea and then to a small forest nearby. There's a museum in the forest that has a very nice garden to walk in. We came across a little lake there, surrounded by flowers.'

Composition

'Composition with the Diana is simple – always have your subject in the middle, or there's a risk nothing will show up,' explains Emil. 'I knew that the water and the flowers would make a nice background, but I didn't know how nice until later. Using the Diana is always trial and error. You have no idea what will come out until the film is developed.'

Lighting and technique

'The Diana camera has, in recent years, reached a level of popularity that is almost absurd,' he says. 'It's a plastic camera that breaks easily, and it just can't take a sharp picture – some people call it the worst camera ever made. The lens is plastic and looks like something cut from a cola bottle, but it takes very soft-focused pictures – almost sharp in the middle but very blurred at the corners. This creates a dreamlike picture that gives an impression of the past. The format is 120 film with 4.5x4.5cm square negatives. There is only one shutter speed, 1/45sec, and three apertures, f/8, f/11 and f/16. Before taking pictures with it, you need to reassure yourself it's lightproof – some duck tape may be handy!'

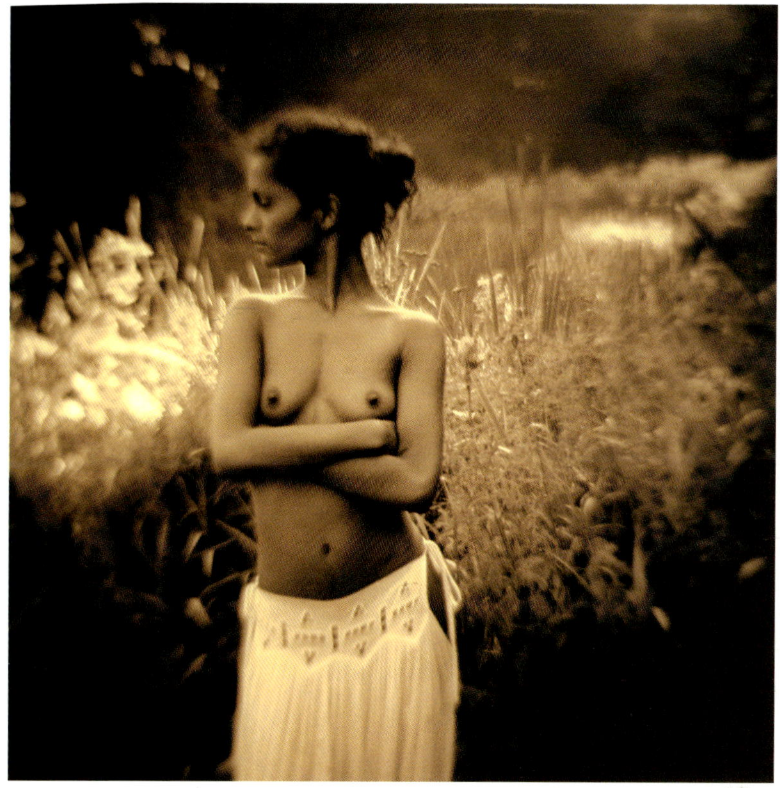

Another 'Diana special' from the same morning shoot. 'Early morning light is very beautiful. The sun is not too hard, and the light makes nice low and long shadows,' says Emil. The highlights on the model's body and parts of the background give a warm glow, which Emil enhanced in the darkroom with his self-invented mixture of toning and re-development (see pages 94–95). ▲

Fact file

Photographer: Emil Schildt
Model: Kala
Location: Aarhus, Denmark
Time of day: Early morning, June

Technical details

Camera: Diana
Lens: Fixed
Film: Kodak Tri-X pan
Exposure: 1/45sec at f/11

The concept

'This was taken during a photography workshop on nudes in the outdoors,' explains Darwin. 'With this particular image, we were trying to meld the shape and tones of the human body into the shape and tones of the landscape.'

The location

Areas of amazing natural beauty, including two national parks, Arches and Canyonlands, surround the town of Moab, in Southeast Utah. The sandstone landscape has been eroded to create a striking environment of contrasting colours, textures, land forms and canyons.

Composition

Taken in a small canyon, with a stream running along the floor, Darwin and his colleagues on the workshop chose a background of the water-carved canyon walls. Their patterns and textures contrast with the smooth skin of the models but the colours and tones are complimentary. Darwin used a fairly wide 55mm lens to make the models a part of their surroundings rather than the dominant element.

Lighting and technique

The models were placed on the shaded side of the canyon because the light was more even and less contrasty than on the sunny side. The sun was above the rocks that shaded them, but there was fill light provided by natural reflection from a wall opposite them.

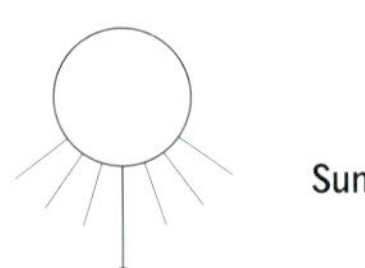

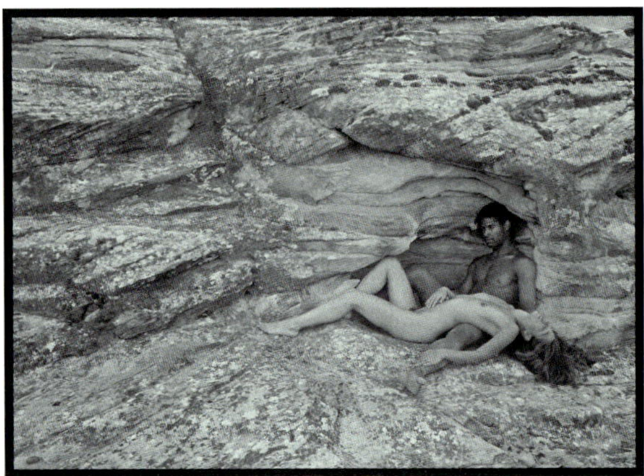

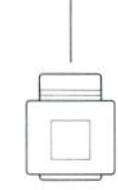

Fact file

Photographer:	Drawin Wiggett
Models:	Saphyre and Jamie
Location:	Near Maob, Utah, USA
Time of day:	10am, June

Technical details

Camera:	Mamiya 645 Pro TL
Lens:	55mm f/2.8
Film:	Fuji Velvia
Exposure:	Not recorded

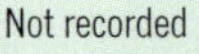

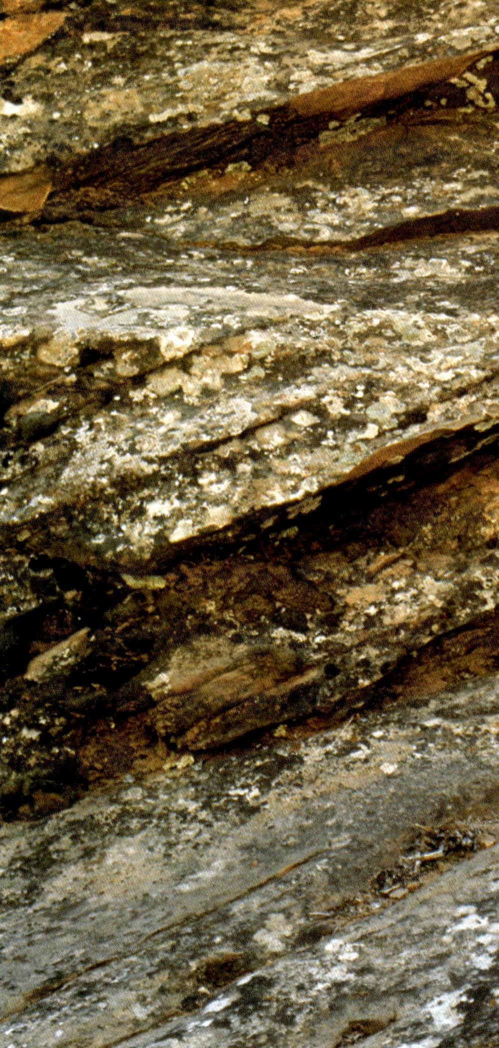

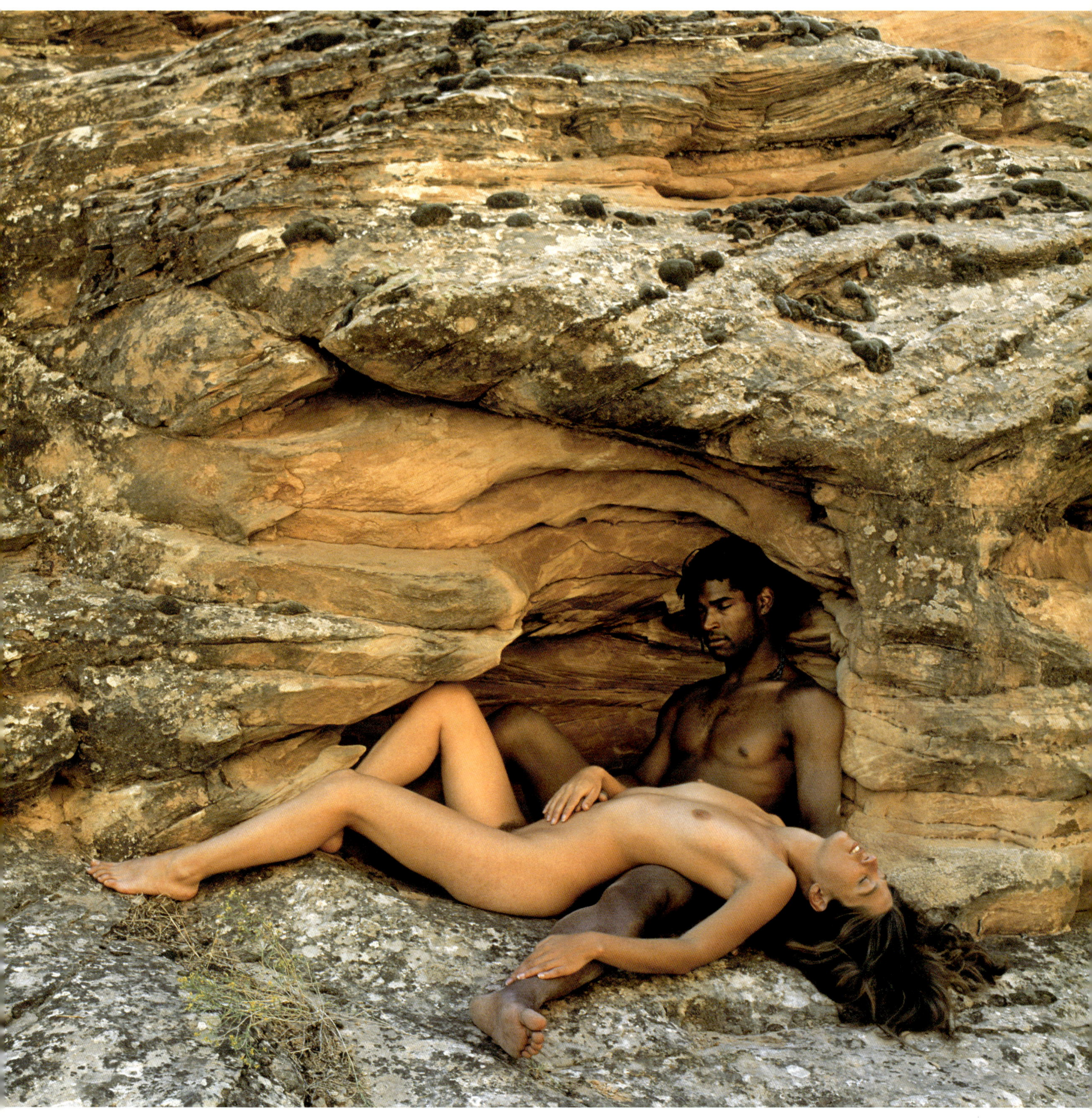

' The warm colour of the reflected light from the opposite canyon wall counteracted the normally blue cast one would get in shaded light with Fuji Velvia film.'

Darwin Wiggett

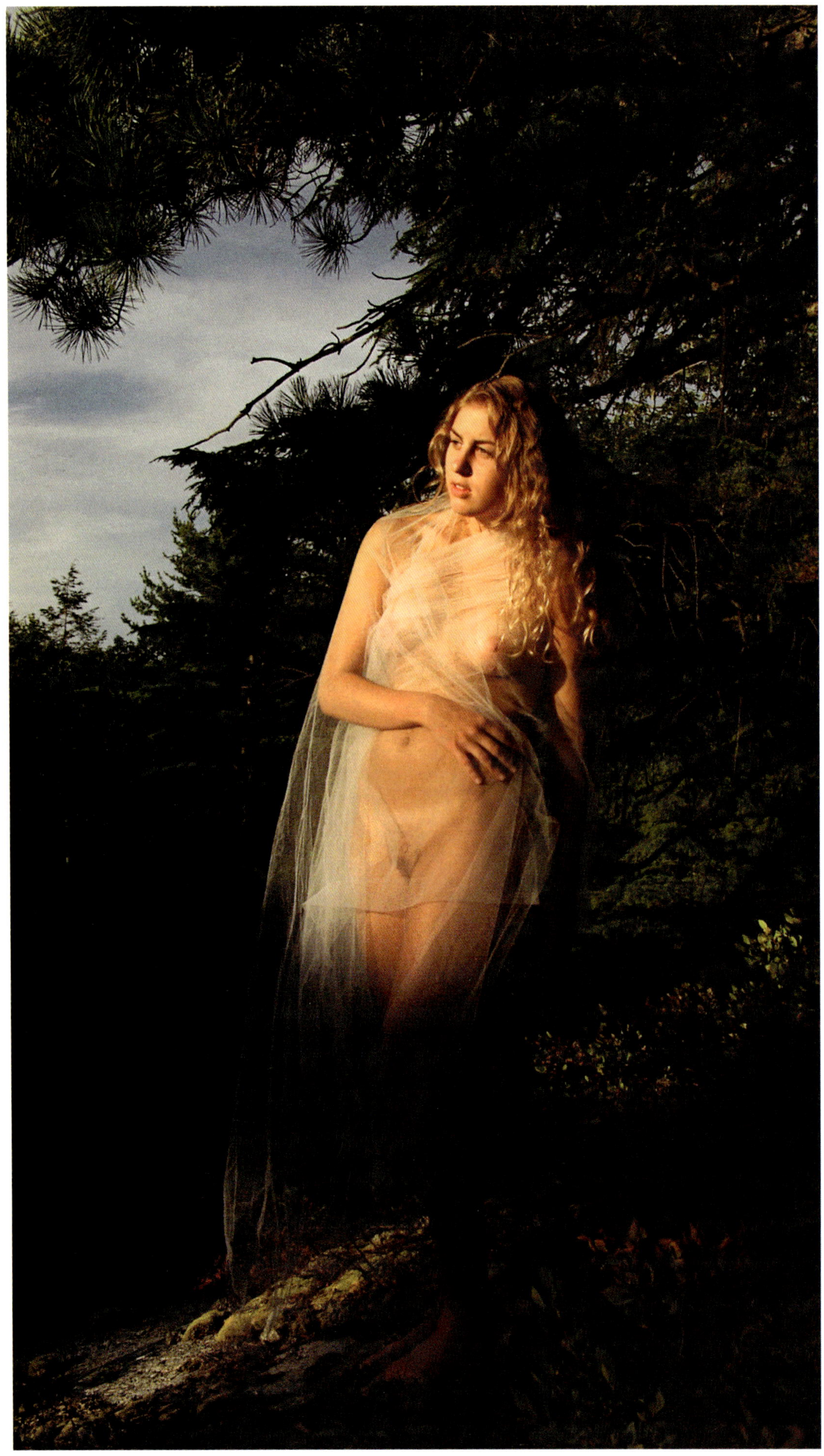

'Of all my images, this was truly a case of being at the right place at the right time, and being ready. The window of opportunity is very small for shots like this. A different month and the lighting is completely different as the sun changes direction all the time. I have certain spots where I can only shoot at particular times of the year.'

Dale Lehmer

Fact file

Photographer: Dale Lehmer
Model: Lauren
Location: Minnawaska State Park, New York, USA
Time of day: Just before sunset, August

Technical details

Camera: Olympus E10 (digital)
Lens: 35mm
Film: n/a
Exposure: 1/640sec at f/7.1

The concept

'I was interested in creating an image that looked like a Pre-Raphaelite painting, as well as attempting to convey the vision of oneness of nature,' says Dale. 'I wrapped the model in the fabric to add delicacy and elegance.'

The location

Dale is fortunate to live close to Minnawaska National Park in New York State, which provides him with numerous beautiful, natural locations. This spot was on the side of a mountain, on a rock ledge, with pine trees, moss and low underbrush growing on the rocks. 'I tried to find a place which had all these elements, as well as some sky and good evening sun,' he says.

Composition

'I think the natural slope of the mountain added to the overall composition, but it made it a little difficult for Lauren to stand in a relaxed pose. She was the perfect model, though. This was the first time she had ever posed and her gestures were very natural and innocent – exactly what I was looking for.'

Lighting and technique

'This was taken five minutes before the sun disappeared below the horizon. It was to my left, and almost horizontal to us, with trees between the sun and Lauren creating the shaded areas around her. When the light is this low, it changes extremely fast and we just happened to catch the perfect time to bathe her with warm light, but put the surrounding trees and bush in shade. It only lasted for about three minutes.'

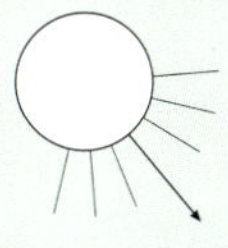

Sun

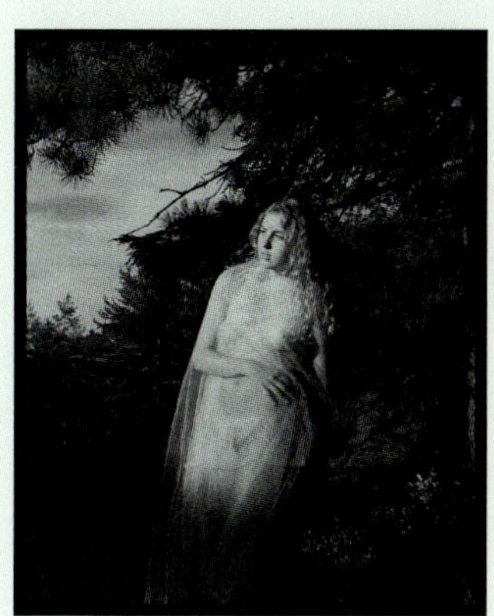

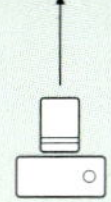

Digital SLR camera

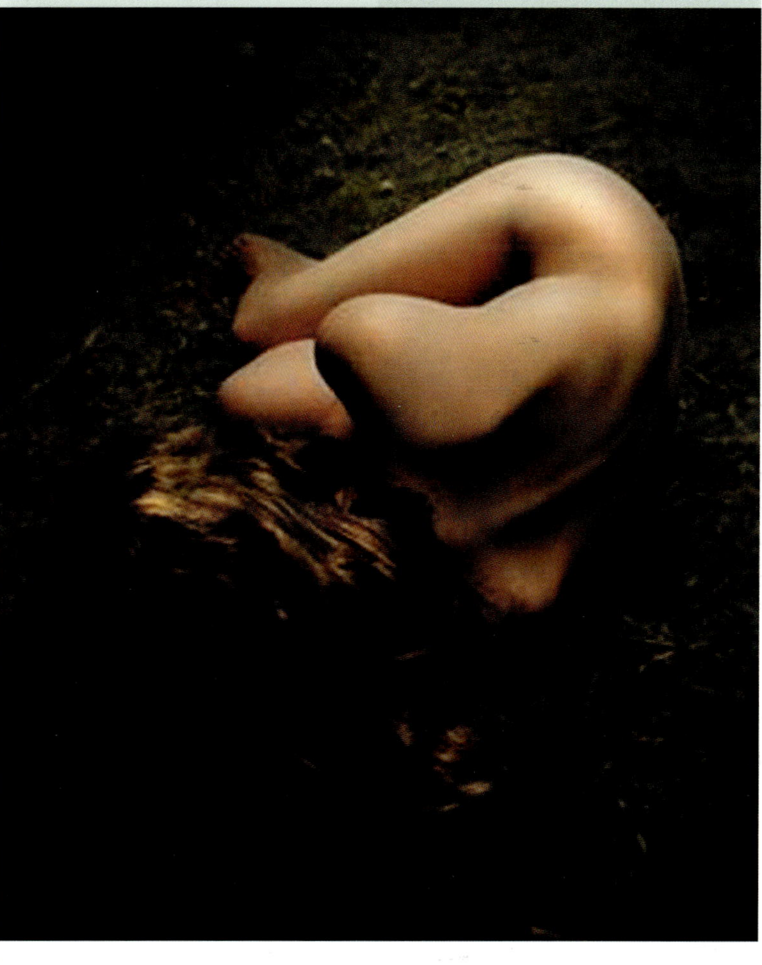

'This was taken in a small clearing of a wood, so the light was from a small area of sky directly above,' recalls Jonathan. 'This is especially good for modelling the subtle curves of the body, along her back. The surrounding greens and browns of the wood have affected the colour of the light, giving these warm, muted tones.'

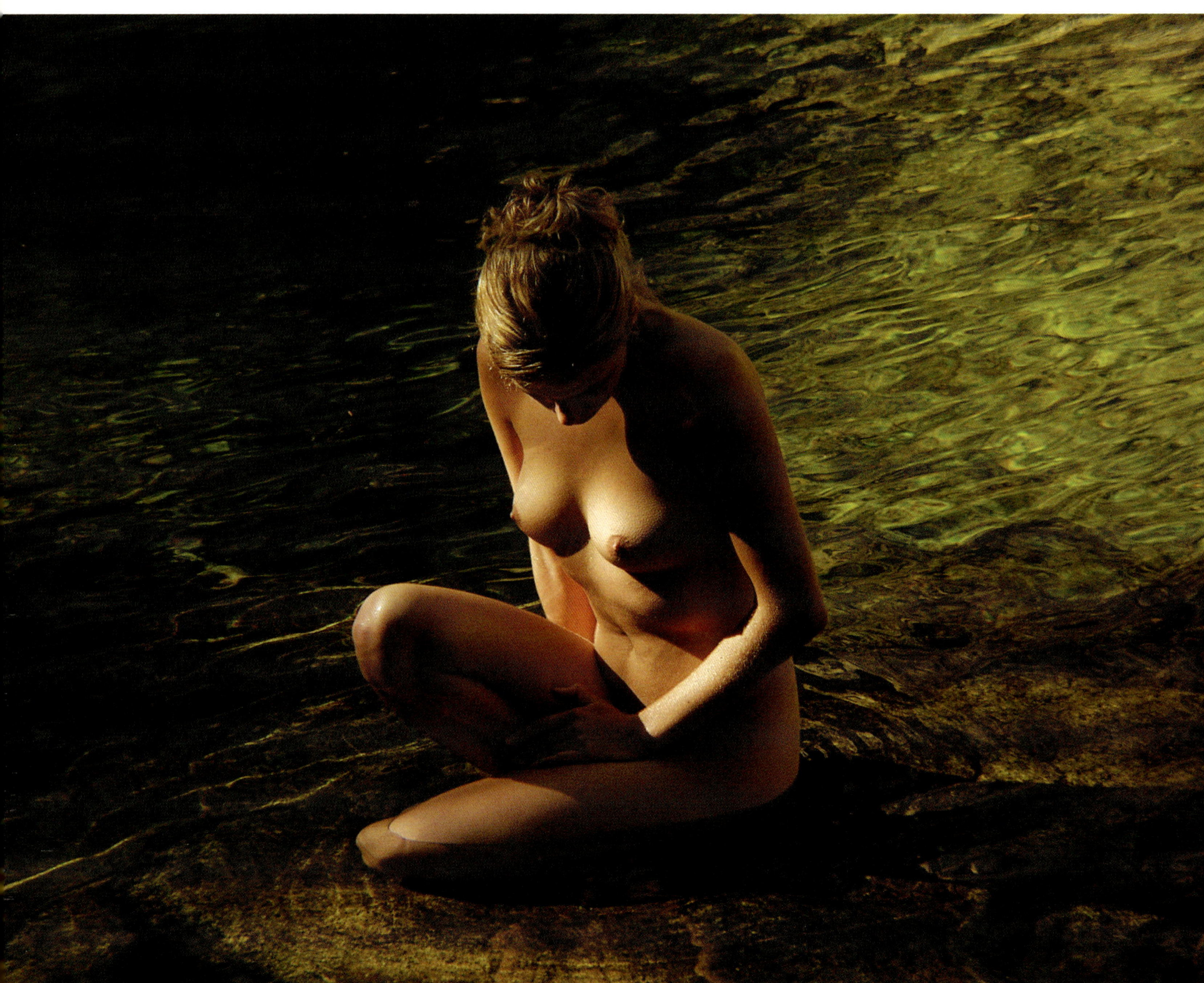

Fact file

Photographer: Dale Lehmer
Model: Helen
Location: Minnawaska State Park, New York, USA
Time of day: 5pm, June

Technical details

Camera: Olympus E10 (digital)
Lens: 35mm
Film: n/a
Exposure: 1/320sec at f/4

'The warm evening sun, for about two hours before sunset, is the best time for the caressing light that I seek. It's soft and has an increasingly red glow to it as it goes down.'

Dale Lehmer

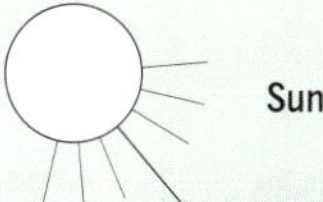

The concept

Dale calls this picture 'Alone' and his idea was that the model was alone with the beauty of nature. 'Her pose and gesture is one of submission and almost reverence to her surroundings,' he says. The timing and location were planned carefully so that the water would be this beautiful green colour and Helen a warm, golden brown tone.

The location

This was taken below a 20-foot waterfall of an exceptionally clear and cold mountain stream. 'It was a mile-long hike to get to this spot, which I selected from numerous previous hikes studying the light and the landscape.'

Composition

'I didn't want anything else in the composition except the water and Helen and I placed her centrally in the frame – against the usual rules – to emphasise the idea that she is stationary, content and secure, with no clear exit from her position in the image.'

Lighting and technique

'I had found out from previous visits that this location has good sun for about 45 minutes at this time of day,' explains Dale. 'The severe angle of the light entering the water is what creates these wonderful emerald colours and the soft, warm skin tones. I positioned myself so the sun was to our left. The cliff of the waterfall, and some trees, provided the sun block that created the darker tones in the water in the upper left-hand corner.'

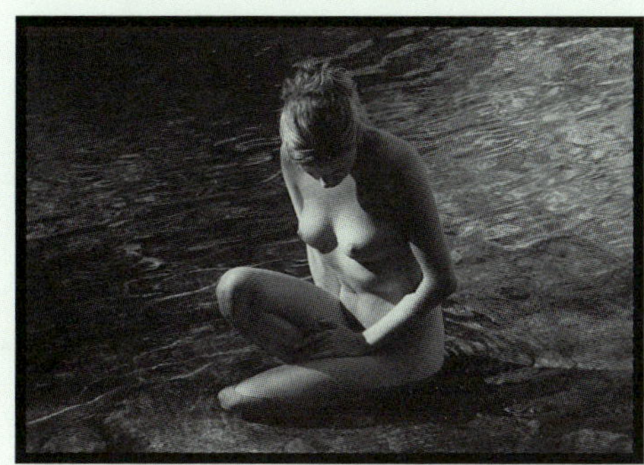
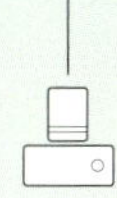

Fact file		Technical details	
Photographer:	Dale Lehmer	Camera:	Olympus E10 (digital)
Model:	Helen	Lens:	35mm
Location:	Minnawaska State Park, New York, USA	Film:	n/a
		Exposure:	1/500sec at f/4
Time of day:	5.45pm, June		

'Taken during the same shoot as the main picture, this was at the tail end of the sun's light in the area. The sun was coming through the trees, lighting up her face and highlighting other areas of her body. I underexposed the image to make it very dark, but soft and warm.' ⧨

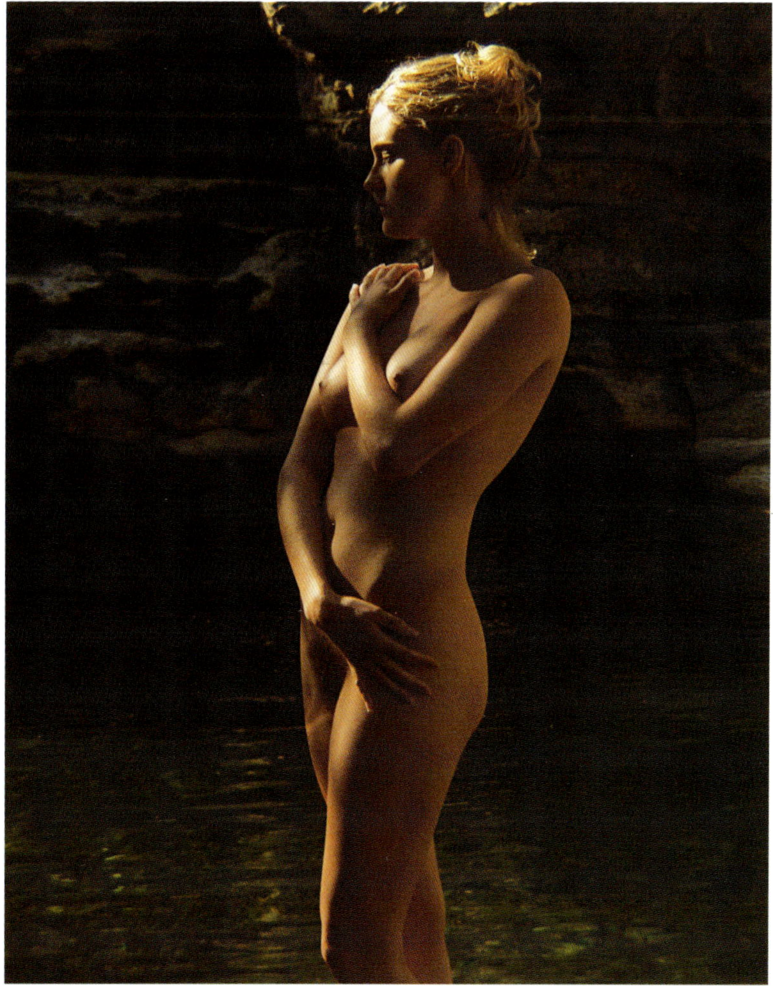

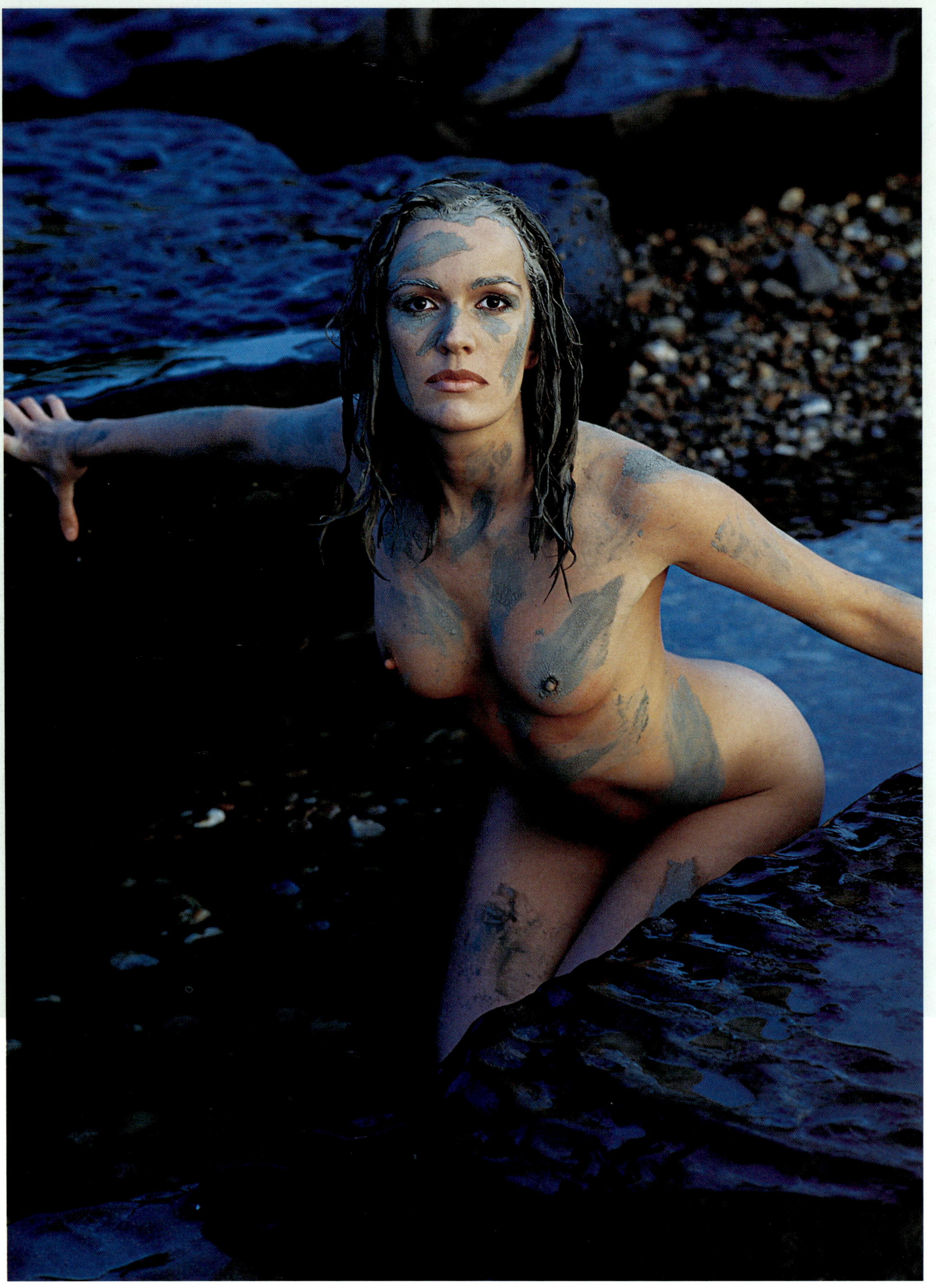

The concept

This was taken for a glamour calendar – a project that presents its own set of challenges. The 12 pictures often have to have a unifying theme, which could be the model, the location or both. Within the theme, each image has to be individually strong and sufficiently different from the others to bear scrutiny and, hopefully provide enjoyment for the whole of the month that it will hang on the wall. Arnold and the rest of the calendar team, wanted this picture to be simple, eye-catching and sexy.

The location

For this calendar, the beach and the 'primitive' look of the model provide the unifying theme. This beach was an ideal choice because it had many different rock structures, as well as the sea, which could be used in different creative ways.

Composition

Again, for a calendar, each pose must be different. Here Arnold has placed the model centrally and gone for direct eye contact from the model to engage the viewer's attention. The dark tones and texture of the rocks contrast with her body.

Lighting and technique

The overriding tones in this picture are cool and almost sombre. It looks like dusk, but was actually shot in the middle of the day. The model was in open shade, provided by the cliffs, and the rocks, wet with seawater, reflected the blue sky. The light from open shade is often slightly cool in tone and photographers often feel the need to warm it slightly using a reflector or fill-in flash. Arnold liked the atmosphere it created here and even darkened the image slightly by deliberately underexposing.

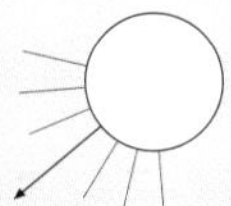

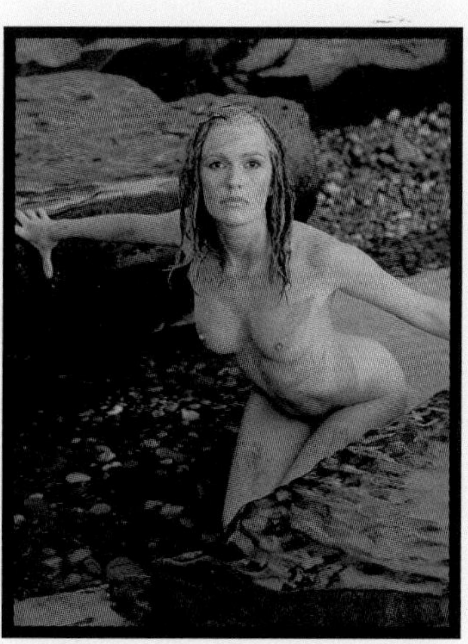

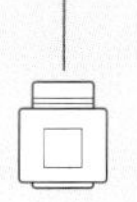

'This coastal location gave a tremendous choice of effects because of the way the light hits the rocks. I could use direct sun or shade as I wanted.'

Arnold Henri

<table>
<tr><td colspan="2">Fact file</td><td colspan="2">Technical details</td></tr>
<tr><td>Photographer:</td><td>Arnold Henri</td><td>Camera:</td><td>Mamiya RZ67</td></tr>
<tr><td>Model:</td><td>Jacqueline</td><td>Lens:</td><td>110mm</td></tr>
<tr><td>Location:</td><td>North coast of France</td><td>Film:</td><td>Kodak Ektachrome 100</td></tr>
<tr><td>Time of day:</td><td>Midday</td><td>Exposure:</td><td>Not recorded</td></tr>
</table>

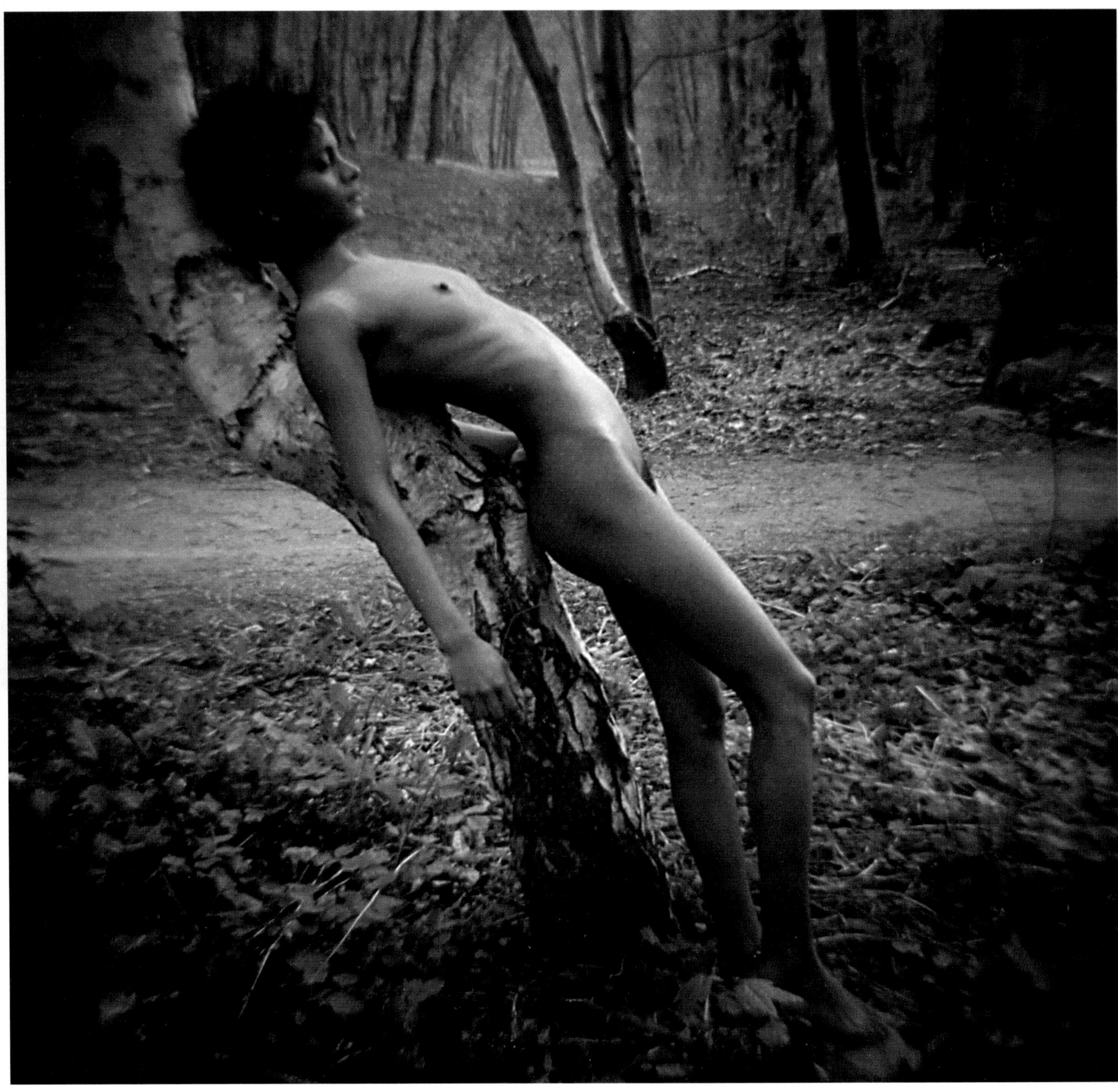

' The Diana is a fun camera that takes beautiful pictures. One of the advantages is that no one minds you taking their picture with it, and no one cares to steal it... unless, of course, they know about it!'

Emil Schildt

<table>
<tr><td colspan="2">Fact file</td></tr>
<tr><td>Photographer:</td><td>Emil Schildt</td></tr>
<tr><td>Model:</td><td>Kala</td></tr>
<tr><td>Location:</td><td>School grounds, Vraa, northern Denmark</td></tr>
<tr><td>Time of day:</td><td>2pm, May</td></tr>
</table>

<table>
<tr><td colspan="2">Technical details</td></tr>
<tr><td>Camera:</td><td>Diana</td></tr>
<tr><td>Lens:</td><td>Fixed</td></tr>
<tr><td>Film:</td><td>Kodak Tri-X pan</td></tr>
<tr><td>Exposure:</td><td>1/45sec at f/8</td></tr>
</table>

The concept

'Kala was a model at the school where I teach photography. It was May 1st so all the students wanted to drink beer and party rather than take pictures,' recalls Emil. 'It was a beautiful day so Kala and I decided to try the difficult thing of taking pictures outside.'

The location

This was taken in the grounds of the school. With the Diana plastic camera (see pages 84–85), Emil always looks for places with lots of nuances and details, with some distance between the background and the main subject. 'That way the special effect of this camera – the distortion made by the lens – becomes much clearer.'

Composition

The vignetting around the edge of the picture is caused by the plastic lens. It means that Emil always has to place the subject right in the middle of the picture or else the distortion is too great. It works perfectly in this image, where the tree trunk serves as a natural prop for the model to follow with her body shape. The tree-lined path in the background draws the eye into the picture, giving it depth.

Lighting and technique

The sun was to the right of the camera, so the model was facing into it. Although quite bright, it was diffused through the leaves of the trees all round. The coolness of the black and white film works well here. It allows attention to focus on the model rather than all the subtle detail of the foliage and also gives the picture a vintage quality, particularly with the dark corners. Emil has invented his own combination of toning and redevelopment. 'First I bleach the picture, then I redevelop it in a bath with a very thin dilution of developer and a little sepia toner,' he explains. 'The developer gets "confused" and doesn't know whether to tone or develop. If I'm lucky some very fine and subtle tones appear.'

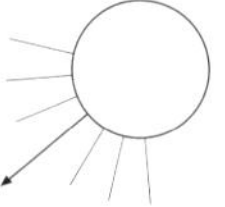

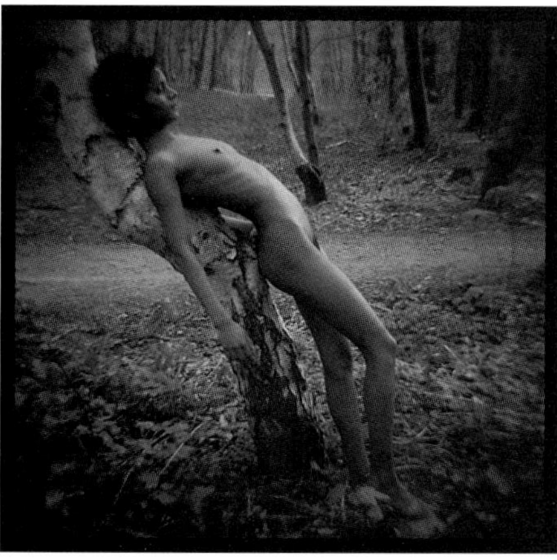

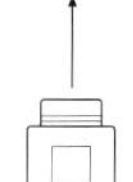

The concept

'It was sunny in the morning so we drove two hours to this location,' recalls Carsten. 'Well, weather can change, and it did, so we made the most of it with this image.'

The location

Carsten is always on the look out for different places for nude photography and, in his eyes, they don't necessarily have to be natural. The hard but undulating rock in this man-made quarry provides a stark contrast to the soft form of the female body.

Composition

Carsten avoided the temptation to go in too close here. Sometimes a composition can have much more impact if the subject has room to 'breathe'. The vast majority of the frame is taken up with the brooding sky and it gives the impression that the model is gazing up at it and enjoying the space and the freedom. 'I love the drama in the image,' adds Carsten. 'The difference in textures, the dangerous clouds. It feels like a kind of sacrifice – give the body to God...'

Lighting and technique

Carsten didn't alter the natural light or use any filters on this image. The cool blue tone is from the thundery clouds and the rock below reflects this colour, saturated further by the use of Fuji Velvia film, which has this characteristic.

Fact file

Photographer:	Carsten Tschach
Model:	Sabrina
Location:	A quarry, Germany
Time of day:	3pm, August

Technical details

Camera:	Nikon F100
Lens:	28–70mm
Film:	Fuji Velvia
Exposure:	1/15sec at f/5.6

'You don't always need good weather to make a good image – just let the weather become part of it.'

Carsten Tschach

Fact file

Photographer: Carsten Tschach
Model: Kati
Location: Factory building, Berlin, Germany
Time of day: 1pm, August

Technical details

Camera: Nikon F100
Lens: 80–200mm
Film: Kodak Elite 160T
Exposure: 1/60sec at f/5.6

This was taken at an old factory building on an intermittently cloudy day. Carsten used tungsten-balanced film, which gives this blue cast when used in daylight. He felt the coolness was appropriate to the cold steel of the industrial setting. ⏬

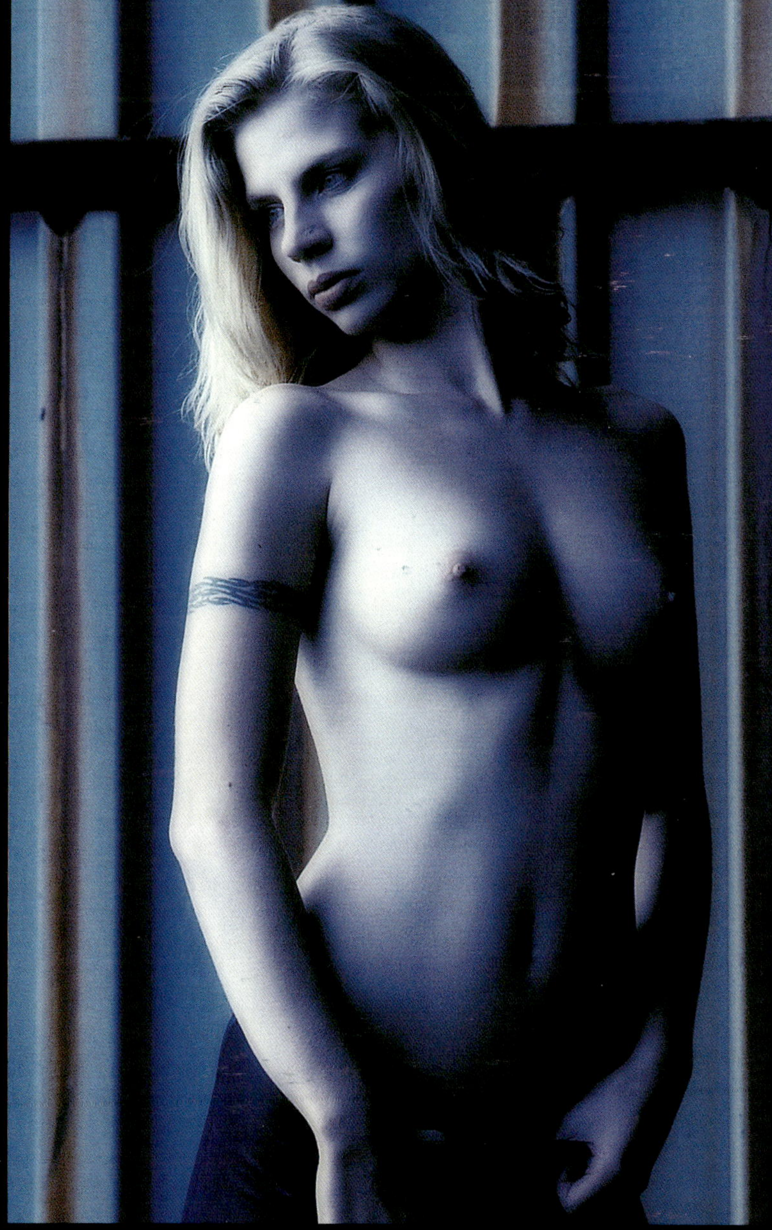

Fact file		Technical details	
Photographer:	Björn Oldsen	**Camera:**	Canon F1
Model:	Karin	**Lens:**	135mm
Location:	Black Forest, Germany	**Film:**	Agfapan 100
Time of day:	Late afternoon, June	**Exposure:**	Not recorded

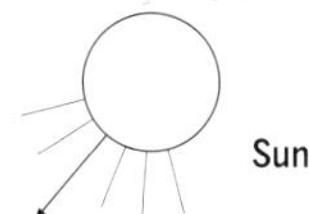

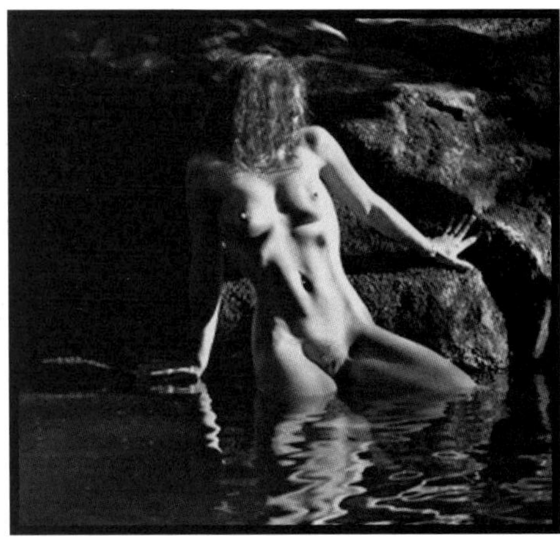

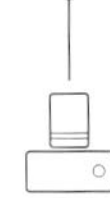

The concept

'I had been taking pictures of the river as part of a commercial job for a client and my wife – who modelled for me here – and I decided to take advantage of the fine weather and the beautiful location to do some nude images,' explains Björn.

The location

Björn and Karin live in the middle of the Black Forest in Germany and this river is close by. They used the shade of a bridge, which was about three metres high, for this picture because it added such a dramatic dimension to the light.

Composition

This looks a bit like a water-filled cavern and the dark tones add a real sense of mystery to the image, emphasised by the model's taut, angular pose – as if she's tentatively exploring this place. 'I really like the way the light and shade accents the muscle in her left leg,' he says.

Lighting and technique

In the late afternoon, the sun was at a low enough angle and it filtered under the bridge through rocks and bushes. This strong side light provides excellent modelling on Karin's body and highlights on the rocks, leaving other areas in deep shade. The well-lit areas have also cast bright reflections, lifting the dark water in the foreground. Björn took a meter reading from a grey mid-tone and then bracketed his exposures around it. In such contrasty light, there is a fine line between under- and overexposure.

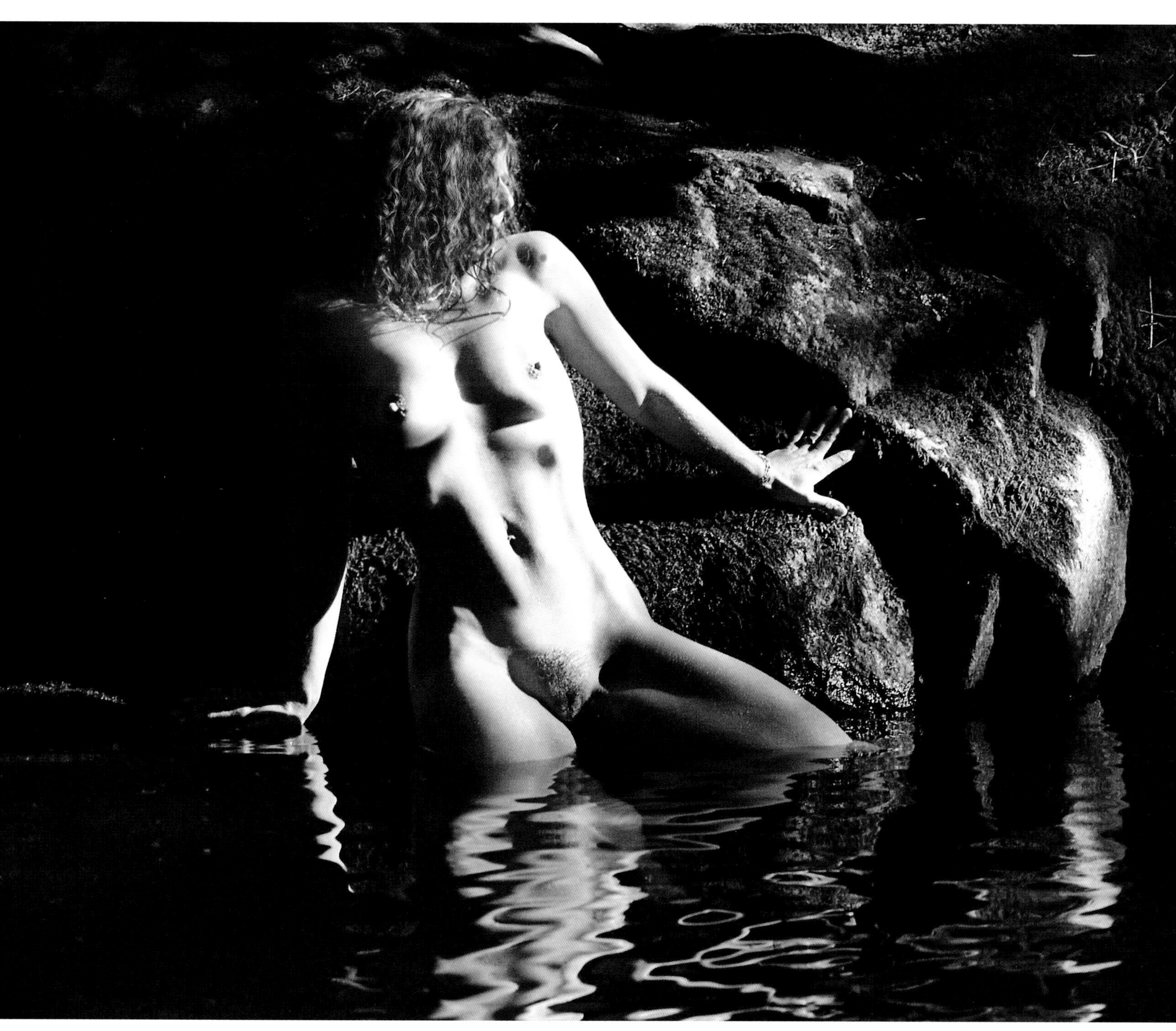

'I love the magical mood from the light and the reflections on the water. It fits in with my idea of the Black Forest in summer.'

Björn Oldsen

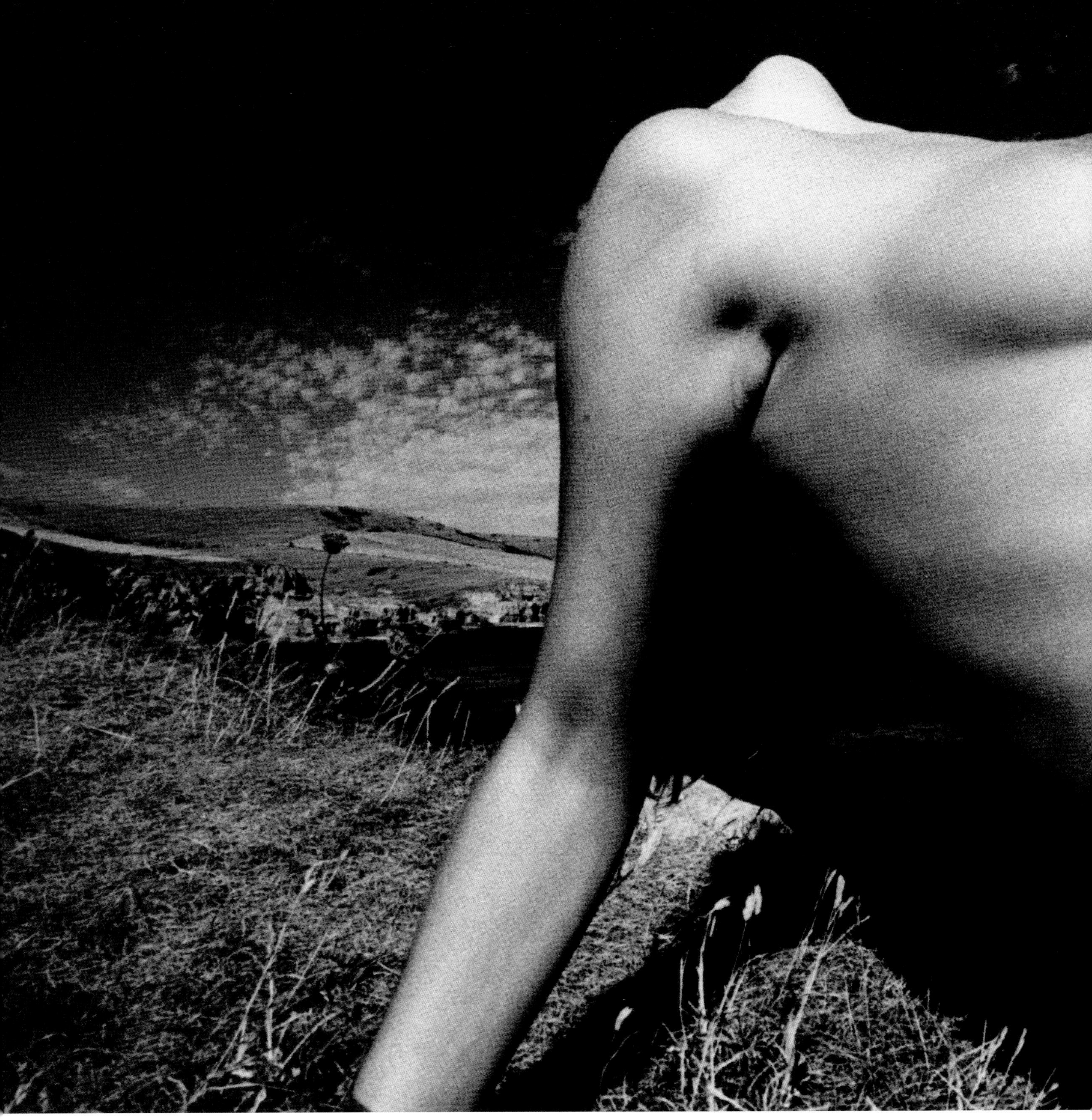

' I use a red filter because I like to have tone in the sky and a definition of the edge of a photograph. A few photographers can work with pure white bleeding, but I can't think of many.'

Nic Tucker

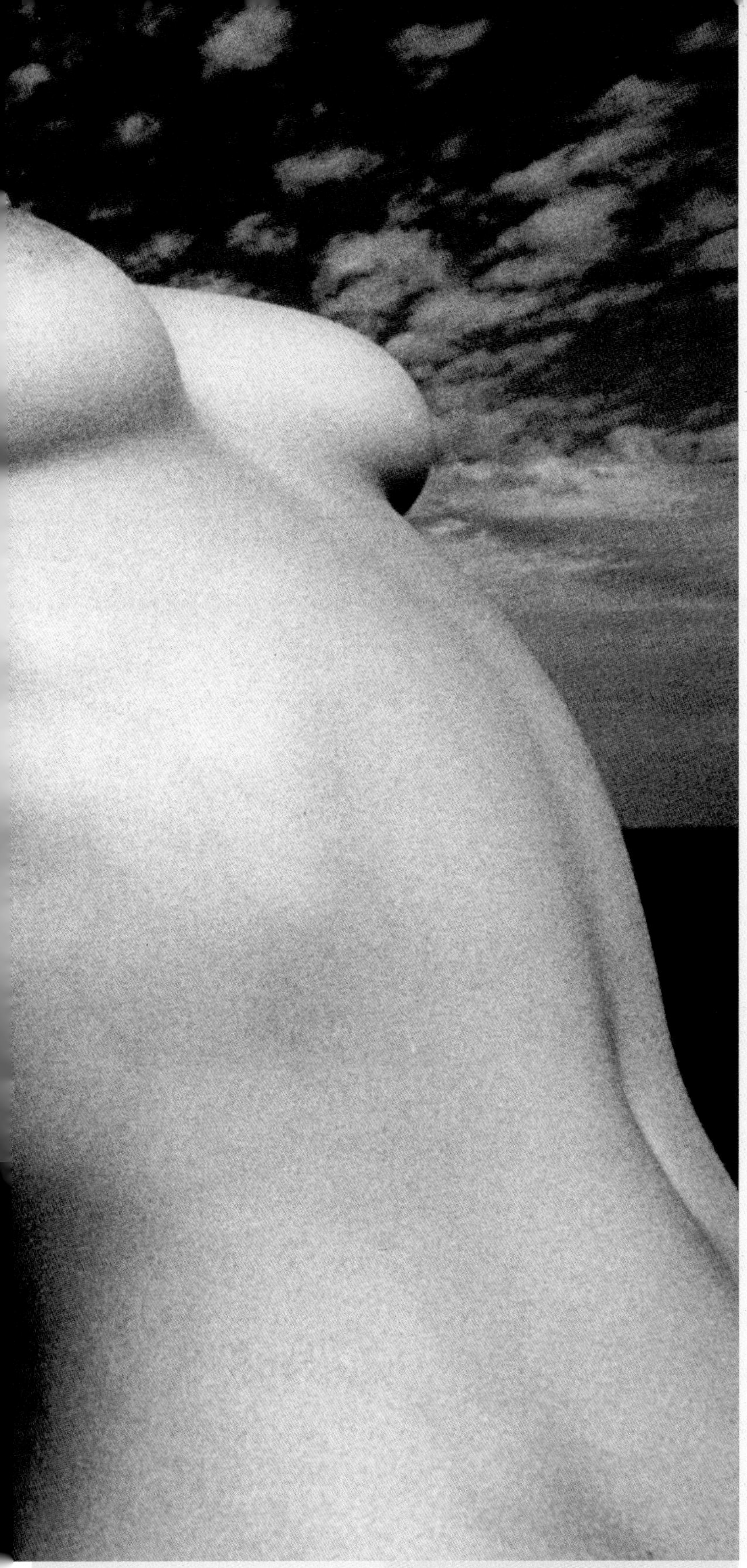

The concept

This was taken for a design consultancy, which was producing a promotional brochure to drum up more business. Nic wasn't given a specific brief, other than to take the kind of strong, graphic image his personal and commercial work is known for.

The location

'I shot the picture in a place called Worth Matravers on the Dorset coast, where there had been extensive quarrying,' explains Nic. 'It's a fair walk from the nearest road and the rocks and coastline are splendid. It's quite a popular spot for walkers, though, so we attracted one or two raised eyebrows during the afternoon!'

Composition

Nic's use of a wide-angle lens is very dramatic here, making the body seem monumentally large against the detail of the landscape in the background. The placing of the body on the right side of the frame was important to allow for this space on the other side which gives such a strange and distorted sense of scale.

Lighting and technique

'The sun was shining so, happily, no extra light was needed,' says Nic. 'I often use a Norman flash outside, but prefer to keep things simple if possible.' The sun was high and to the left of the camera, lighting up the top of the model's body and creating a deep shadow underneath. Nic intensified the contrast between the highlights and the background by using a Wratten 25A red filter on the lens, which significantly darkened the sky.

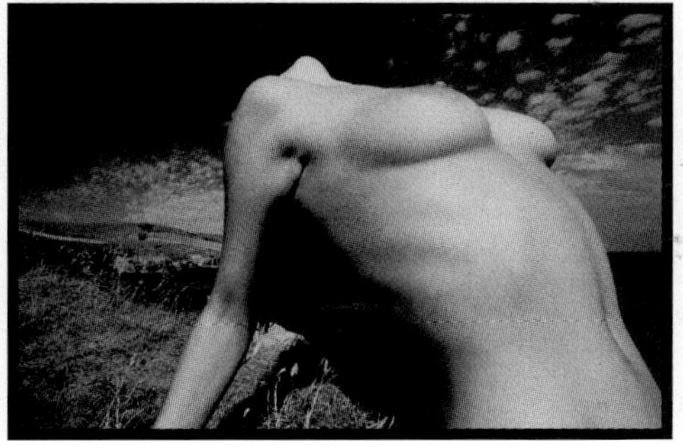

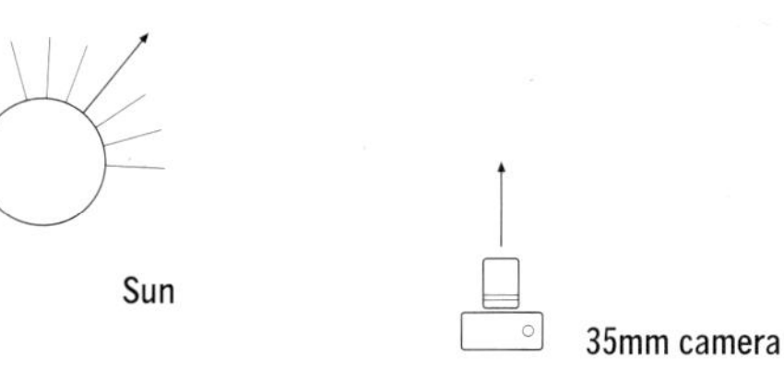

Fact file

Photographer: Nic Tucker
Model: Claire
Location: Dorset coast, UK
Time of day: Early afternoon, August

Technical details

Camera: Nikon FA
Lens: 20mm
Film: Fuji Neopan 400
Exposure: Program mode

Fact file		Technical details	
Photographer:	Nic Tucker	Camera:	Nikon FA
Model:	Laura	Lens:	20mm
Location:	La Jara beach, Spain	Film:	Fuji Neopan 400
Time of day:	Late morning, September	Exposure:	Program mode

The concept

I had gone to Spain with a girlfriend and we'd driven all the way down south from Madrid. We were exploring parts of the coast, near Sanlucar and decided to take some pictures, using the interesting architecture and the sea.

The location

La Jara beach on the Atlantic Ocean is a few miles from the town of Sanlucar de Barrameda – famous for Manzanilla sherry and fine seafood. 'The beach was very lovely, with old seafront villas. There was a particularly beautiful one behind this doorway but, I've been back to the beach since then and sadly that villa is no longer there.'

Composition

Nic used a wide-angle lens to include both the building, the sandy beach, and a hint of the sea in the frame. The crumbling walls of the building provide an interesting textured background, contrasting with the model's smooth skin. The overhanging part of the building is an important part of the composition. Its round shape breaks up the strong diagonal of the wall, and the deep shadow contrasts with the bright, sunlit areas of the image.

Lighting and technique

The sun, from the left of the camera, was very strong and bright and full on the model's back and the wall behind her. Nic wanted a really strong contrast between the sky and the model, beach and building to make these well-lit areas stand out. He used a red filter on the lens, which has rendered parts of the sky almost black, contrasting with the white clouds to dramatic effect.

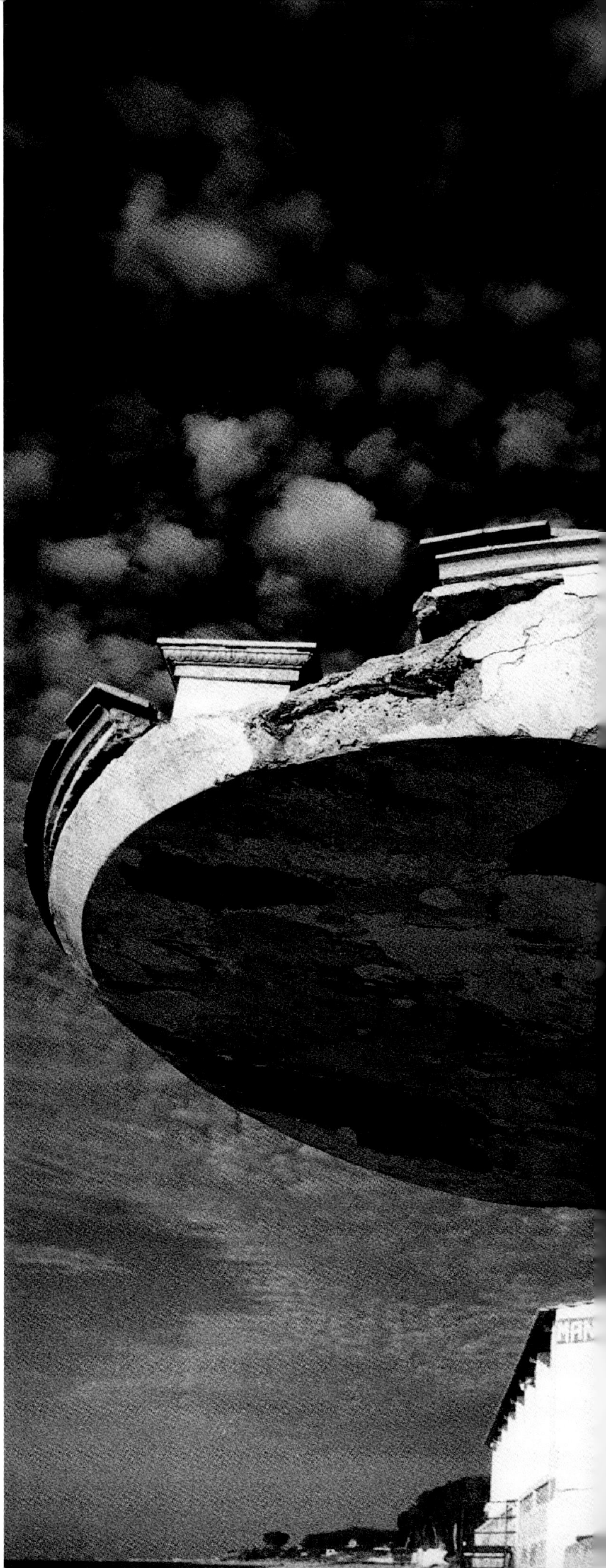

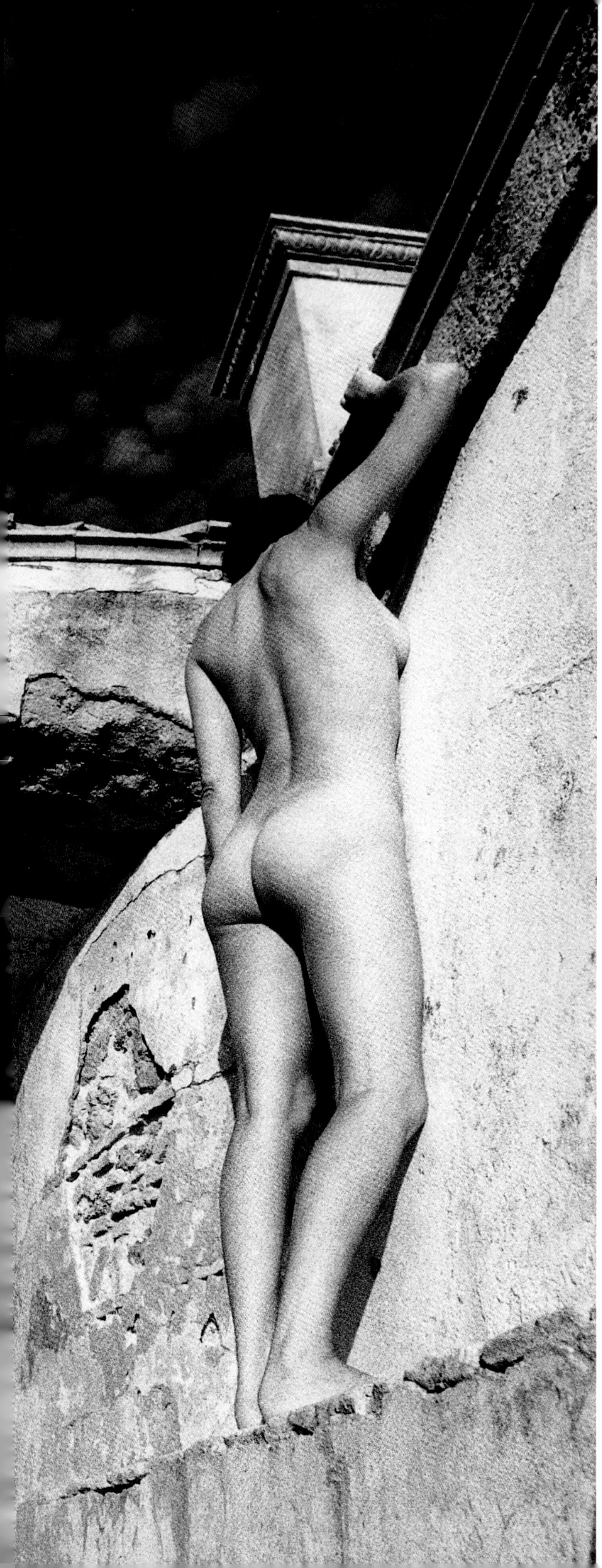

Fact file

Photographer: Jonathan Charles
Model: Marie
Location: Near Plymouth, Devon, UK
Time of day: Late afternoon, July

Technical details

Camera: Olympus OM2
Lens: 100mm
Film: Ilford HP5
Exposure: Not recorded

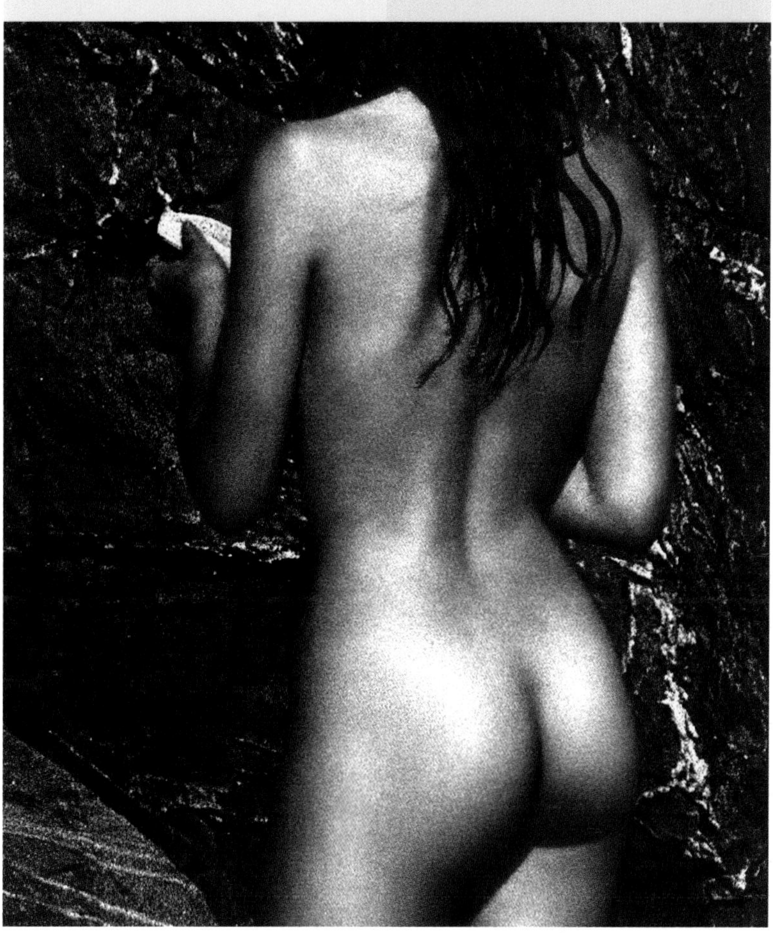

'This wasn't a planned shot,' recalls Jonathan. 'Marie was drying in the hot sun after a swim and I had climbed higher up the rocks. Looking down with the sun behind me, I was struck by the gleaming reflection from her skin and the marbling of the dark stone rocks. I slightly underexposed and printed dark to create a shiny, almost metallic tone which contrasts with the rough rock background.' ♠

'We thought the villa was completely deserted, until a boy came out, playing with a tin drum. He was rather surprised to see a naked girl at his gate to the beach!'

Nic Tucker

Fact file

Photographer:	Björn Oldsen
Model:	Maren
Location:	Southern Germany
Time of day:	6pm, August

Technical details

Camera:	Canon F1
Lens:	135mm
Film:	Kodachrome 100
Exposure:	Not recorded

'Knowing the model well helps a lot. Communication is much easier and the situation is altogether more relaxed than it is with a stranger.'

Björn Oldsen

The concept

Björn and his sister, Maren, worked together on a number of pictures of her when he wanted to build up his portfolio and she was happy to pose in return for her own set of prints. The concept behind this shot was simple and inspired by the location.

The location

The wall was outside a former studio of Björn's in southern Germany, near Switzerland. Far from being annoyed by the graffiti, he was attracted by the colours and the abstract shapes against the texture of the rough concrete and old brickwork.

Composition

Björn and Maren planned the picture together, deciding on accessories that would go well with the setting. The colour and texture of the coat co-ordinate perfectly with her hair, and the golden tones work well with the yellow writing in the background. Björn placed the figure centrally, allowing just the right proportion of the wall around her. It's a straightforward full-length composition, but striking for the range of colours and textures – and the model herself.

Lighting and technique

Björn waited for a cloudy day to take the shot to ensure low contrast and a lack of hard shadows. Overcast, diffused lighting is perfect for producing even skin tones and soft subtle colour, although it can sometimes be a little cool in tone. If that is the case, then a carefully placed reflector or fill-in flash can be used to add warmth.

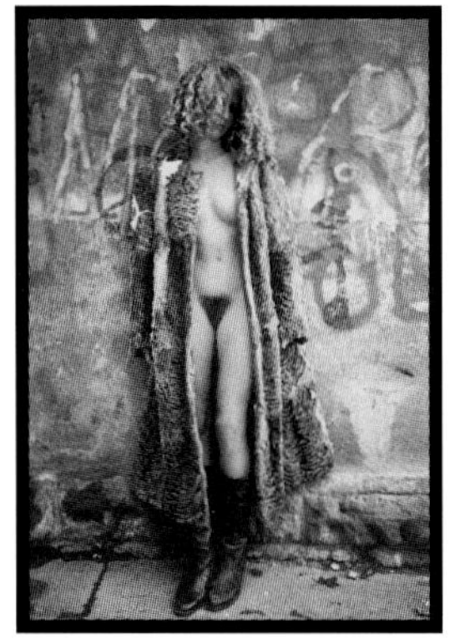

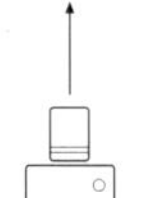

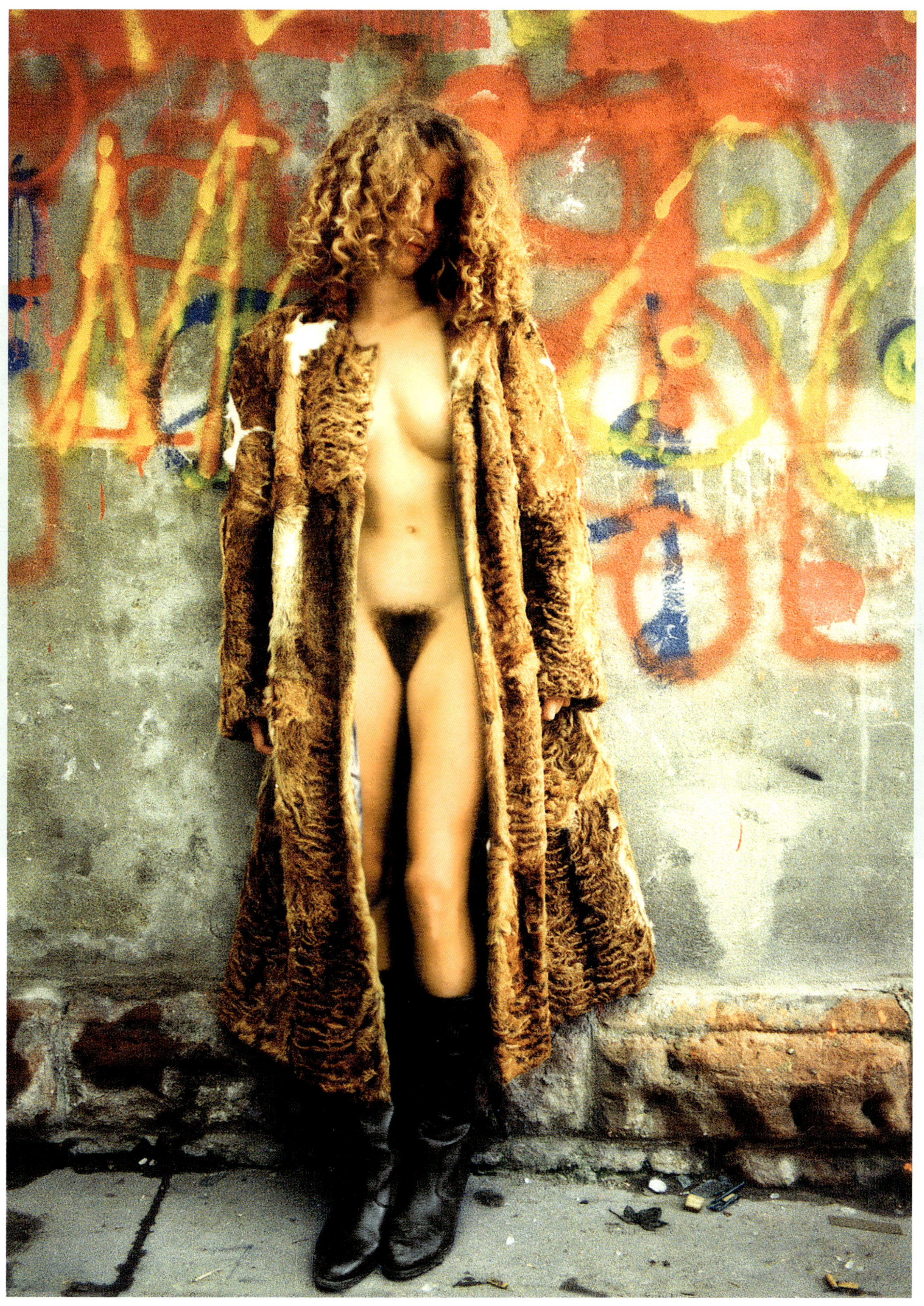

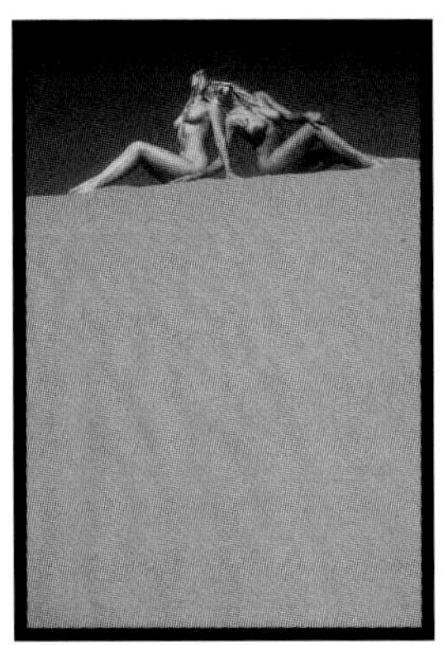

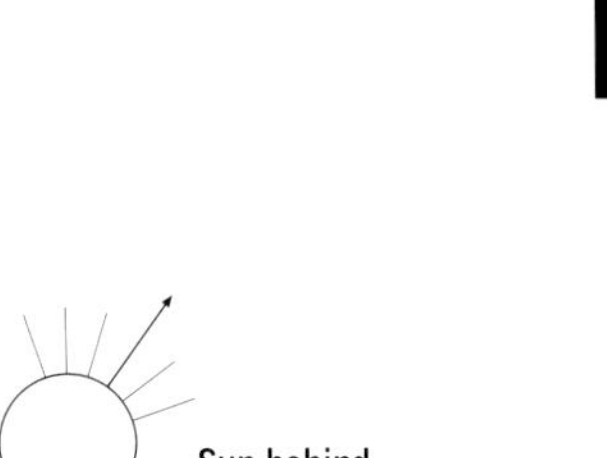

Sun behind
photographer's shoulder

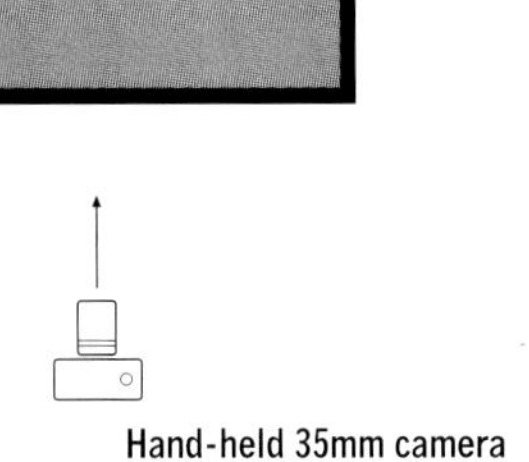

Hand-held 35mm camera

The concept

'This was simply a composition in colour,' explains Mark. 'I asked the two models to give me a sense of camaraderie, enjoy the sand and sun on their bodies and connect with each other. That is what they gave me.'

The location

These huge expanses of rippled dunes make a natural partnership with the nude form, especially in this light when the orange tone of the sand is similar to that of tanned skin and the stunningly blue sky forms such a dramatic contrast.

Composition

'The simplicity of colour, lines and lovely shapes were what made this scene so special. This shot composed itself,' says Mark. The graphic camera angle he chose makes it look as though the models are sitting on a giant wall of sand, which is given texture by the shadows of the ripples.

Lighting and technique

'The low, late afternoon sun was coming over my left shoulder. It was casting a very warm light on an already warm scene, so the colours were just explosive,' says Mark. He used Fuji Velvia film, which tends to saturate colours well and a polarising filter on the lens turned the blue sky an even deeper shade.

' It was a stunningly gorgeous day... an orange sand dune, a brilliant blue sky, and two close friends rolling around in the warm, sensuous sand.'

Mark Esposito

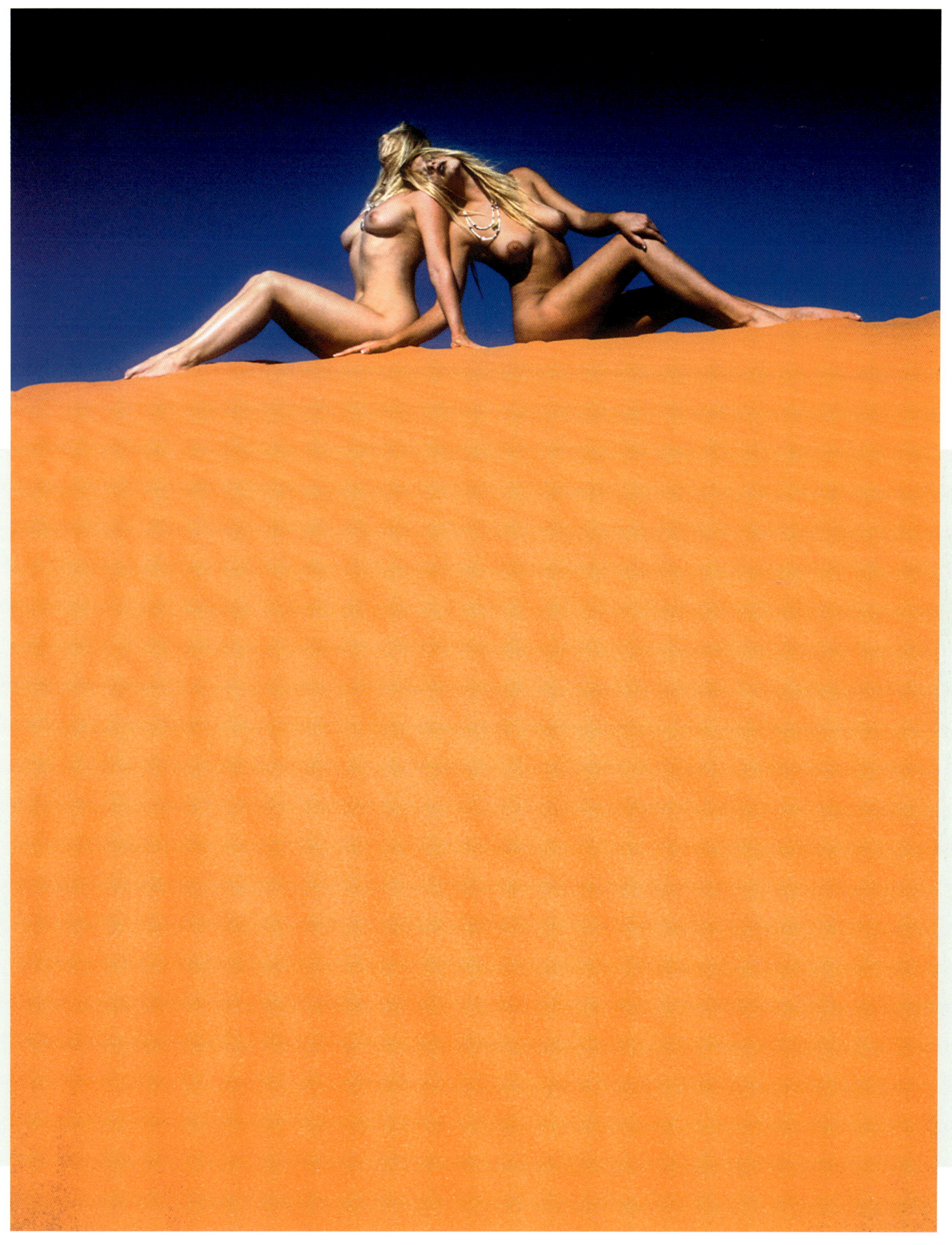

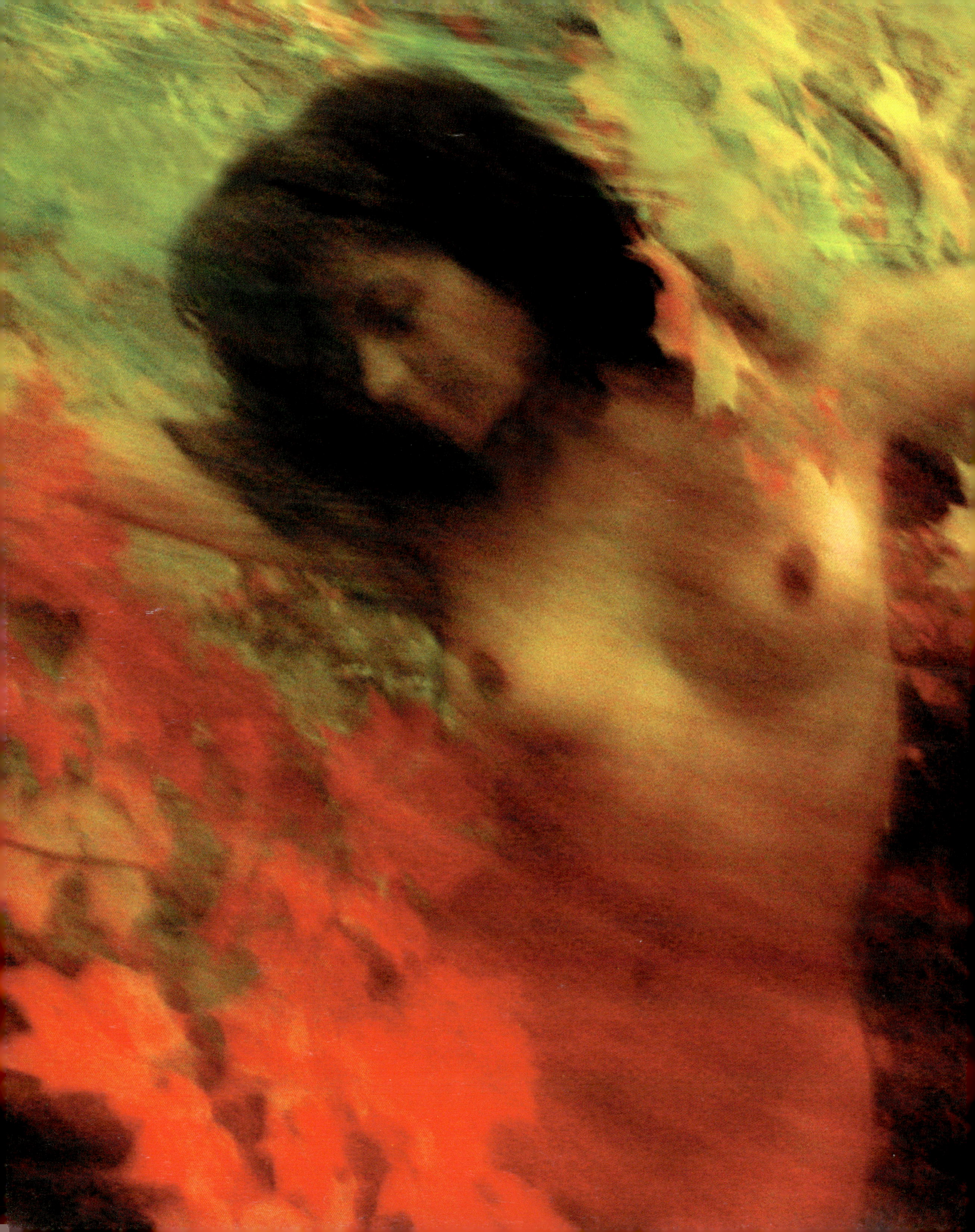

' I've been working on this technique for about a year now and it's still very difficult to get right. This is my favourite result so far.'

Dale Lehmer

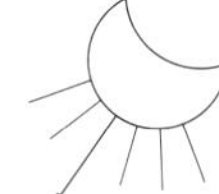

Sun behind clouds

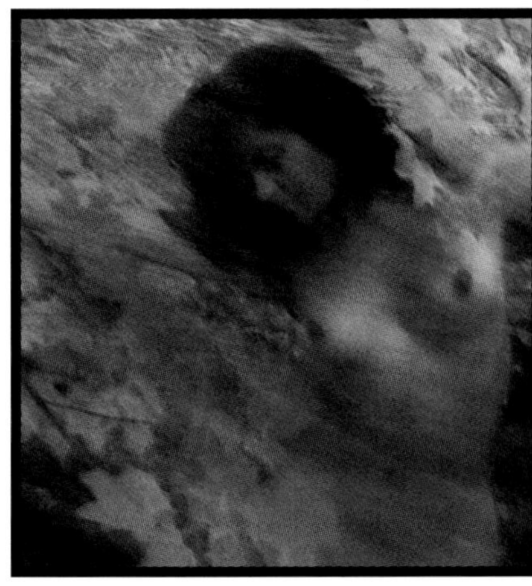

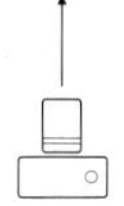

Hand-held 35mm camera

The concept

'I've been experimenting with a technique I created – as far as I know – that I call "painting with the camera". Similar to panning, it's an attempt to blend all the different components into one organic image, as it is in nature,' explains Dale. 'I call this picture "Surrender", as I'm trying to express the feeling of yielding to nature, which we all do eventually when we die.'

The location

Dale didn't have to go far to take this shot – the maple tree was right outside his own home. Having seen the beauty of its autumn colour many times, he was able to plan the image and wait for the opportunity to achieve it.

Composition

The model took her pose among the leaves and branches of the maple tree but the composition was fairly hit or miss because of the nature of Dale's technique. In this case it worked perfectly – a beautiful melting pot of colour with just the right blend of blur and subject detail to create plenty of atmosphere.

Lighting and technique

It was a cloudy day in the late afternoon, providing low enough light to allow a shutter speed of one second, but just bright enough to give the colours some zing. 'During the exposure I focus on the subject for a split second – done by feel – and then I sweep the camera in a smooth and consistent direction, usually sideways and up,' he explains. 'You can't drag it over any area that has direct sky or very bright areas, as you'll get streaks of just very bright light over the whole image. Done correctly the colours blend into each other, giving a watercolour painterly feel but still with some focus on the subject.'

'It was only when I made the prints that I was struck by the richness of the colours from the seaweed – like a painter's palette.'

Sergey Ryzhkov

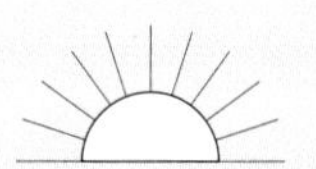

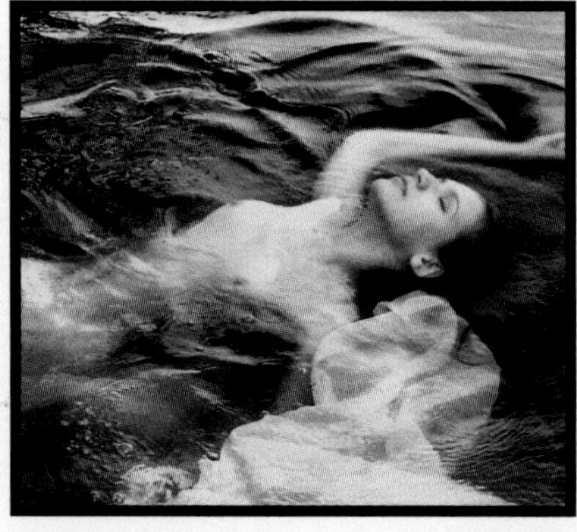

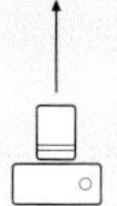

The concept

'I didn't have anything particular planned for this shoot,' says Sergey. I started the day with the model very early and took about 120 photographs on the coast or in the water – it was really successful. This was the first image I took and I just wanted to combine the human body with the beauty of nature.'

The location

Sergey is based in Kiev, the capital of the Ukraine, and took this from a bank of the Dnipro River which runs adjacent to the city. Like many photographers working with the nude, he loves using water because of its elemental nature and the way that it changes the solid appearance of the human body into something more transient.

Composition

Cropped down from 35mm, the square format really suits this image. Sergey used a piece of fabric in the foreground to add a different texture and draw the eye towards the model, who is placed centrally in the frame for added impact. It's the movement of the water and the wonderful mixture of so many colours, contrasting with the pale skin that are the real key to the picture's success.

Lighting and technique

This was taken with only natural light. Sergey is not a fan of using flash, even indoors, because he believes it kills natural colours. At 5am the sun was low above the horizon, producing a soft quality to the light. 'I like to photograph early in the morning because everything in nature seems so fresh at that time,' he says.

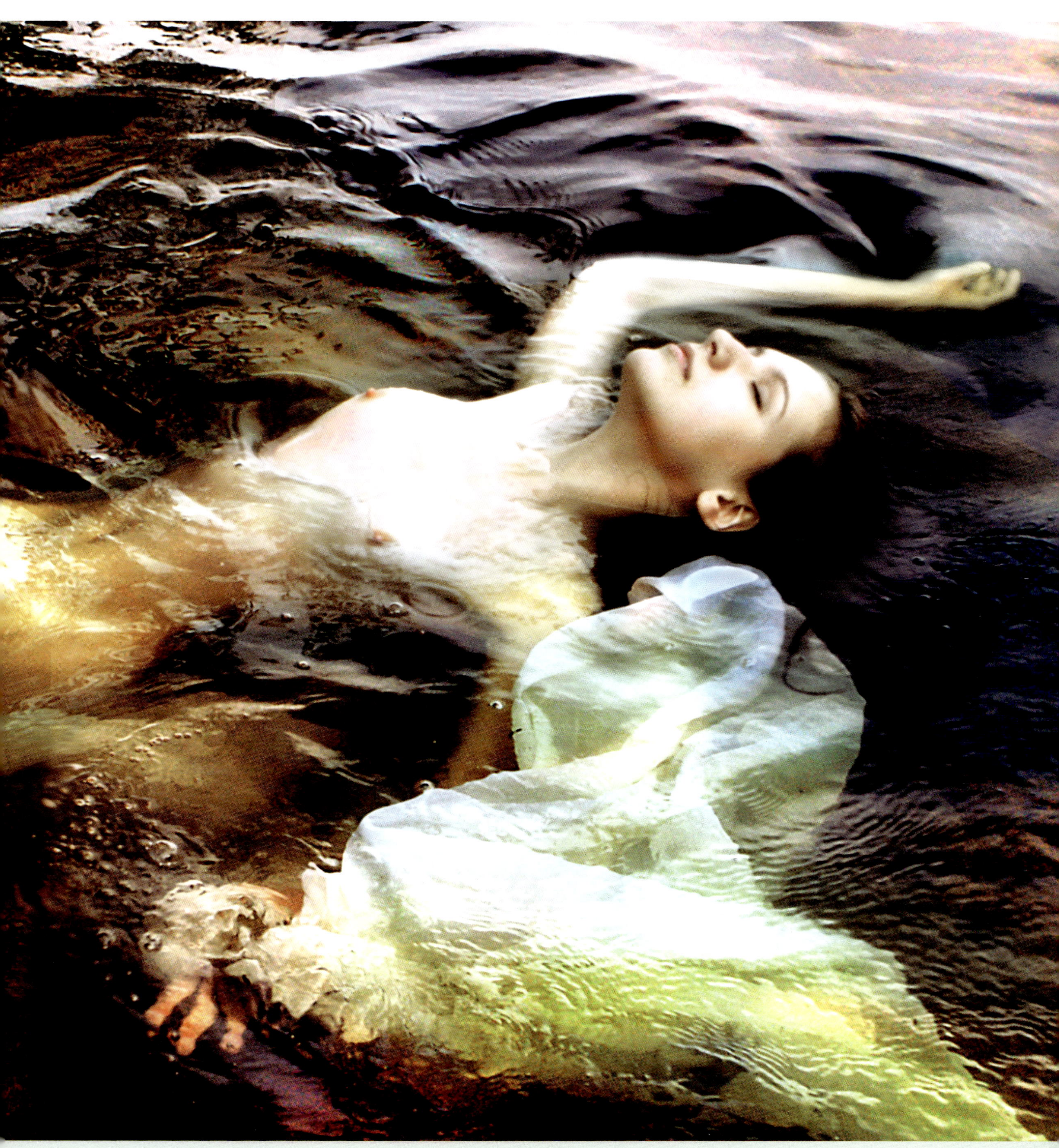

The concept

This is part of a personal body of work by Wade, which he aims to publish eventually as a coffee table book. He wanted the picture to look like it was taken somewhere warm and exotic, despite shooting it in the middle of winter!

The location

For practical purposes, Wade wanted to take the shot in New York where he lives, but cityscapes where not part of his plan. After scouting around for possible places, this spot in the famous Central Park provided the ideal solution, although, even early in the morning, it didn't offer much privacy. 'The park was crowded, but there was some cover to hide. As people walked by, the model covered herself with a blanket I provided,' he says. 'She was a good sport.'

Composition

The lake in the background provides the water element, which so often goes hand in hand with nude photography. The rock and the plant also add interest, colour and texture and make it hard to guess that this was taken in the middle of one of the busiest cities in the world.

Lighting and technique

On a bright day, the early morning light is warm in tone, even in December. The sun was still very low in the sky and behind the model, to the right of the camera, creating a rim-light effect around her hair and body. Wade could have used a reflector to bounce light back on to her face but he preferred the subtlety of the soft shadow. You can see how the water itself has acted as a reflector lower down, creating highlights on her thighs and the edge of her arm. There was quite a contrast between the brightness of the background and the shadier foreground so Wade used a Minolta light meter to take a reading from both areas and then worked out the average for a correct exposure.

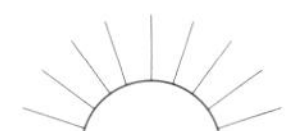

Low sun behind model and
to her right

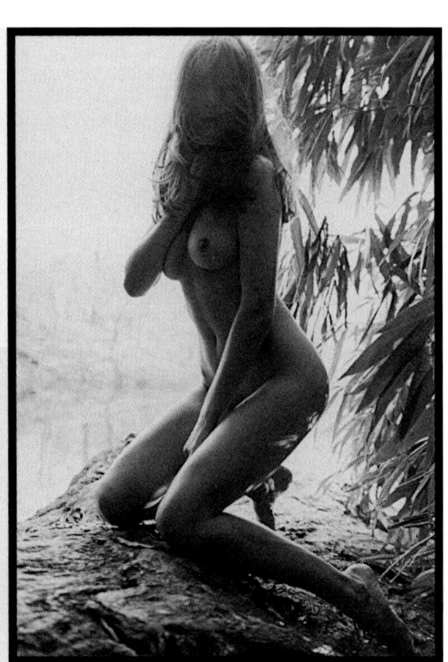

Fact file

Photographer: Wade Schields
Model: Anonymous
Location: Central Park, New York
USA
Time of day: Early morning, December

Technical details

Camera: Nikon F5
Lens: 50mm f/1.8
Film: Fuji 160 NPS
Exposure: 1/30sec at f/4

'Colour photography is about colour and black and white is about everything else.'

Wade Schields

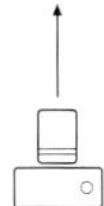

Hand-held 35mm camera

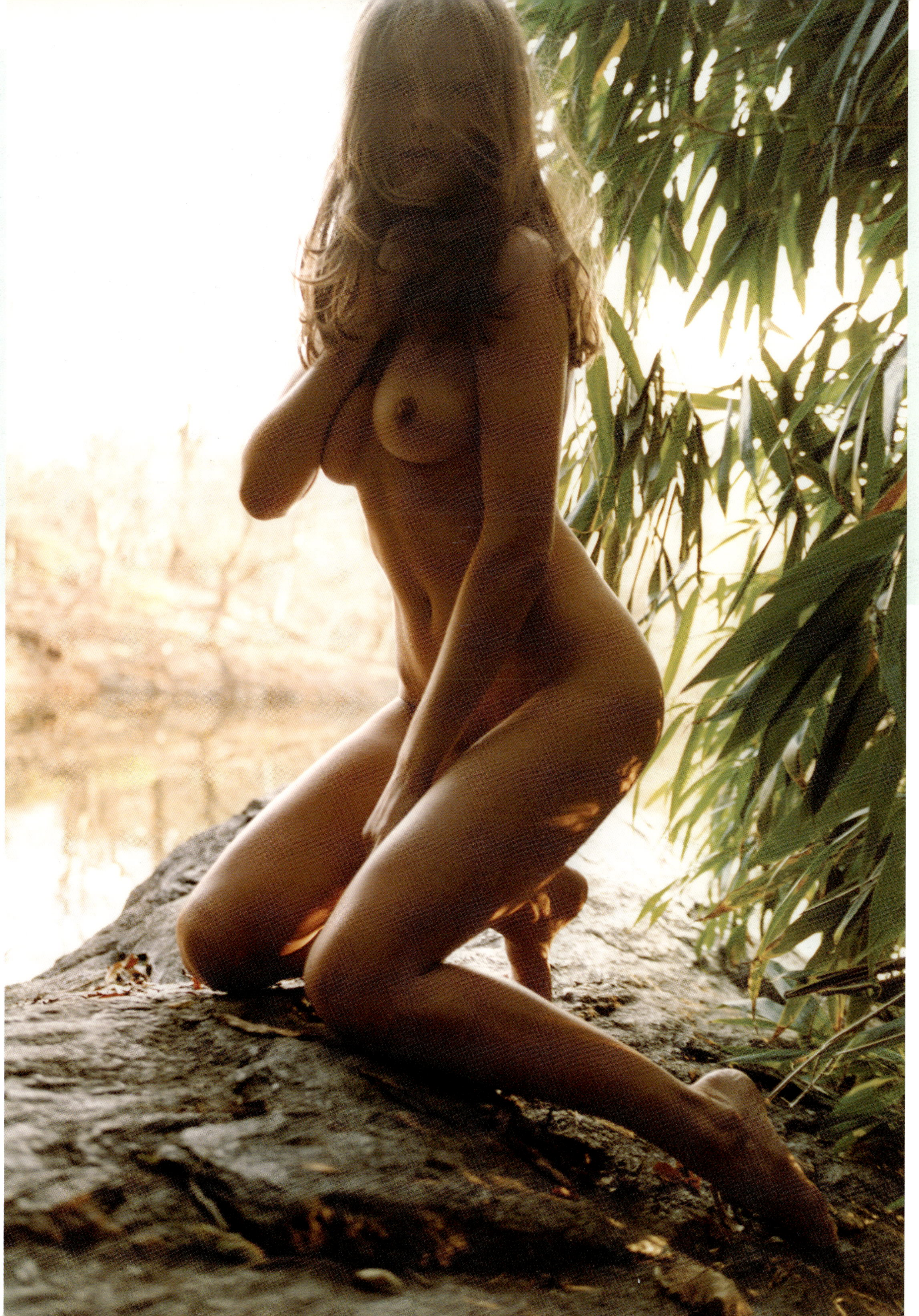

Chapter 5: **Adapting the light**

Unless you're shooting candids, it's pretty rare in photography that you have to accept whatever light that nature throws at you. There are always adjustments that can be made, even if it's only changing the angle of the model, finding a nearby structure that will provide some open shade, or simply being patient and waiting until it changes.

The following pages look at some of the numerous options for enhancing the effect of the light on nude images. They include the use of flash to fill in shadow areas and reduce contrast, and the way tungsten film in daylight can create atmosphere on an otherwise dull and uninspiring day. A fold-up reflector is another useful tool in the kit bag of any photographer of people, allowing extra flexibility when the light is lacking on part of the subject. Finally, Dale Lehmer explains how he produces the magic lighting in his pictures by using trees and other foliage to filter the sun's rays.

Fact file

Photographer:	Dejan Dizdar
Model:	Larisa
Location:	Ashkelon, Israel
Time of day:	Late afternoon, April

Technical details

Camera:	Minolta 800si
Lens:	28–80mm
Film:	Kodak Gold 400
Exposure:	1/90sec aperture not recorded

'Most of the girls I work with are, or become, good friends. Our shooting is based on a mutual interest in creating something.'

Dejan Dizdar

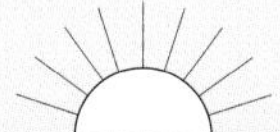

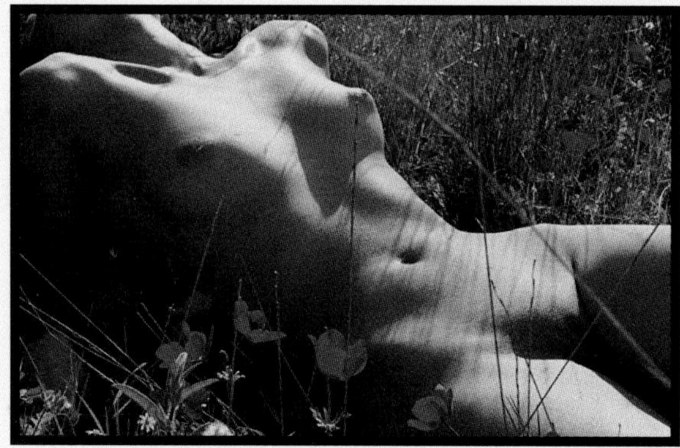

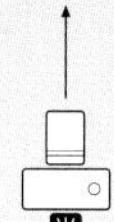

The concept

Dejan has been working on a personal project, photographing the nude in natural outdoor environments for many years. 'It is an "opus", never to be finished,' he says. 'It grows and develops with every new landscape I discover. The first 20 years of black-and-white nudes in nature I have published in a monograph. The next one will be in colour. The overall feeling is one of close interactivity between a woman and her femininity and that of nature.'

The location

'Ashkelon is the town where I live, on the edge of the desert. There are a lot of secluded and unspoilt places around it, with sand dunes, sea, eucalyptus groves and fields, and I often explore them, either to take pictures or just to have fun with my kids. I chose this spot because of the lightness and translucency of the grass and my own childhood memories of the scents of spring.'

Composition

Dejan finds that once he becomes familiar with a location and gets a 'feel' for the place, composing the nude photograph comes relatively easily. He never uses a tripod so he can change his position easily and work more quickly. This shot has a relaxed, peaceful quality to it. The model's reclined pose looks as though she is enjoying soaking up the sun on her body. It was important to include poppies both in the foreground and background because their contrasting splash of colour really lifts these areas of the image.

Lighting and technique

The late afternoon sun was quite low and the model was in semi-shade. Dejan used a camera-mounted flashgun, covered with a diffusing material and set as fill-in to create areas of highlight on the body. This was preferable to shooting earlier in the day, when the sun was very strong and harsh and the excessive contrast would have created metering difficulties.

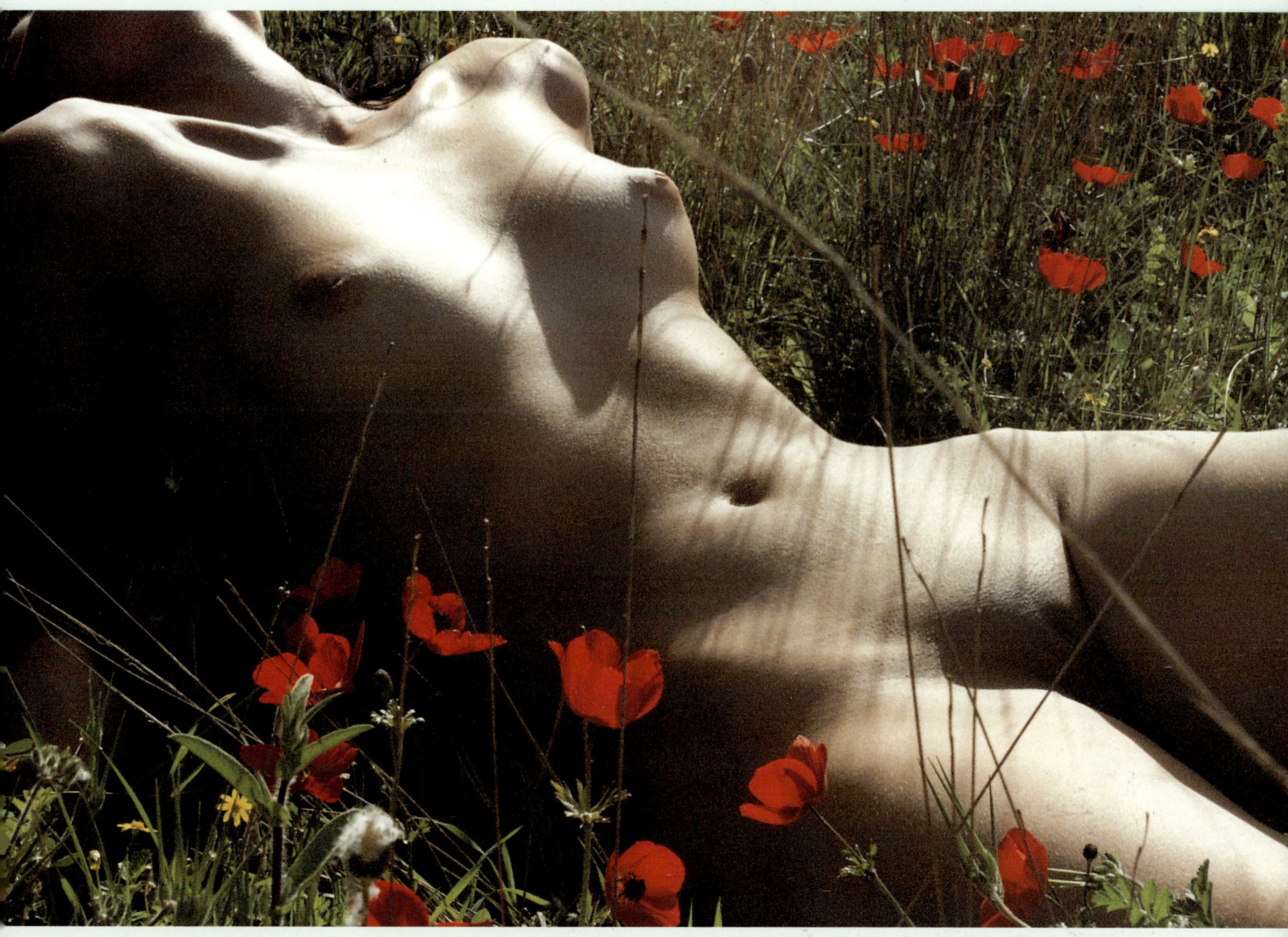

'The light in Israel is not like European light. It is very strong, so I often need to use either a reflector or flash in order to make the image appear more balanced and normal.'

Dejan Dizdar

Fact file

Photographer: Bob Carlos Clarke
Model: Oris
Location: River Thames, London, UK
Time of day: Mid-morning, January

Technical details

Camera: Pentax 6x7
Lens: 400mm
Film: Ilford HP5
Exposure: Not recorded

The concept

'Oris had been caught in a carjacking in New York and had six bullets in his torso. I took some extraordinary pictures of his scars in the studio and then we went down to the river for a few more shots, just as personal work,' recalls Bob.

The location

Oris was standing up to his knees in the mud of the riverbank and the background is the sunlit river behind him, dramatically overexposed.

Composition

In contrast to the previous pictures showing Oris's scars on the front of his body, Bob chose a more conventional three-quarter-length rear view here to show the contours and strength of the body in a sculptural way.

Lighting and technique

On a bright but overcast day, the water in the background was around three stops brighter than the model's very dark skin. Bob exposed for the latter, leaving the background to blow out, and then bleached it further in the darkroom with potassium ferrocyanide. He took the picture standing on some steps, looking down slightly on the model, and used a 400mm lens to compress the perspective. A Lumedyne flash unit was supported on a boom, held by an assistant, about four feet above Oris to provide fill-in light on his neck and shoulders.

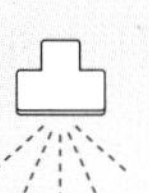

Lumedyne flash

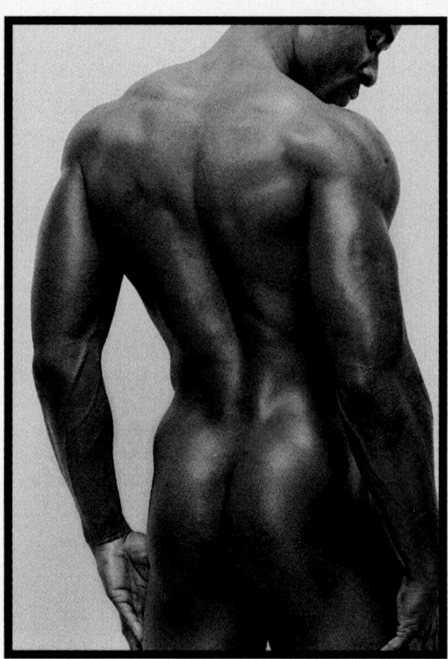

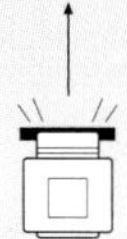

Medium format camera
with ringflash

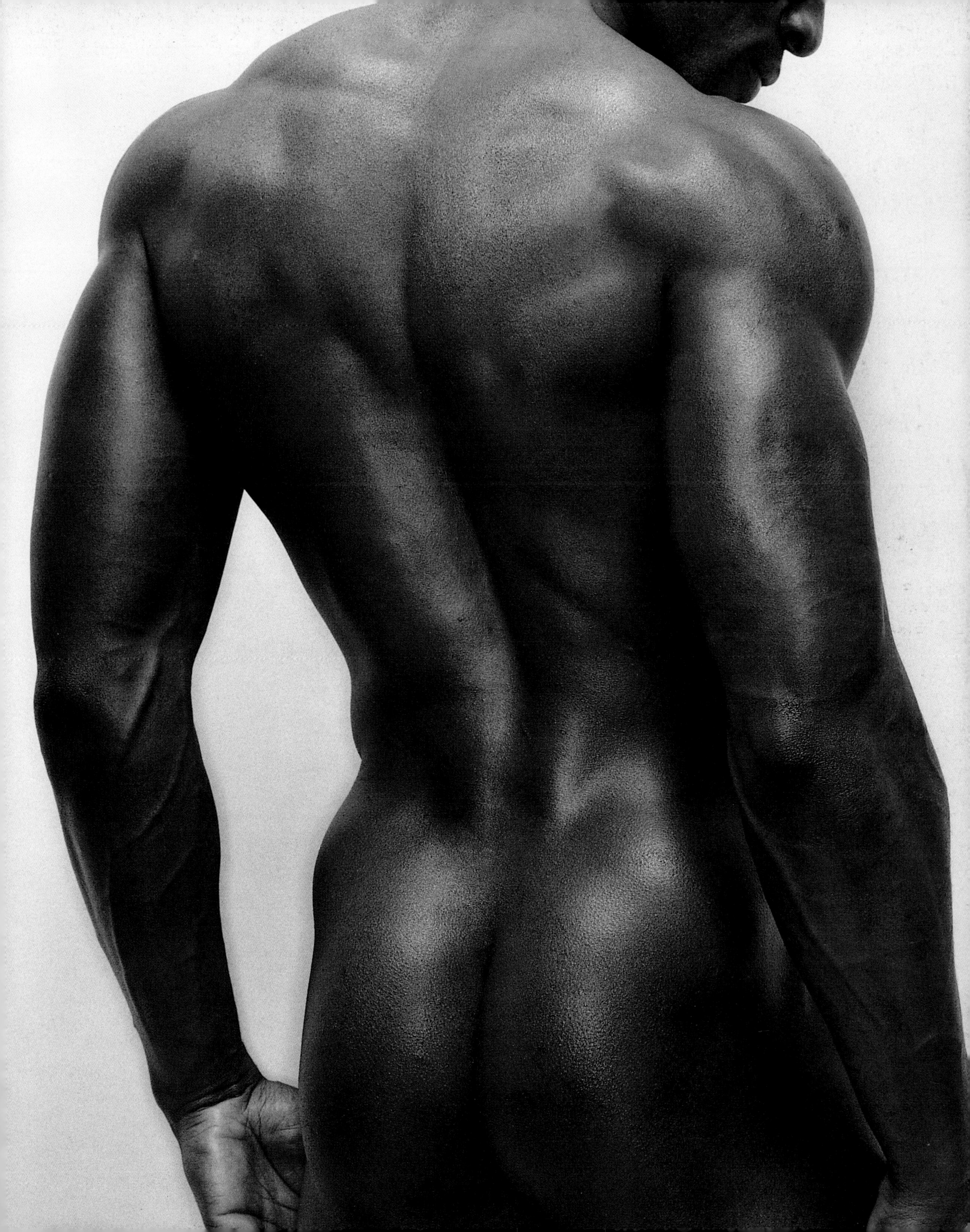

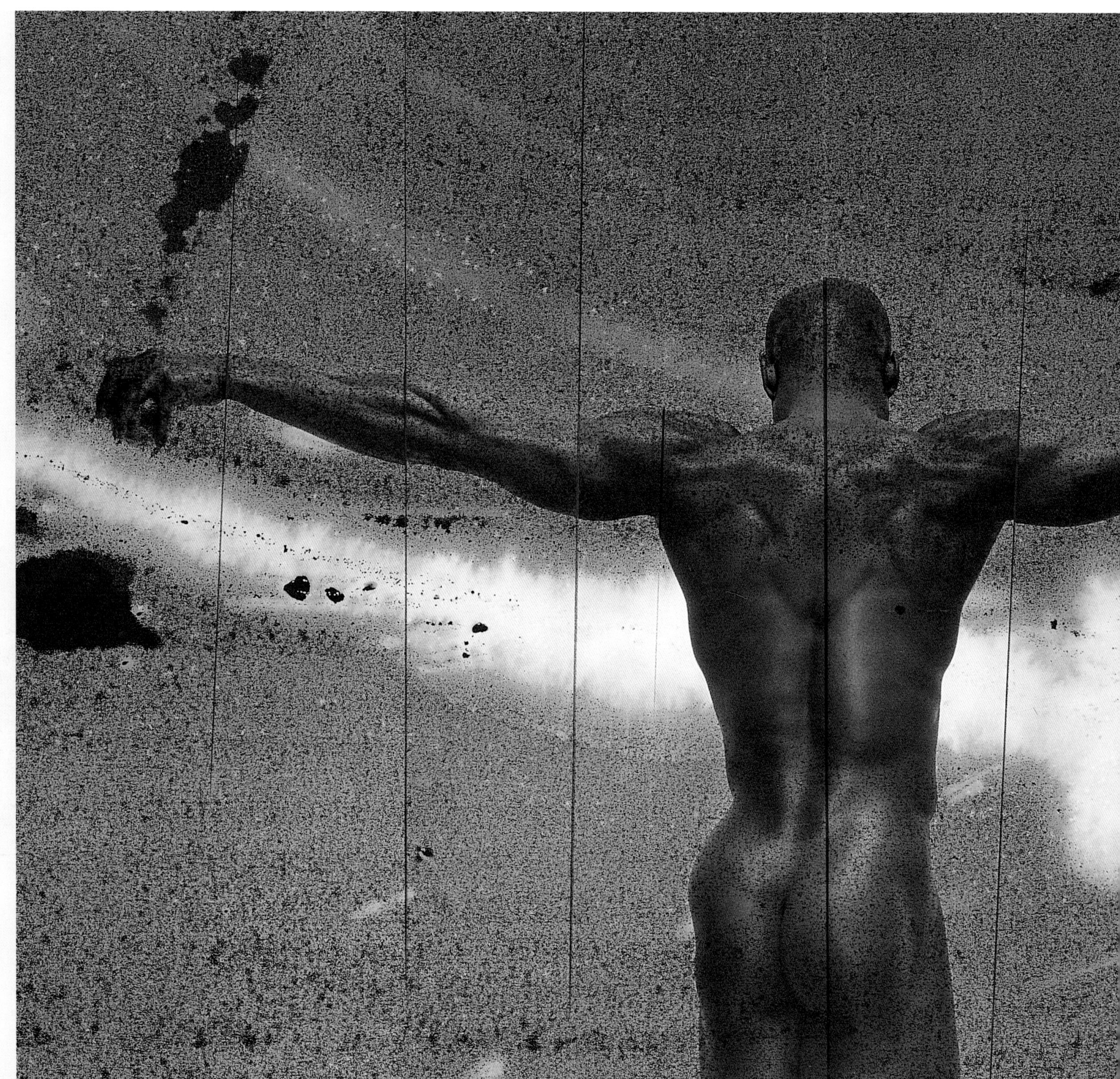

Fact file

Photographer:	Bob Carlos Clarke
Model:	Oris
Location:	River Thames, London, UK
Time of day:	Mid-morning, January

Technical details

Camera:	Pentax 6x7
Lens:	400mm
Film:	Ilford HP5
Exposure:	Not recorded

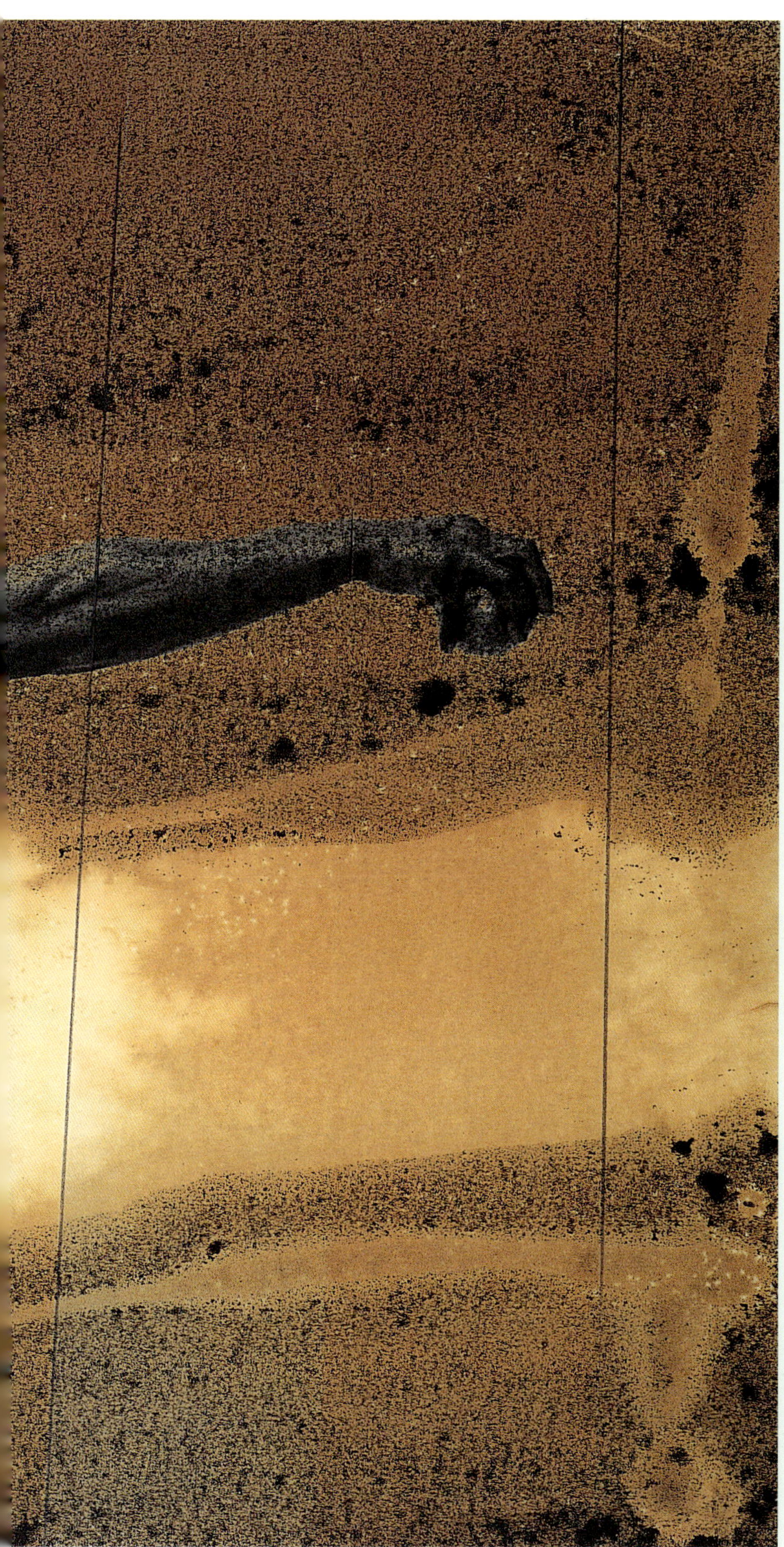

The concept

This was from the same shoot as the picture by Bob Carlos Clarke on the previous spread. As before, it was not commissioned work but prompted by Oris's fantastic physique, his entertaining personality and his willingness to pose.

The location

Most of the shots from this session show the Thames-side location in more detail, with Oris up to his thighs in the mud of the riverbank. For this image, Bob used a long lens and overexposed the water in the background to make Oris the sole focus.

Composition

The emphasis here is on the strength and muscle tone of the model's back, shoulders and particularly arms which, outstretched like this, seem to have a huge span.

Lighting and technique

The winter sun was bright, but diffused by cloud cover. A little more light was required on Oris's body to give the muscles definition so Bob used fill-in flash in the form of a Lumedyne head, supported on a boom above the subject by an assistant. The background was originally the river and this toned and textured effect was achieved by contaminating the straight print with another that had been pre-soaked with developer before the final fixing.

'As a rule I hate shooting male models. Men who make a living from their looks can be quite dull, but Oris is an exception. Most of the guys I shoot are strong personalities in their own right, like Keith Richards, Marco Pierre White or Vinnie Jones.'

Bob Carlos Clarke

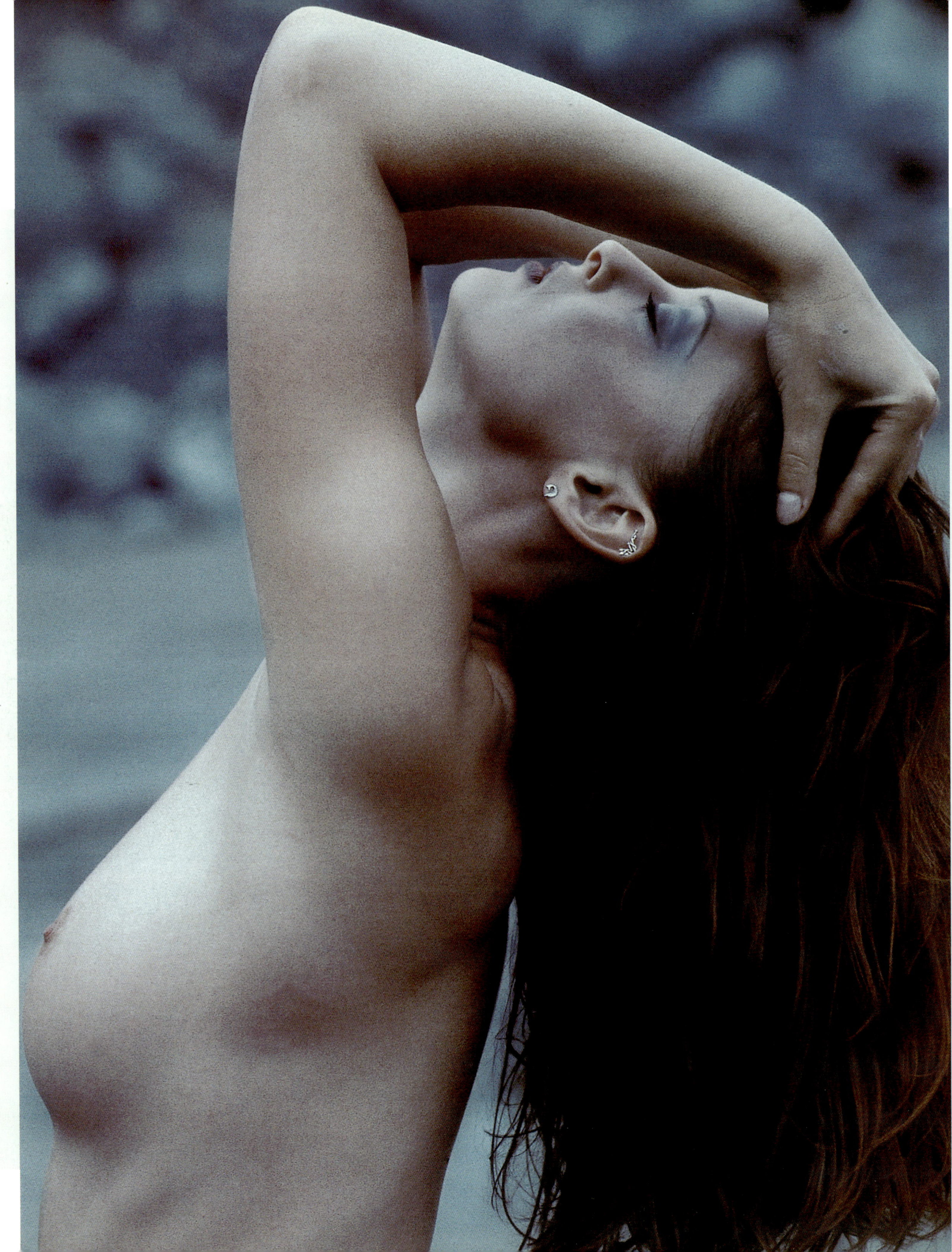

'Hikers like to say that it's never the wrong weather, just the wrong clothes you're wearing. With photography, it's not the wrong weather, but the wrong film you're using.'

Carsten Tschach

The concept

'We set up the date for this shoot but sadly it turned out to be cloudy, boring light with rain from time to time,' says Carsten. 'We didn't want to lose the day so we tried to make the best of it.'

The location

This disused quarry is a favourite place for Carsten. He likes the combination of the hard rocks with the soft female form and, because the environment is without any vibrant colour, it works particularly well for cool-toned images.

Composition

Carsten used his zoom lens at the longest end – 200mm – to frame in tightly on Ramona and put the background out of focus, giving just a hint of the rocky texture. The pose is striking, especially because of the model's hair, which provides a strong colour contrast to the overall blue tone.

Lighting and technique

'It was a very dull day with no contrast and no shadows – just very diffused light from the sky above,' recalls Carsten. 'To make the picture more interesting we used blue make-up, with tungsten-balanced film to give the blue colour cast. This film is my favourite choice for grey, cloudy days, but you have to be careful if you have sunlight in the picture as it will burn out and create a dull image. I always take a spot meter reading on the brightest part of the model's skin and then underexpose this by one stop. Black-and-white film is another option for grey days, but I prefer shooting in colour.'

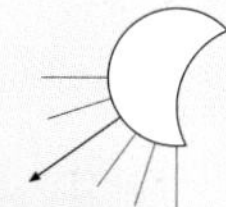

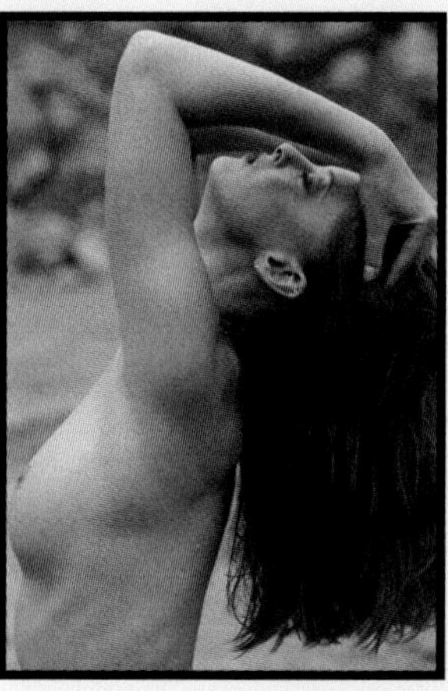

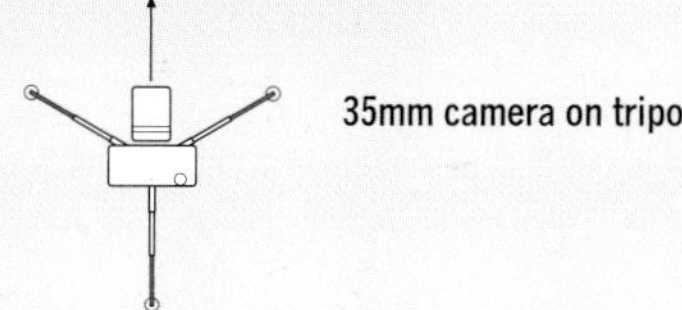

Fact file

Photographer:	Carsten Tschach
Model:	Ramona
Location:	A quarry in Germany
Time of day:	2pm, August

Technical details

Camera:	Nikon F100
Lens:	80–2100
Film:	Kodak Elite 160T
Exposure:	1/60sec at f/2.8

Fact file

Photographer: Dale Lehmer
Model: Claire
Location: Caves, Rosendale, New York, USA
Time of day: 3pm, August

Technical details

Camera: Olympus E10 (digital)
Lens: 35mm
Film: n/a
Exposure: 1/80sec at f/2.8

The concept

'I wanted the combination of the harsh rocks in the background and the delicate, soft beauty of Claire to encompass the entire yin-yang spectrum of masculine/feminine, soft/hard, and beautiful/ugly,' says Dale. 'I believe this whole unity of opposites to be an integral part of the natural world.'

The location

Dale was after a rugged natural background, and found it by some caves, not far from where he lives.

Composition

The fabric here is a fine, mesh bed cover and Dale had two reasons for using it. 'I wanted to tone down the bright sun so I could shoot at different times of the day, other than early morning or evening. I also thought it would add some elegance and delicacy for interest and effect.' The glimpse of rocks in the background provides an important contrast in texture.

Lighting and technique

Although it was a clear, bright, day, the sun was partly obscured by foliage and Dale found that his model was not well enough lit underneath the fabric. He rarely uses a reflector but found it the answer here. 'I used a gold reflector, inside the opening of the material, to catch a few rays of sun shining through the leaves and reflect them on to Claire,' he explains. 'One problem with such fine, sheer cloth shot digitally, is that it becomes very "noisy" and blurred when seen on the screen and printed. It was ruining my pictures and I was trying to get rid of it in Photoshop. I just tried blurring it more and, to my surprise, it actually cleared it up so the image could be used. Work that one out!'

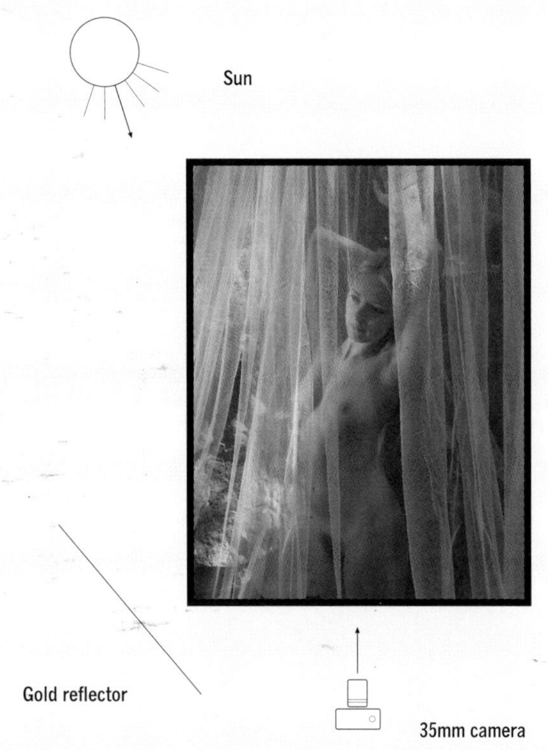

'The reflector was just enough to highlight the model with a beautiful gold colour, which worked well with the light brown cloth.'

Dale Lehmer

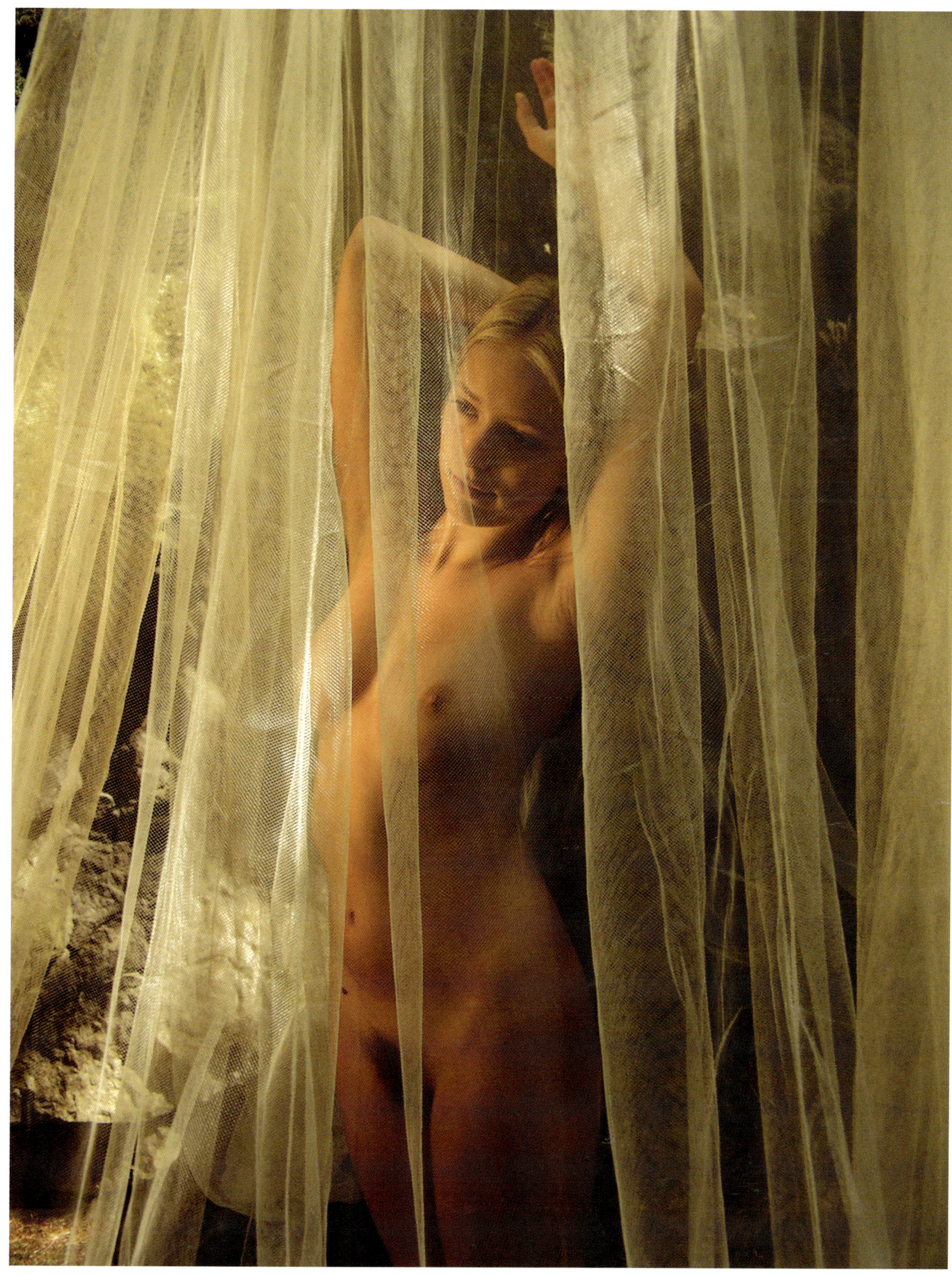

 125

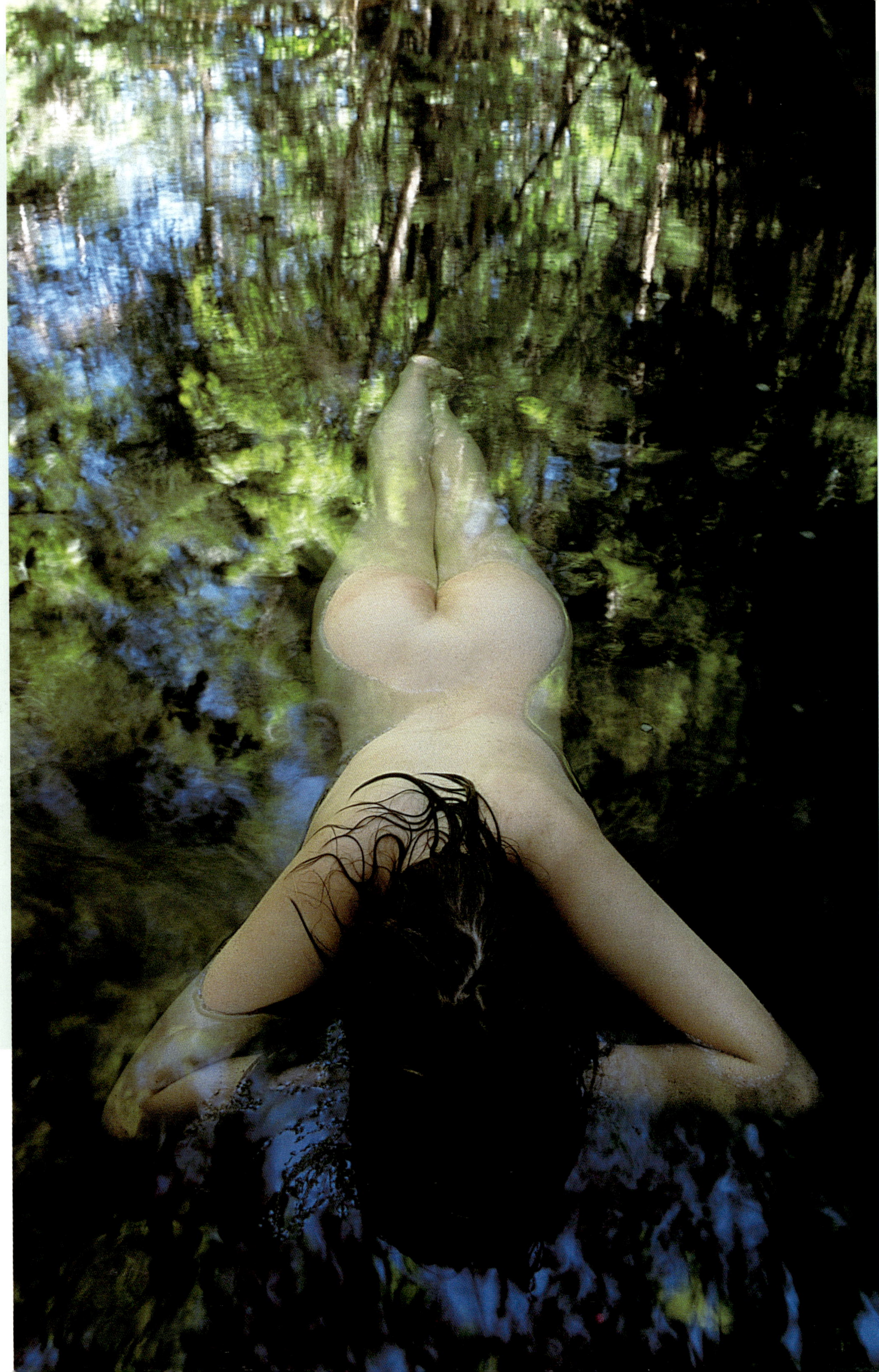

Fact file

Photographer: Eric Boutilier-Brown
Model: Romina
Location: Woodland brook, Nova Scotia, Canada
Time of day: 1.30pm, June

Technical details

Camera: Nikon F3
Lens: 17mm, f/2.8
Film: Fuji Astia RAP
Exposure: 1/30sec at f/8

The concept

Having decided to create an image using the water, the picture developed as a result of finding suitable lighting in tricky conditions, as well as catching the beautiful colours of the reflections.

The location

'Both the model and I really enjoy working with water, for the extra complexity and random element it lends to images,' explains Eric. 'This particular place is relatively remote, ensuring long, uninterrupted sessions.'

Composition

'The brook where we worked filled a broad, shallow rock-shelf and looked more like ice, or standing water than a moving stream,' says Eric. 'The real magic, however, came from the reflections of the trees and sky above the pool, reflected into the water.' The use of an ultra wide-angle lens was important to draw the eye along the figure and create a flow to the image.

Lighting and technique

'Because the session was in the middle of the day, the biggest problem we had was overcoming the incredible contrast caused by the bright sunny day,' recalls Eric. 'In the deep woods, the bright shafts of sunlight were almost blinding against the shadowed undergrowth and open shade of the forest. Fortunately, one of the better spaces to work in was totally in shade, providing the low light I prefer for river work to permit longer shutter speeds to blur the water. It also created a nice, even light which gives such a glow to Romina's pale skin.'

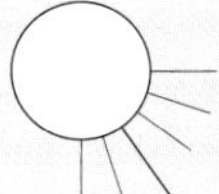

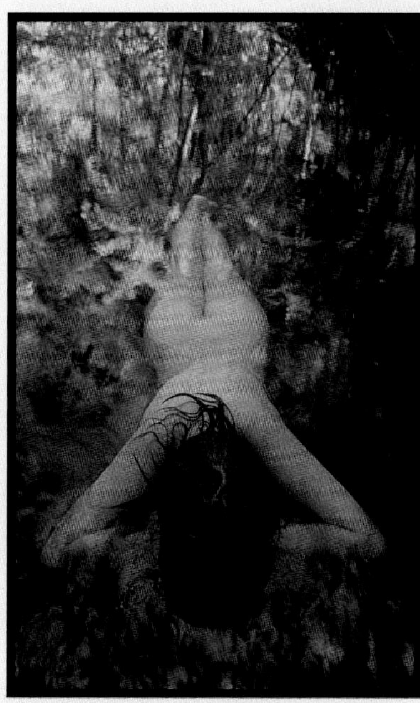

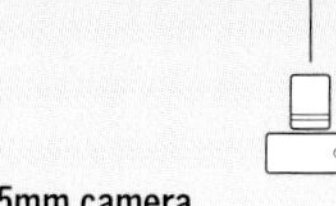

'When Romina moved into the pool and let the water around her settle, everything just came alive. The dance of the eye between the figure and the reflection, and back again, is a real pleasure.'

Eric Boutilier-Brown

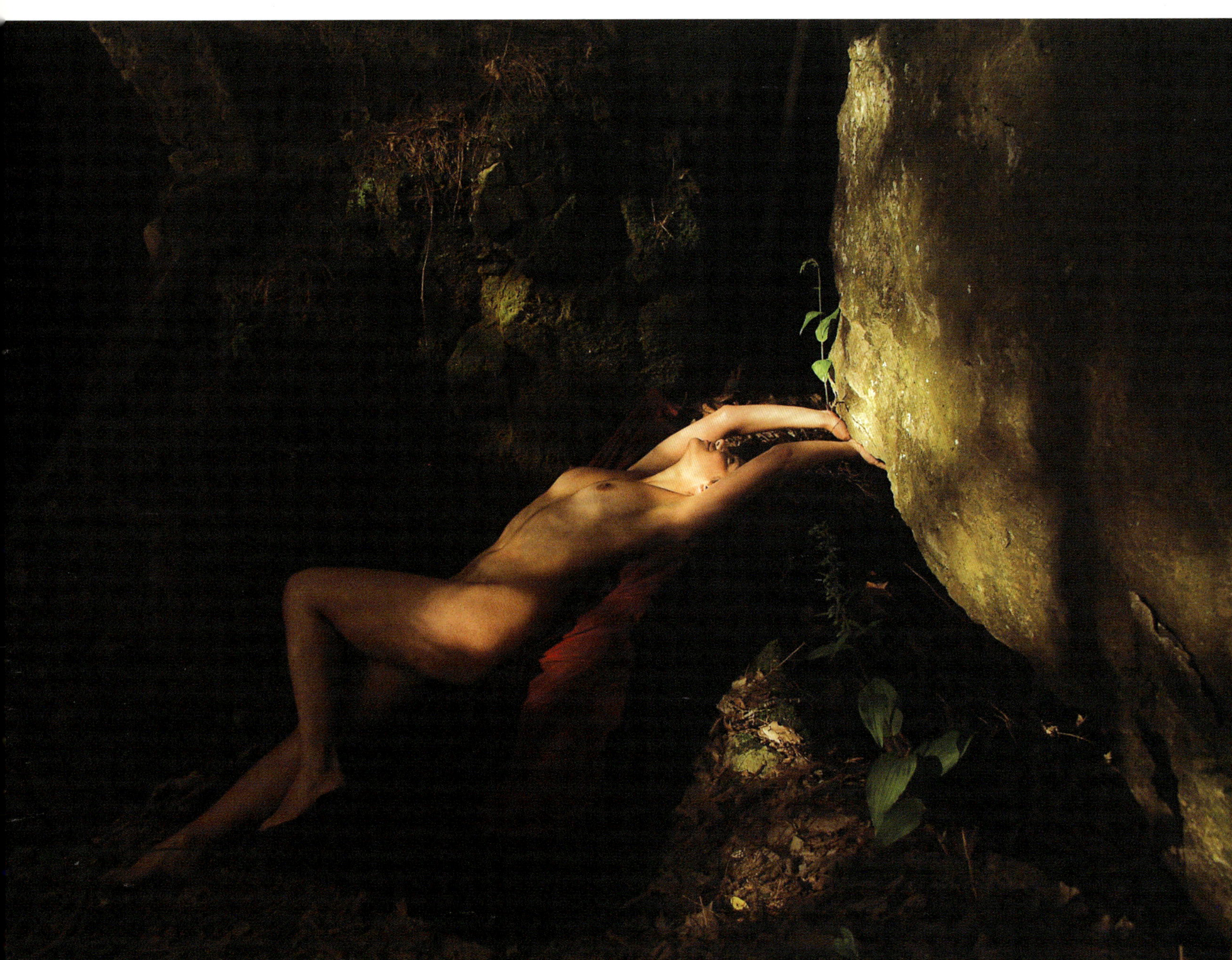

Fact file

Photographer: Dale Lehmer
Model: Angela
Location: High Falls, Woodstock, New York, USA
Time of day: 4pm, August

Technical details

Camera: Olympus E20n (digital)
Lens: 35mm
Film: n/a
Exposure: 1/125sec at f/4

'I am trying to develop the skill of looking at varied landscapes through my lens and seeing what elements will be shaded or highlighted and what will become negative space when I underexpose an image. I then frame with that composition in mind.'

Dale Lehmer

The concept

'This shot is about eroticism and passion, giving birth to light and new growth,' says Dale. 'I kept the image dark and atmospheric to emphasise the mystery of birth and creation.'

The location

Dale was shooting in caves near his home in the late afternoon sun. He favours locations where natural filters, particularly leaves, help to soften the effect of the sun. 'I find that pine and hemlock trees that have needles are best as they tend to filter out the light in small portions, so there are no heavy shadows on the models. Here there were oak leaves in different degrees of density, so the light came through in varying levels of intensity.'

Composition

'The sun had just moved to this spot in the area we were shooting,' he recalls. 'I placed the rock in the right-hand side of the image with Angela in a diagonal position, more or less underneath the rock, to give the feeling she is holding it up, sustaining it. The small green plant growing from her hands signifies new life and the red cloth she is lying on adds some colour and eroticism.'

Lighting and technique

The sun was coming from behind Dale's left shoulder, mostly through leaves, and you can see how the light on the model's body changes according to their density. A small gap in the leaves allowed the sunlight to come through directly, highlighting the area around the large rock. Dale underexposed the image to darken everything except the areas he wanted to focus on – the rock, the plant and Angela's upper body.

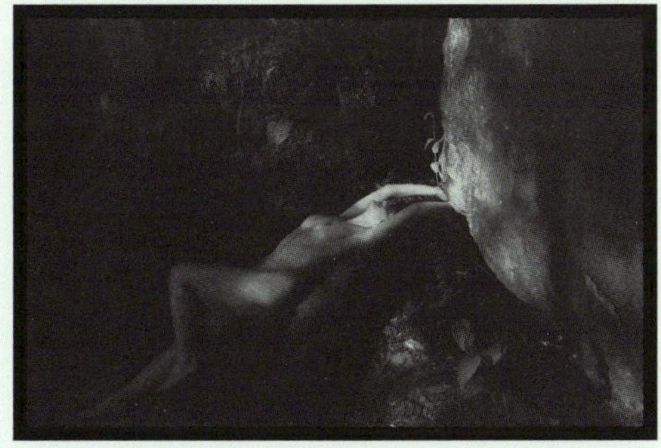

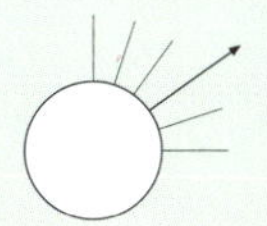

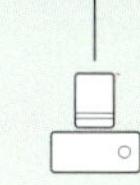

Fact file

Photographer: Dale Lehmer
Model: Angela
Location: Minnawaska State Park, New York, USA
Time of day: 2pm, August

Technical details

Camera: Olympus E20n (digital)
Lens: 35mm
Film: n/a
Exposure: 1/640sec at f/4.5

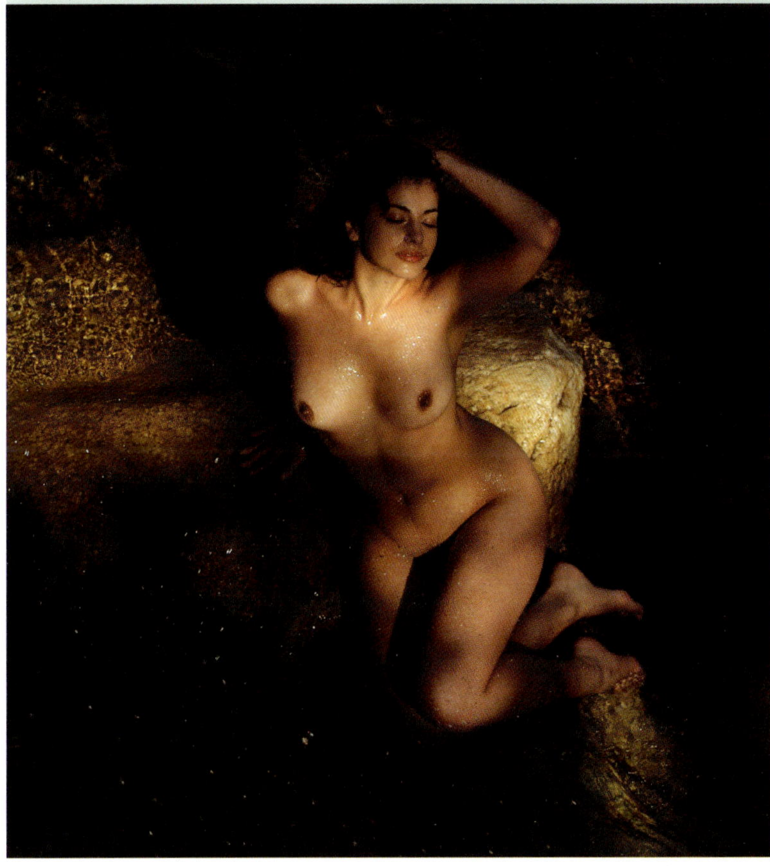

In the middle of the afternoon, the direct sunlight was partially filtered through clouds. Dale underexposed greatly to darken the shadow areas and make the highlights stand out. 'The low, shadowy light and glistening spray help to create a mysterious and sensuous image of a very beautiful woman,' he says. 'Her erotic-looking expression of satisfaction was a response to the cool spray that showered her on an extremely hot day.'

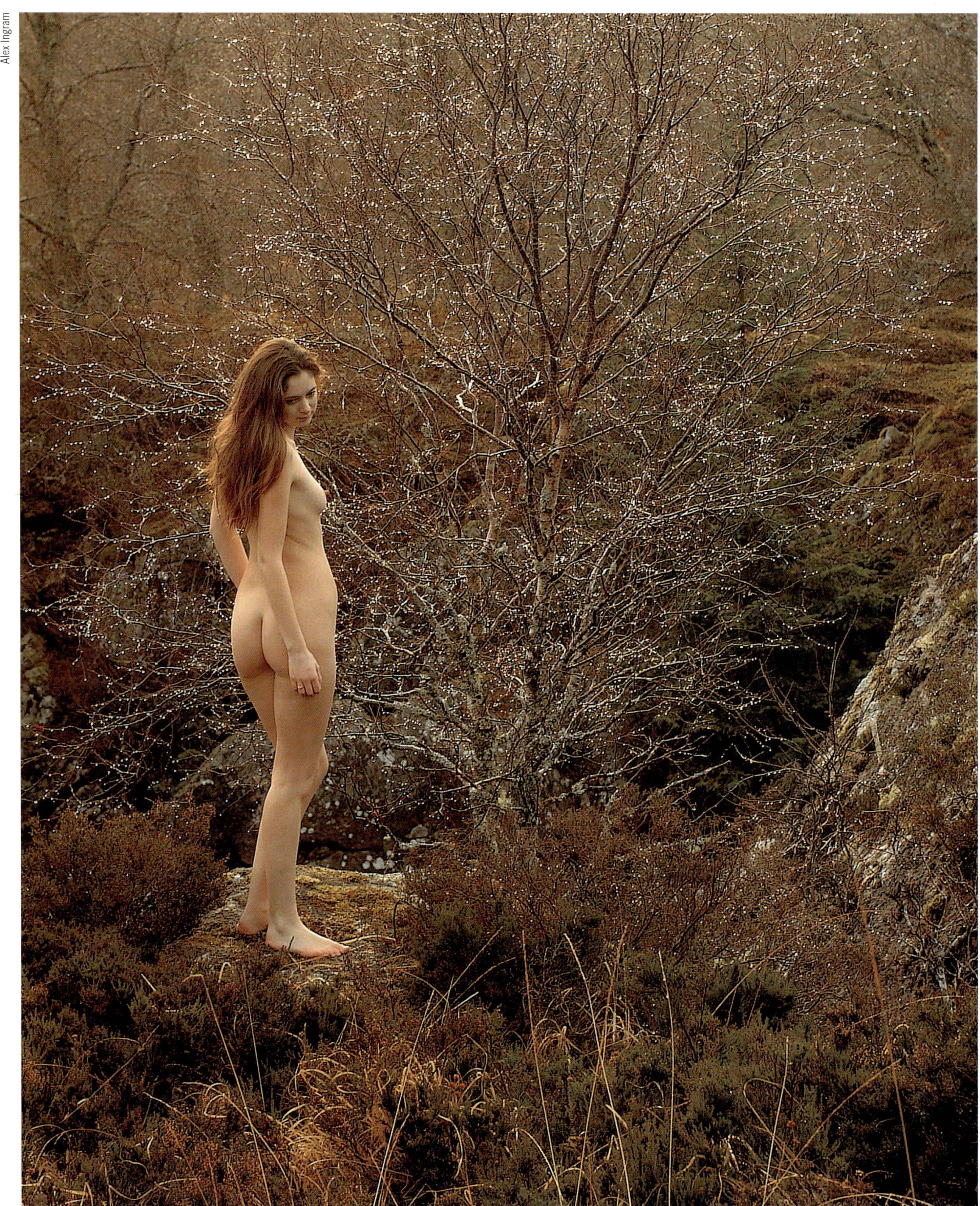

Chapter 6: **Landscape & the body**

Many photographers have a dual interest – they love the form and shape of the human body and have equal passion for nature and the environment. The two combined makes a compelling partnership, but a challenging one if the nude is to look in harmony with the landscape rather than an incongruous addition.

The starting point is to find the location. Some photographers do this on treks prior to the shoot, perhaps taking Polaroids or digital pictures as a record. Others find that inspiration comes while exploring a promising area on the day. Either way, once the place has been found, the light is the next hurdle – it has to enhance both the nude and the landscape.

Again, photographers have different approaches. Some plan carefully ahead, visiting favoured spots at different times of day and year, and taking note of the movement of the sun. Others rely on good fortune or patience. Every landscape photographer will be able to recall countless occasions when they have had to wait for a break in the clouds or for the sun to rise a little further to make their pictures come alive. Then there are the lucky breaks, when the perfect light presents itself and you just have to catch it before your chance is gone. When all the variable ingredients come together, the effects can be stunning, as the following pictures demonstrate.

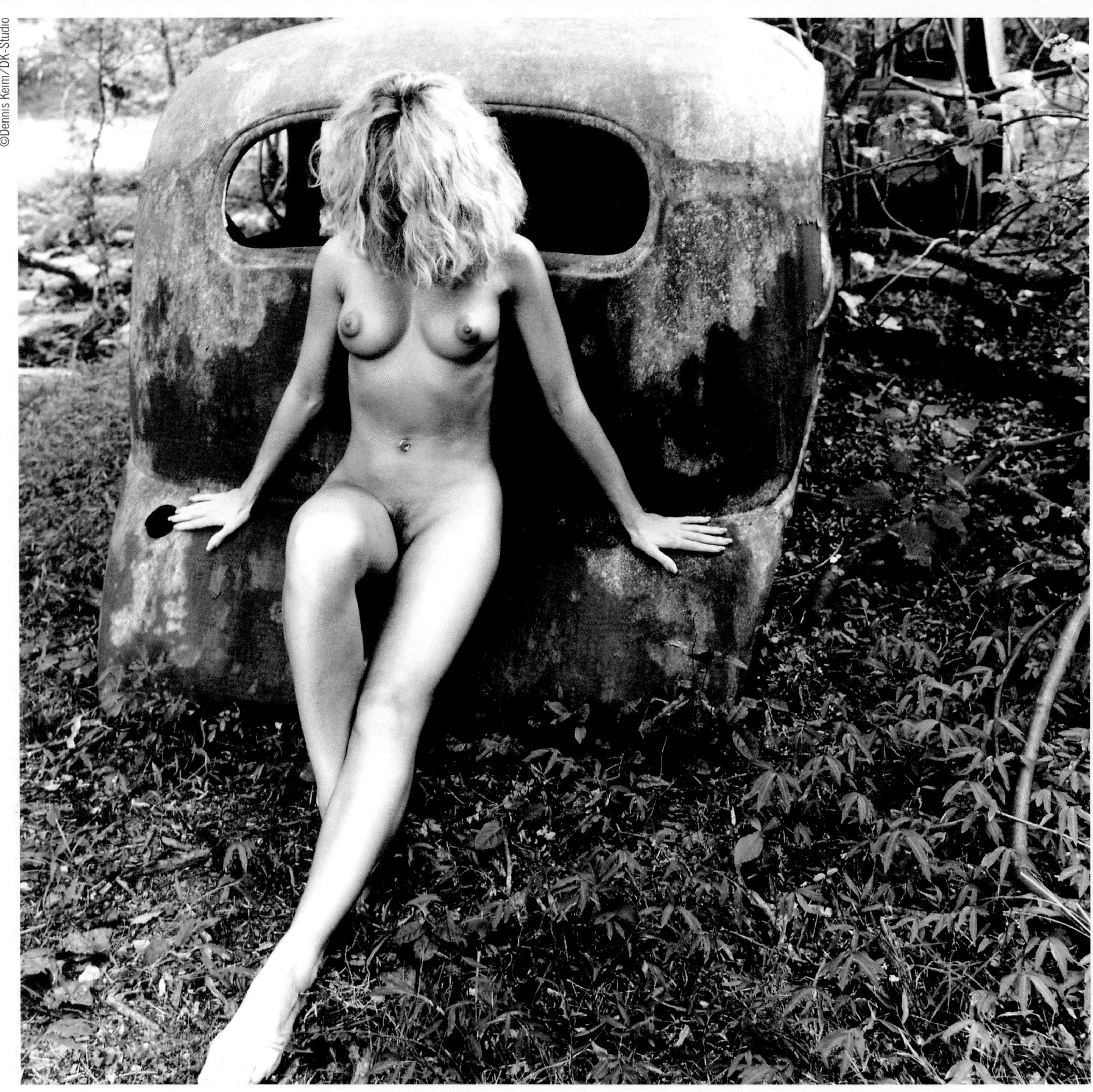

' I always scout the location before asking the model to participate because it's important to have a clear understanding and vision of the type of shots you want to accomplish. That way you have a more invigorated model who will actively help you achieve the desired results.'

Dennis Keim

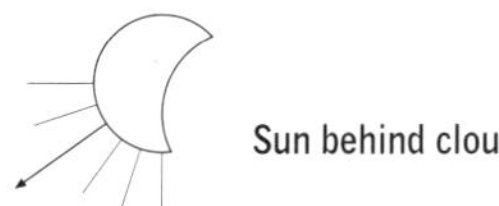

Fact file

Photographer: Dennis Keim
Model: Anonymous
Location: Moontown, Alabama, USA
Time of day: Mid-afternoon, October

Technical details

Camera: Bronica SQA-M
Lens: 55mm
Film: Ilford PanF
Exposure: 1/60sec at f/5.6

The concept

This is part of an on-going fine art photography series, entitled 'Abandoned', that Dennis created for a gallery exhibition. 'In this particular image I was trying to capture the interaction of the individual as it related to the junk cars, and the potential of the naked body to seem to merge with the automobile,' explains Dennis.

The location

'In the "Abandoned" series I've used numerous locations, including deserted houses, warehouses and junk yards,' says Dennis. 'This location is one of three private resources I have access to for shooting nudes outdoors. It offers various settings including waterfalls, rock formations and the array of abandoned vehicles.'

Composition

Dennis followed the classic rule of thirds for this composition, with the model positioned just to the left of centre and the eye drawn from the lower left of the image to the top right. He used a wide-angle lens to include a good part of the surrounding foliage on the ground which, together with the decay of the vehicle, adds a sense of harsh reality to the picture.

Lighting and technique

No reflectors or other accessory lighting equipment were used here. The sun was directly above and slightly behind the model and, due to the slightly overcast autumn day, the light is beautifully diffused. Dennis measured the exposure by taking an incident light reading from the model's position.

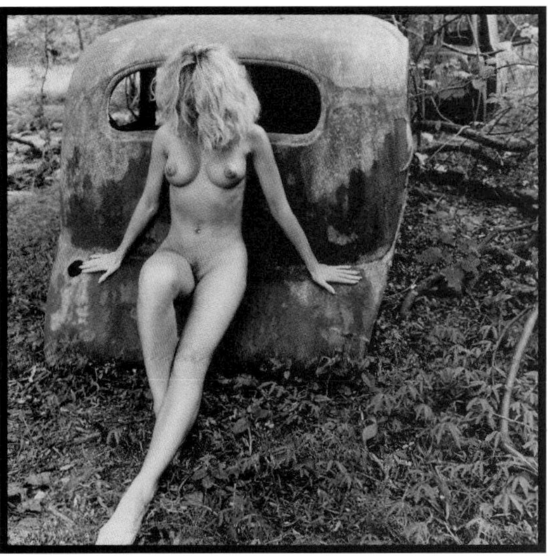

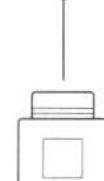

Medium format camera

'When I first stood on this road, I was so impressed by this landscape and the sheer scale of nature,' says Sylvie. 'The challenge was to find a way of bringing together the monumental landscape and the model so that I kept the sense of space without the nude appearing too small in the picture.'

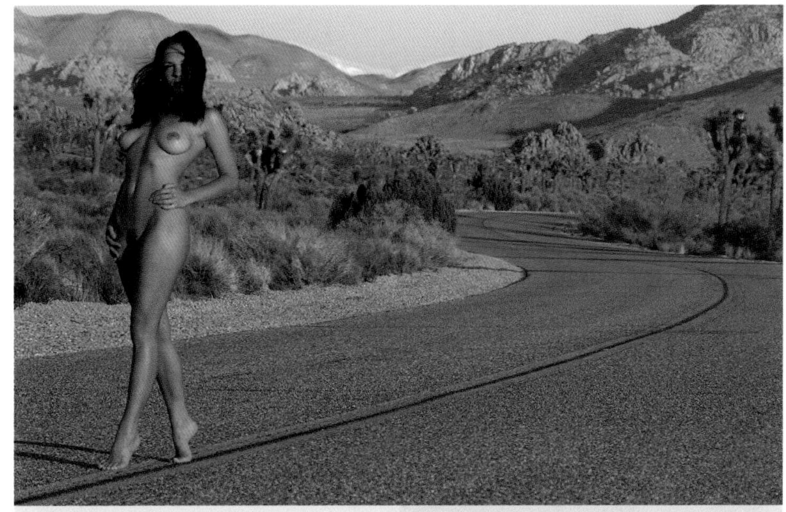

Fact file

Photographer: Sylvie Blum
Model: Natalie
Location: Joshua National Park, California, USA
Time of day: 8pm, June

Technical details

Camera: Hasselblad 500 CM
Lens: 80mm
Film: Ilford FP4
Exposure: Not recorded

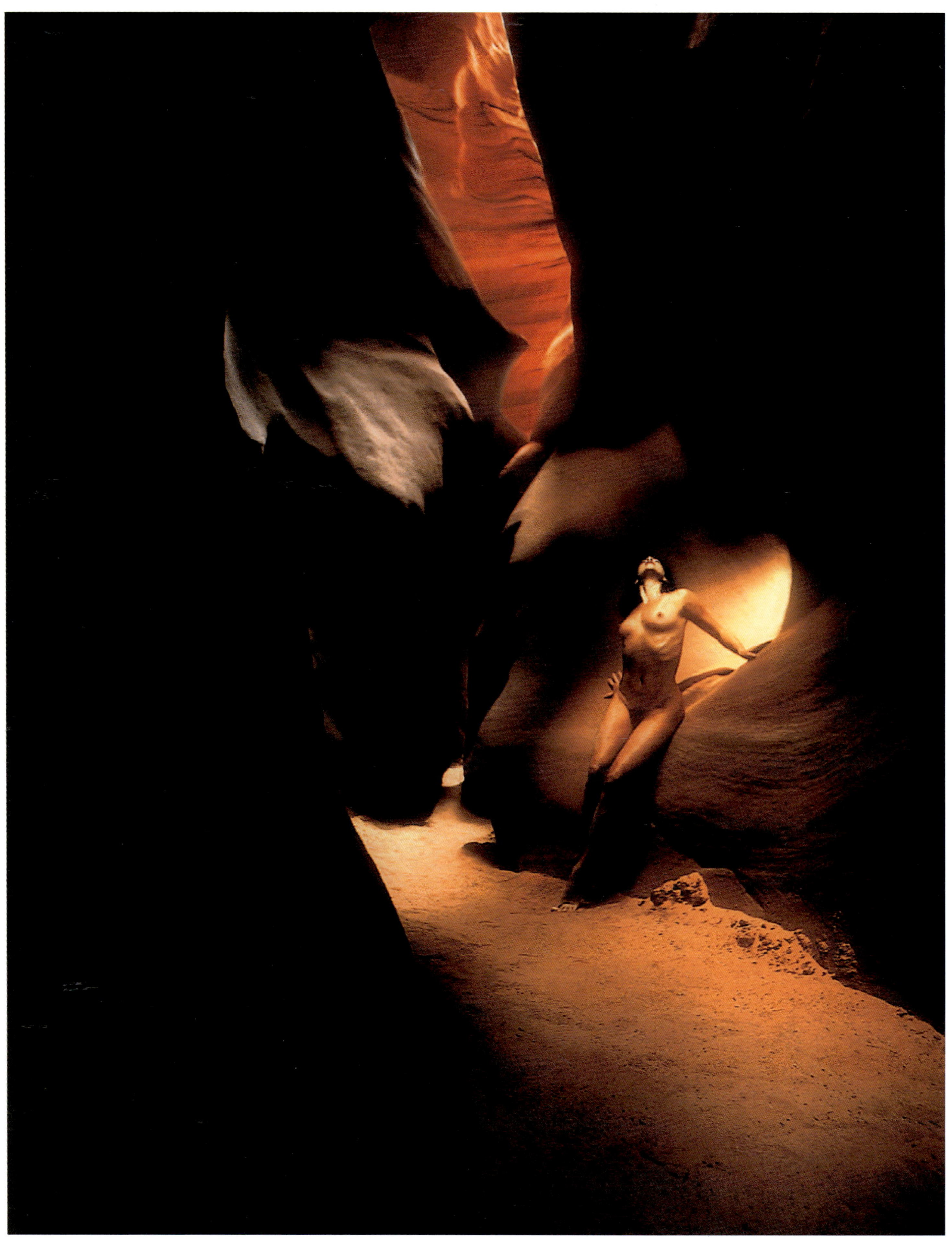

Fact file		Technical details	
Photographer:	Mark Esposito	Camera:	Olympus OM-1
Model:	Karina	Lens:	35–70mm
Location:	Antelope Canyon, Navajo Nation, USA	Film:	Fuji Provia 100
		Exposure:	1/8sec at f/8
Time of day:	Mid-afternoon, late September		

The concept

'I was looking to capture a sense of emotion from my model that would integrate nicely with the drama of the landscape,' says Mark. 'Clouds were drifting across the sky so shafts of light periodically shot through and drifted into the canyon.'

The location

'This canyon is an artist's dream. It doesn't take a rocket scientist to appreciate the stunning natural beauty – and the light. The one thing constant about it is change. If I could live there, I would.'

Composition

Mark found that the most important thing here was to find a balance in the composition. The landscape and the figure had to compliment each other, with neither one dominating the scene. Fortunately he had time to consider this, setting the camera on a tripod and finding the best angle of view and position for the model while they were waiting for the light.

Lighting and technique

'Nowhere is light so fickle, yet so alluring as in the canyons. Midday sun in September is not overhead and, in the canyons, it's a matter of luck anyway, as to when and where direct light will invade. It's not necessarily direct light that is the most interesting or desirable, anyway. Reflected and bounced light is what I look for most of the time. It's soft, flattering and offers wonderful shades of colour.'

' As we were walking through the canyon, we rounded a corner and this scene presented itself. It lasted long enough to say "Wow! Look at that" and it was gone. So Karina and I got set up and waited...and waited...until finally the clouds allowed the sun a quick burst of light. It was just long enough to get this shot and then it vanished.'

Mark Esposito

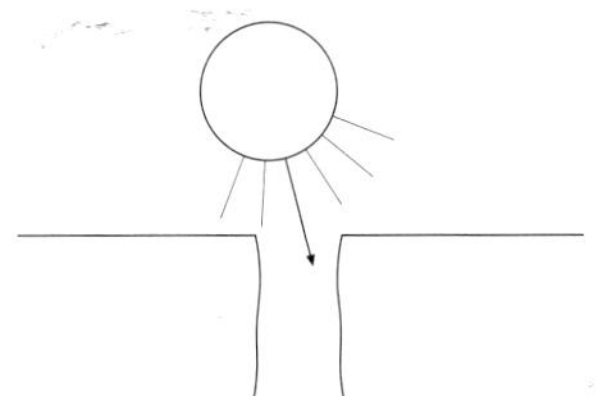

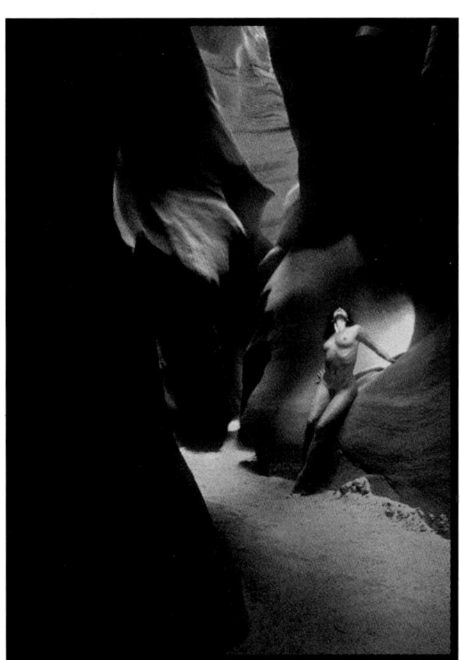

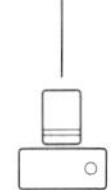

Fact file

Photographer: Björn Oldsen
Model: Karin
Location: Minnewaska State Park, New York, USA
Time of day: 3pm, May

Technical details

Camera: Olympus E10 (digital)
Lens: 35mm
Film: n/a
Exposure: Not recorded

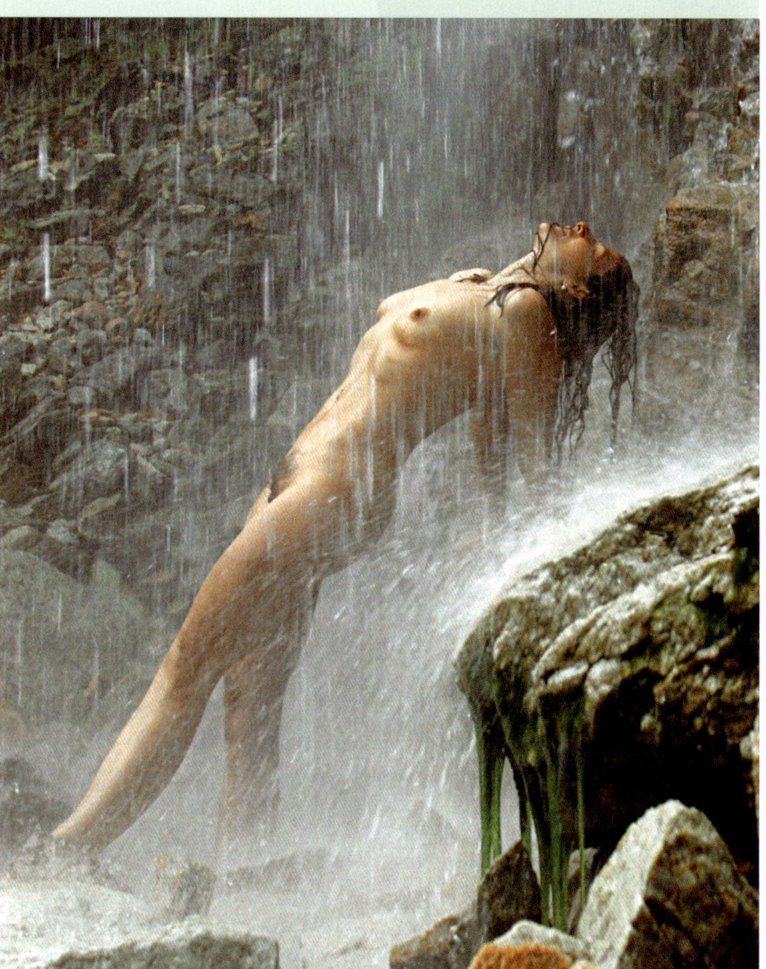

Björn was hiking through the wild and beautiful Minnewaska State Park with another photographer and his wife, who is the model here, when they came across this waterfall. 'As soon as we saw it, we saw that it had potential for some nude shots – despite it being terribly cold that day!' Like Mark Esposito's picture, the weather for this was overcast, with just enough light coming through the clouds to highlight the front of the body. ▲

'The vastness of the scene was overpoweringly beautiful so I had to decide what was the most important element in the composition.'

Mark Esposito

The concept

The amazing natural beauty of the location was the inspiration behind this picture. 'I wanted to match the graceful arc, waterfall and plunge pool of the water with a sense of casual observation, yet still capture the drama of the overhanging cliff,' explains Mark.

The location

Mark is based in Moab, Utah, and so is familiar with the surrounding canyons, although he still finds them a constant source of surprise and inspiration. 'This canyon, Dragon Fly, is one of incredible moods,' he says. 'Most of the time it's dry, and I was working around the next bend when we heard the sound of falling water. A passing thunderstorm left enough rain behind for this small flash flood to create this elegant waterfall.'

Composition

Mark chose his position carefully to ensure the long curve of the canyon rim swept through his picture from corner to corner. This is perfectly balanced by the arc of the falling water. The figure of the model is so small in the frame that she's almost an unexpected detail, but place your finger over her and you'll find that the picture loses much of its impact.

Lighting and technique

A thundercloud was hovering over us at the time of this shot and the soft, diffused light was perfect for saturating the colours and eliminating harsh shadows.

Fact file

Photographer: Mark Esposito
Model: Anna
Location: Moab, Utah, USA
Time of day: Late afternoon, July

Technical details

Camera: Olympus OM-1
Lens: 35–70mm
Film: Fuji Provia 100
Exposure: 1/60sec at f/8

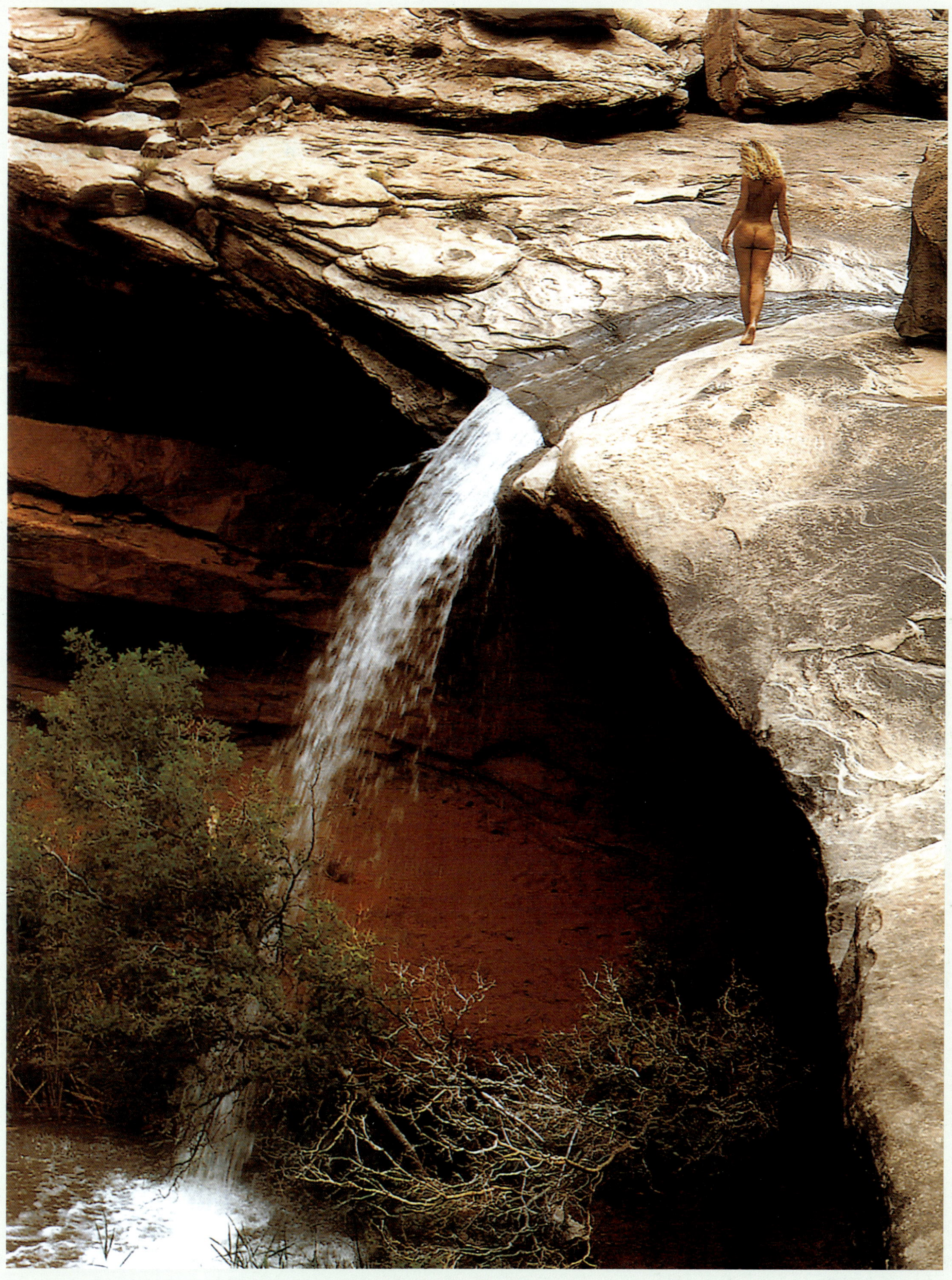

The concept

The unusual, round rock was the starting point for this idea. Eric wanted the shape of the model to reflect that of the rock. 'I seldom have an idea in my head before I begin working with a model or a space. It's more about responding to the setting, and the light,' he says.

The location

'The coastal barrens around Nova Scotia provide rich spaces to work in with the nude,' says Eric. 'Scattered glacial erratics provide beautiful platforms on which to place models and the desolate surroundings lend a sparse, forlorn feeling to the images.'

Composition

Placing this huge, natural boulder centrally in the image makes a strong statement in the composition and the position of the shadow is perfect for defining its shape and texture, as well as providing dramatic contrast with the pale skin tones of the model and the ground behind it. The model's pose is almost childlike and nicely echoes the roundness of the rock. Perhaps what really makes the picture is the way her hair is blowing in the wind. Eric describes that as 'serendipity'.

Lighting and technique

In late autumn, the light was low and angular. Eric placed the model so that the sun was slightly behind her, ensuring rich modelling of her figure. This position also allowed him to include the shadow of the rock, which is crucial to the success of the composition. The 17mm wide-angle lens covered a significant arc of the sky, resulting in the darkening of the sky on the left edge of the image. The infrared film has added to the character of the picture, boosting contrast and grain.

'I have a real affection for straightforward compositions with central focal points.'

Eric Boutilier-Brown

Fact file

Photographer:	Eric Boutilier-Brown
Model:	Ingrid
Location:	Coastal barrens, Nova Scotia, Canada
Time of day:	2.30pm, October

Technical details

Camera:	Nikon F3
Lens:	Tokina 17mm
Film:	Kodak High-Speed Infrared HIE
Exposure:	1/250sec at f/8

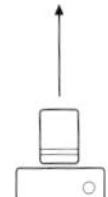

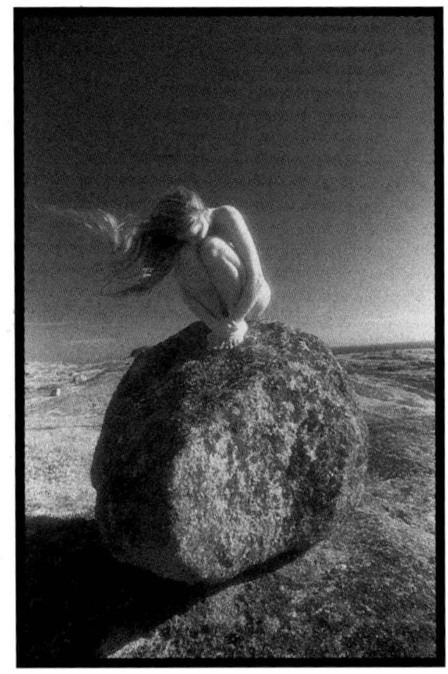

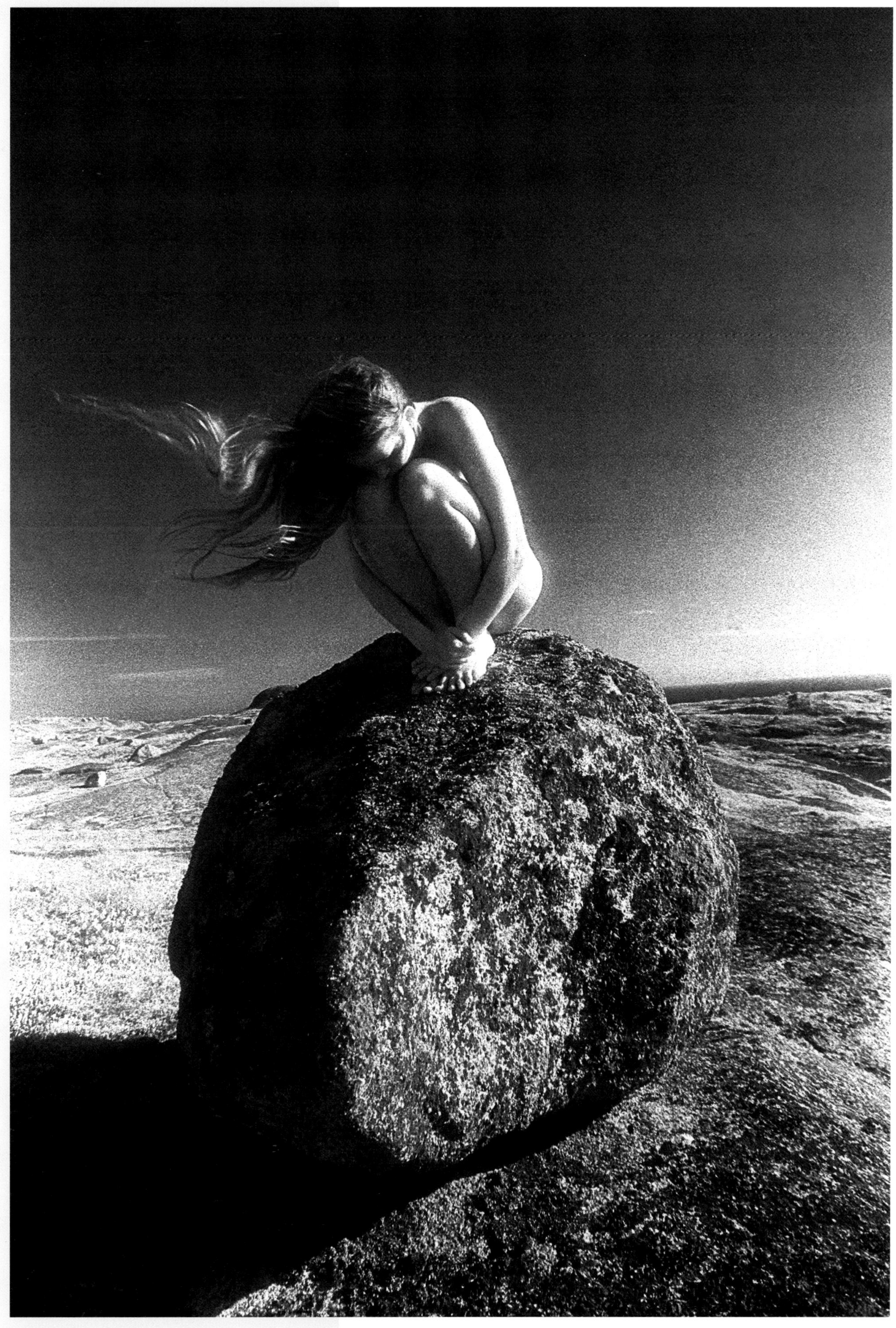

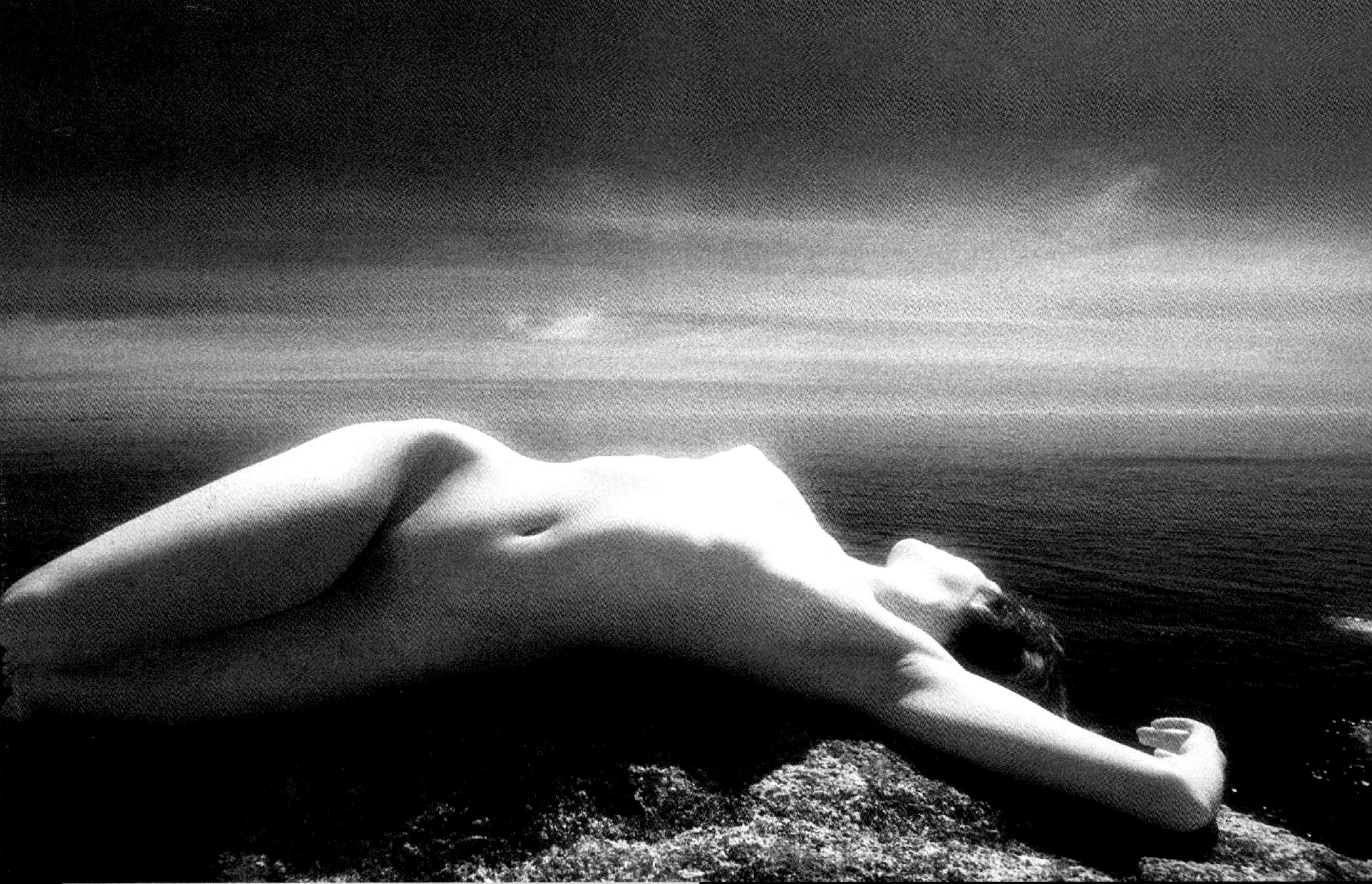

Fact file

Photographer: Eric Boutilier-Brown
Model: Victoria
Location: Chebucto Head, Nova Scotia, Canada
Time of day: 2.30pm, June

Technical details

Camera: Nikon F3
Lens: Tokina 17mm
Film: Kodak High-Speed Infrared HIE
Exposure: 1/250sec at f/11

The concept

'I didn't plan this shot. The model was free that day and so was I, so we went off to the location to make images,' says Eric. 'I worked with what was at the space when we were there and, as it turned out, it couldn't have been better.'

The location

Chebucto Head is a rugged corner of granite and scrub that looks out over the Atlantic Ocean. 'The rock forms run for several kilometres and provide wonderful spaces to work with a model,' explains Eric.

Composition

Eric felt it was important to place the model so that she was emerging out of the bottom of the image, with her body sweeping up to the line of the fog on the horizon. He used a 17mm ultra wide-angle lens, which he had to keep carefully parallel with the model to avoid too much distortion of her figure.

Lighting and technique

'When we arrived at the coast there was heavy fog over the horizon,' recalls Eric. 'I knew this would end up being a light detail above a dark ocean while the full, direct sunlight would give a rich highlight to the figure. The infrared film accentuated this. I always work with infrared in 35mm. I am drawn to it for its magical look and the way it makes the model's skin look like stone.'

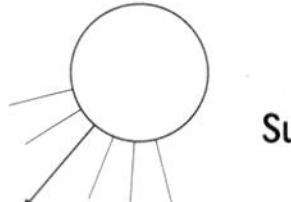

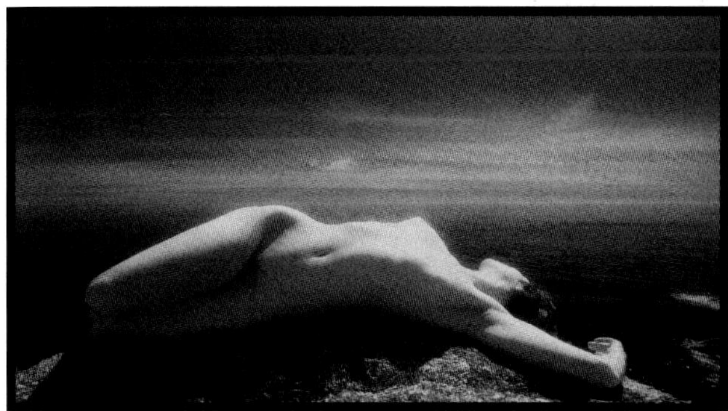

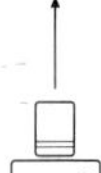

Fact file

Photographer: Jonathan Charles
Model: Liz
Location: Chipstead Lake, Kent, UK
Time of day: Early morning, July

Technical details

Camera: Olympus OM2
Lens: 24mm
Film: Kodachrome 25
Exposure: Not recorded

The concept

'This is part of a personal art project that I call "Eve", on the theme of humanity in an idealised state of harmony with nature,' explains Jonathan. 'The idea here was Eve in the Garden of Eden, being warmed by the sun.'

The location

Chipstead Lake was artificially built and unusual in that the grass goes right down to the water's edge. Jonathan wanted an idyllic-looking spot and was already familiar with this location, having sailed on the lake on previous occasions.

Composition

Jonathan took the shot from the other side of the lake, deliberately keeping the figure small in the frame, 'to give weight to the surrounding tranquil scene and avoid a "glamour" effect,' he says. 'I used the cooler tones of her reflection as a bridge between the bright skin tones and the dominant blue/green of her surroundings.'

Lighting and technique

Jonathan had to time this shot carefully to achieve the natural spotlight effect on the model that is so crucial to its success. 'Direct sunlight is not usually a good way of lighting the nude because of harsh shadows, but in this photo, the early morning sun was low in the sky and directly behind me,' he explains. 'The result was almost as though direct flash had been used on the scene. I liked the way the warm yellow colour of the sun picks up the skin tones and adds to the contrast with the deep green background.'

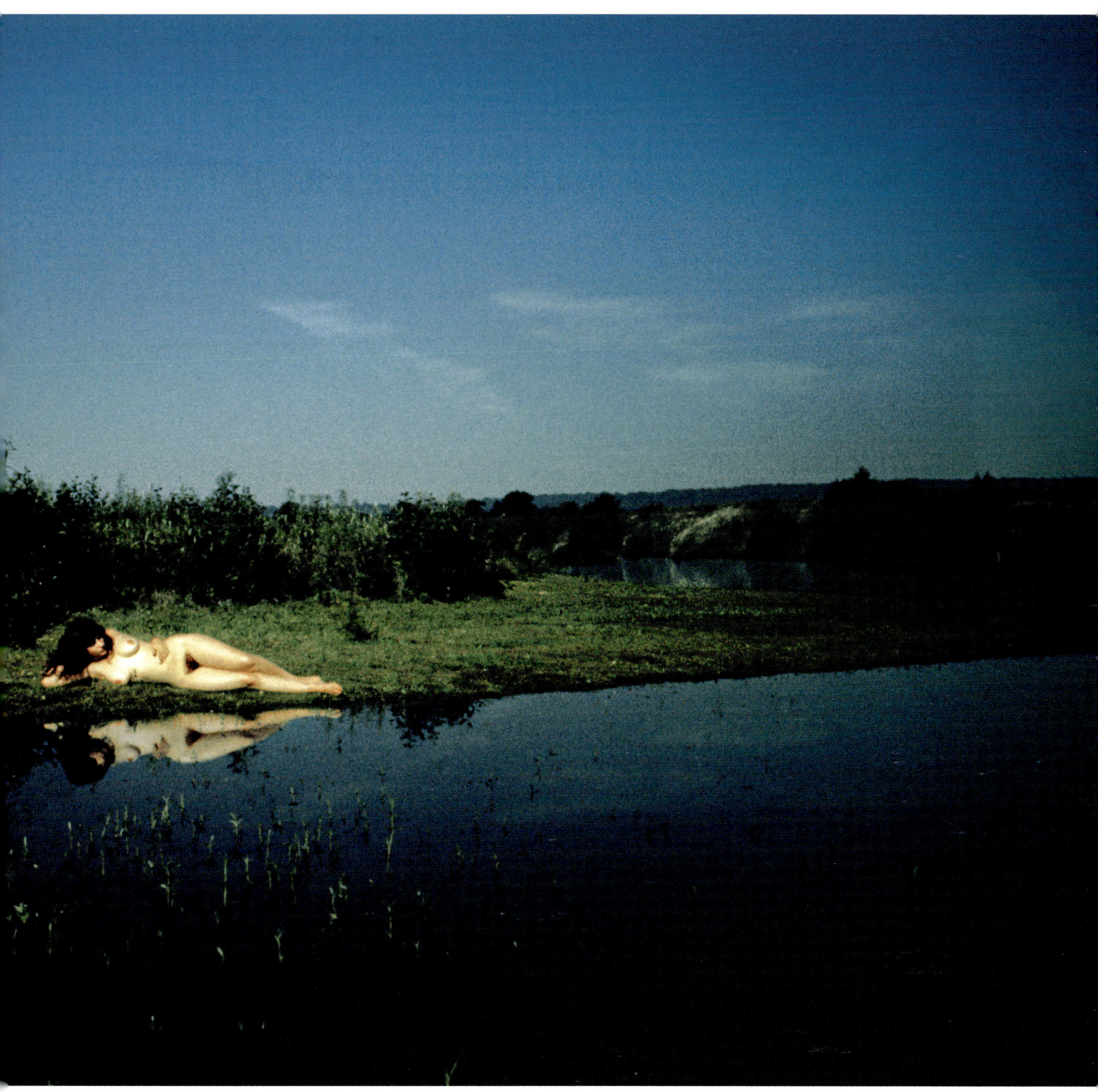

'We arrived before the sun came up and waited for it to rise above the horizon. The first few moments were a little flat, but as it moved slightly higher it produced this wonderful warm colour.'

Jonathan Charles

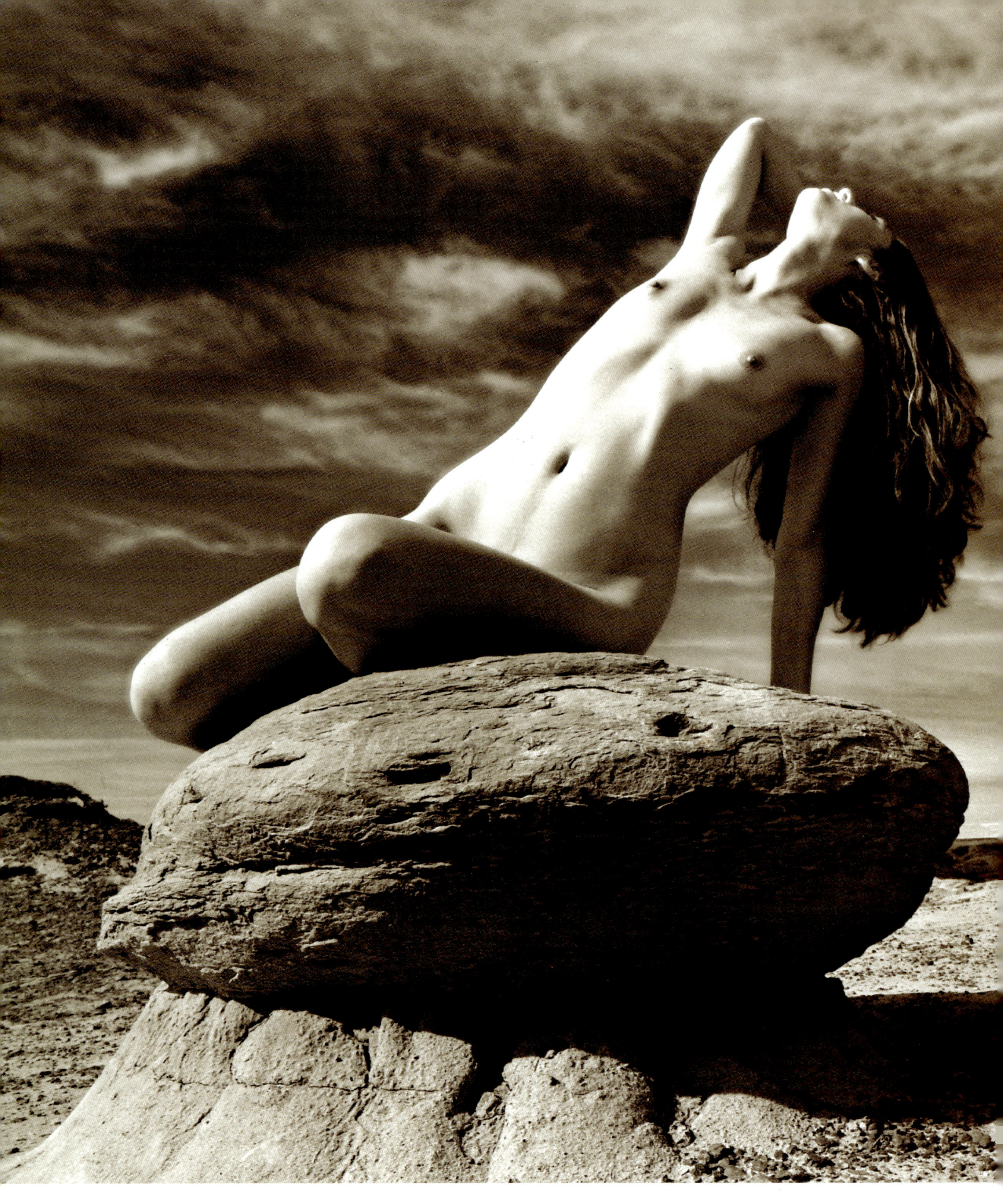

The concept

'I was leading a photography workshop and we were working with three models – two females and one male. I split the groups into three, so each model had only two photographers,' explains Darwin. 'We were looking to get photos of the nude form in landscapes that were "raw" and "elemental", so rocks, sky, earth and water.'

The location

Darwin had taken his group to this spot near Drumheller, Alberta, Canada because he knew there were excellent rock formations that would fit the feel of the imagery they were going for. Drumheller is famous worldwide for its stark 'Badlands'.

Composition

The rock formation or 'hoodoo' was the starting point for the composition. Wiggett set up the shot with the rock in the foreground and asked the model to sit on it. 'We tried out various poses and this is the one we liked best, as it seemed to "flow" with the natural elements in the scene,' he explains. 'I placed the rock and the girl slightly to the left, so that the shadow would form a strong compositional element leading into the rest of the scene.'

Lighting and technique

The scene was strongly side lit, with the light coming from the left-hand side and slightly to the front of the model. This helps to bring out the shape of the model's figure and emphasise the texture of the rock formation and landscape. A polarising filter on the lens darkened the sky to contrast with the wonderful clouds passing overhead. Darwin used a wide-angle lens (35mm in 645 format is the equivalent of 20mm in 35mm format) to distort the size of the rock in relation to the surroundings. He had to rest the camera on the ground and prop the lens up with small rocks to hold the camera steady. He couldn't get his eye to the camera at this angle so used a right angle finder attached to the viewfinder.

Fact file

Photographer: Darwin Wiggett
Model: Jamie
Location: Drumheller, Alberta, Canada
Time of day: 9am, August

Technical details

Camera: Mamiya 645 Pro
Lens: 35mm f/3.5
Film: Ilford XP-2 400
Exposure: 1/250sec at f/9.5

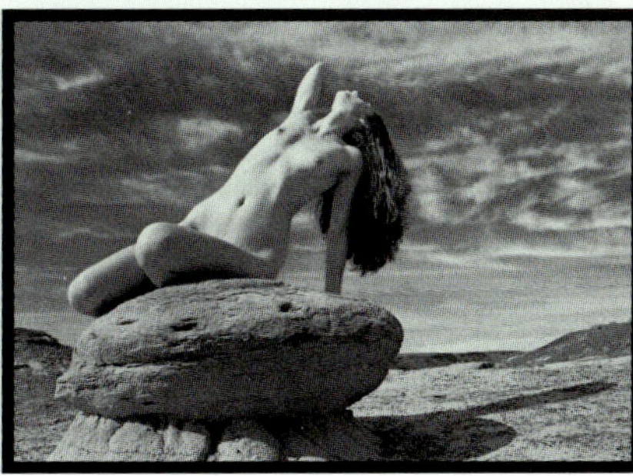

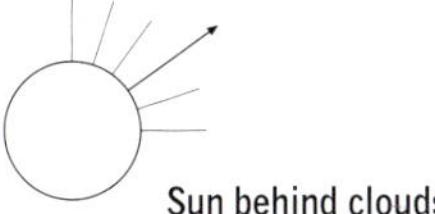

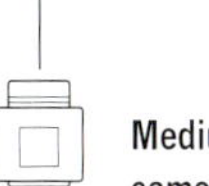

' I am foremost a landscape photographer and for me this shot is as much about the landscape as it is about the nude form.'

Darwin Wiggett

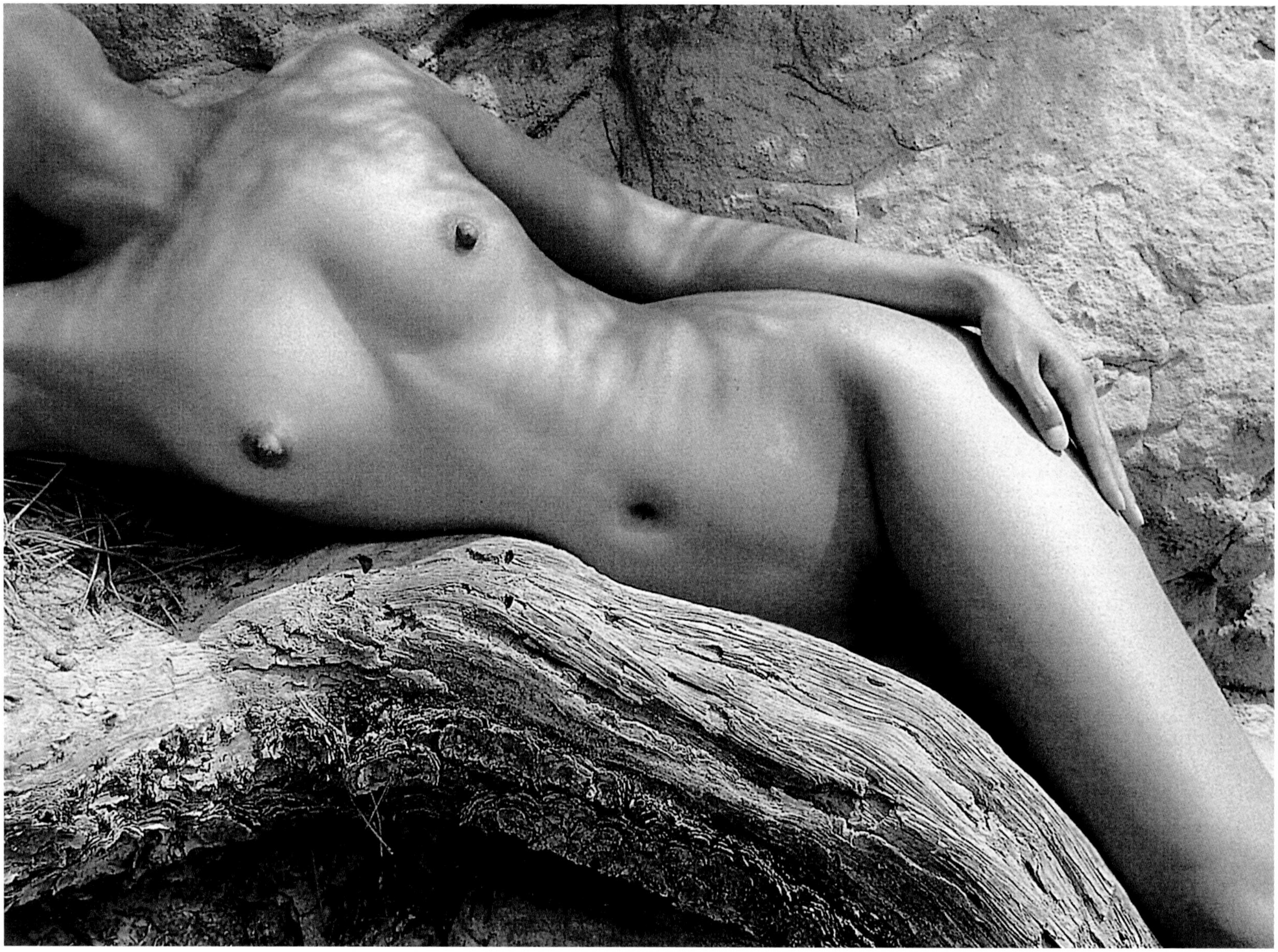

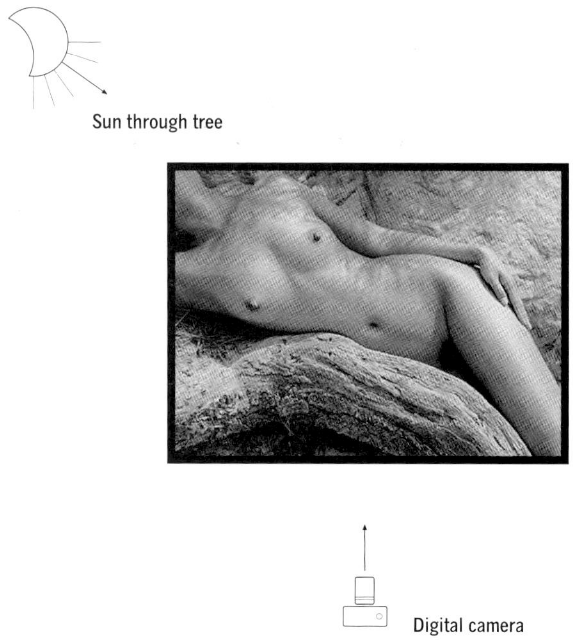

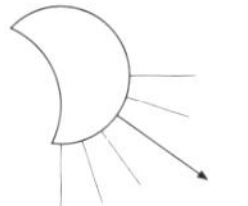

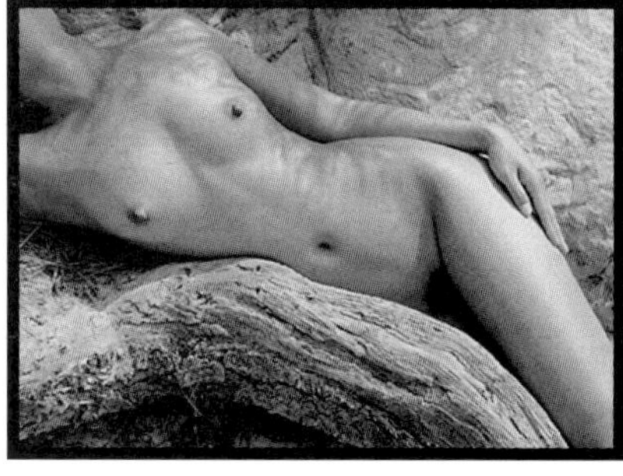

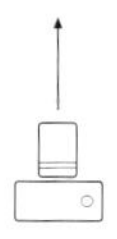

' My models love the digital camera. Sometimes they are posing in uncomfortable positions, wedged between rocks, and they have trouble visualising how beautiful they look. With digital, they can see the results immediately and I can also catch mistakes and re-shoot.'

Blake White

The concept

A personal shot for Blake and his model, this was inspired by the texture and shapes of the rock, which Blake felt would contrast well with the smoothness and softness of a nude. He enjoys the challenge of working outdoors, finding natural features in the landscape that a model can mould herself around.

The location

This city park in Colorado Springs, Colorado, is a favourite area for Blake. 'It's quite large with well-defined paths over steep rocks,' he says. 'I like to get off the park, just out of sight of people passing by, and I've never had a problem with people seeing us. The park has a great variety of boulders, trees and interesting cracks that work well with nude models. It also has great views of Pike Peak.'

Composition

'When I find interesting locations, I usually either show the model what pose I want her to try, or point out a boulder or ledge and ask her to fit herself around it,' explains Blake. 'She tries the pose first with her clothes on and sometimes it works, sometimes not. The key is to try.'

Lighting and technique

At the hottest part of the day, the sun was directly above the model. Blake tried to wait for a cloud to pass over the sun to soften the light, but it would not oblige. There was some shade, however, from a tree above the model and you can see the shadows cast by it on her body. Blake used a 3 megapixel digital camera and converted the image to black and white with Photoshop. He also used this to sharpen the image slightly to bring out the detail in the rocks, then added a slight blur to the model's torso to soften the look of the skin.

<table>
<tr><td colspan="2">Technical details</td><td colspan="2">Fact file</td></tr>
<tr><td>Camera:</td><td>Olympus 3020 (digital)</td><td>Photographer:</td><td>Blake White</td></tr>
<tr><td>Lens:</td><td>32–96mm</td><td>Model:</td><td>Jasmine</td></tr>
<tr><td>Film:</td><td>n/a</td><td>Location:</td><td>City park, Colorado Springs, USA</td></tr>
<tr><td>Exposure:</td><td>1/650sec at f/4</td><td>Time of day:</td><td>Midday, August</td></tr>
</table>

<table>
<tr><td colspan="2">Fact file</td><td colspan="2">Technical details</td></tr>
<tr><td>Photographer:</td><td>Carsten Tschach</td><td>Camera:</td><td>F100</td></tr>
<tr><td>Model:</td><td>Heike</td><td>Lens:</td><td>28–70mm</td></tr>
<tr><td>Location:</td><td>A field, Germany</td><td>Film:</td><td>Fuji Sensia</td></tr>
<tr><td>Time of day:</td><td>5pm, June</td><td>Exposure:</td><td>1/250sec at f/5.6</td></tr>
</table>

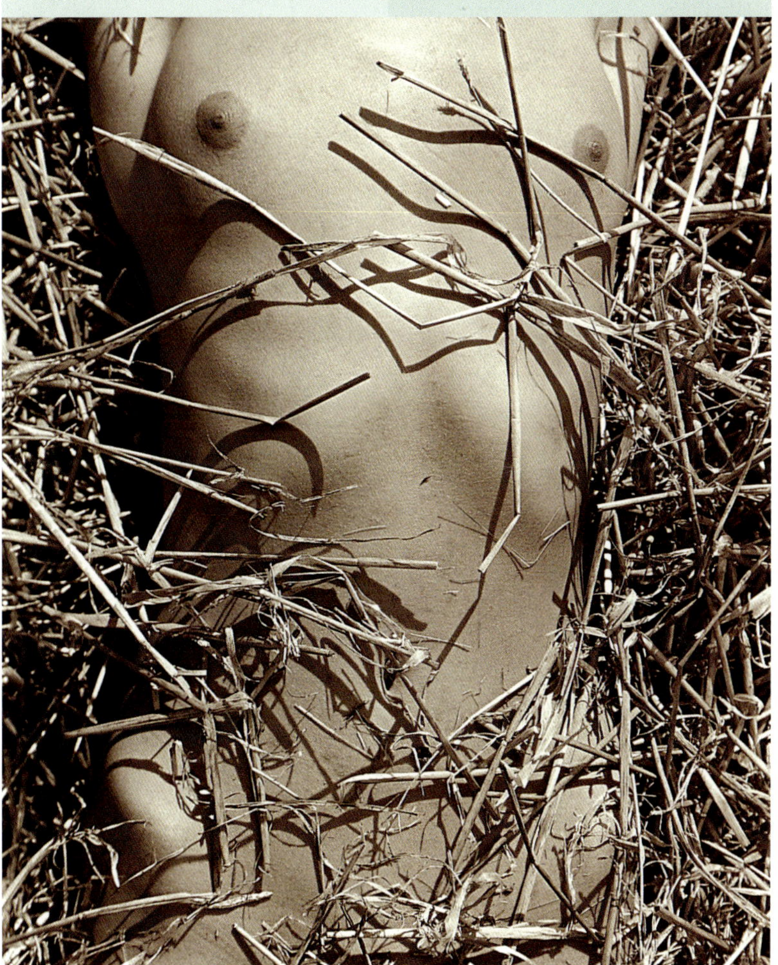

On the way home from a previous shoot, Carsten and his model drove by this field and saw the lovely light of the afternoon sun, which they felt was too good to miss. 'The idea behind the picture was to integrate the female body with nature so they look like they belong together,' he says. The image was converted into black and white and sepia toned using tritone mode in Photoshop. ▲

The concept

Dale had taken some previous pictures of Claire underwater while he was standing on cliffs above. They came out so well he decided to try some with the camera underwater as well. 'I wanted to see what a nude looked like to the brook trout that live in this stream! I don't have a waterproof case for my camera so I bought a small aquarium to get the camera under the surface. I thought there would be some reflections from the underside of the water but I wasn't sure.'

The location

The Woodstock area of New York where Dale lives is full of crystal-clear streams. He had used them many times before as backgrounds to his nude pictures but this was his first attempt at photographing in one of them.

Composition

'Fortunately the Olympus E20 has a monitor that you can pull out at a 90 degree angle so I could compose the image without having to stick my big head upside down in the aquarium,' explains Dale. 'I shot close up so that the sediment we kicked up in the water wasn't an issue.'

Lighting and technique

'This was shot with direct noon sun to get as much visibility as possible under that water. The water was so cold and the air so warm that the glass on the aquarium steamed up all the time. I was able to push the aquarium under the surface of the water a good eight or nine inches, have the camera inside pressed up against the glass, focus, compose and shoot.'

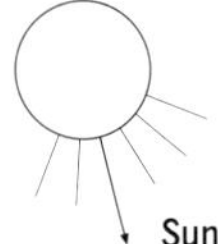

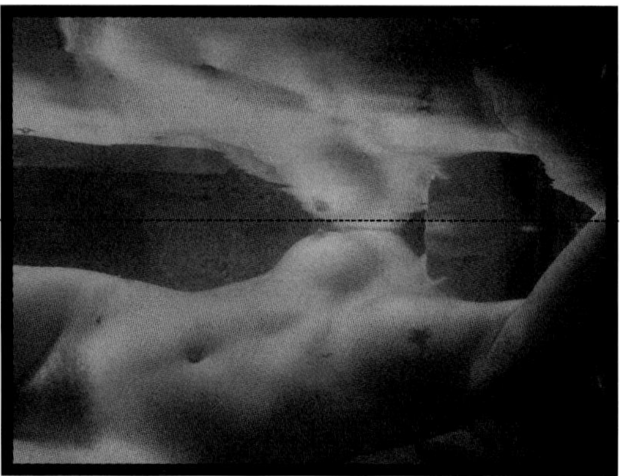

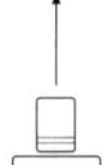
Digital camera in a glass aquarium, pushed underwater

'I was extremely happy with the results and this one reminds me of the Sistine Chapel.
I was also happy I didn't slip on the rocks and take my camera swimming. It hates
cold water.'

Dale Lehmer

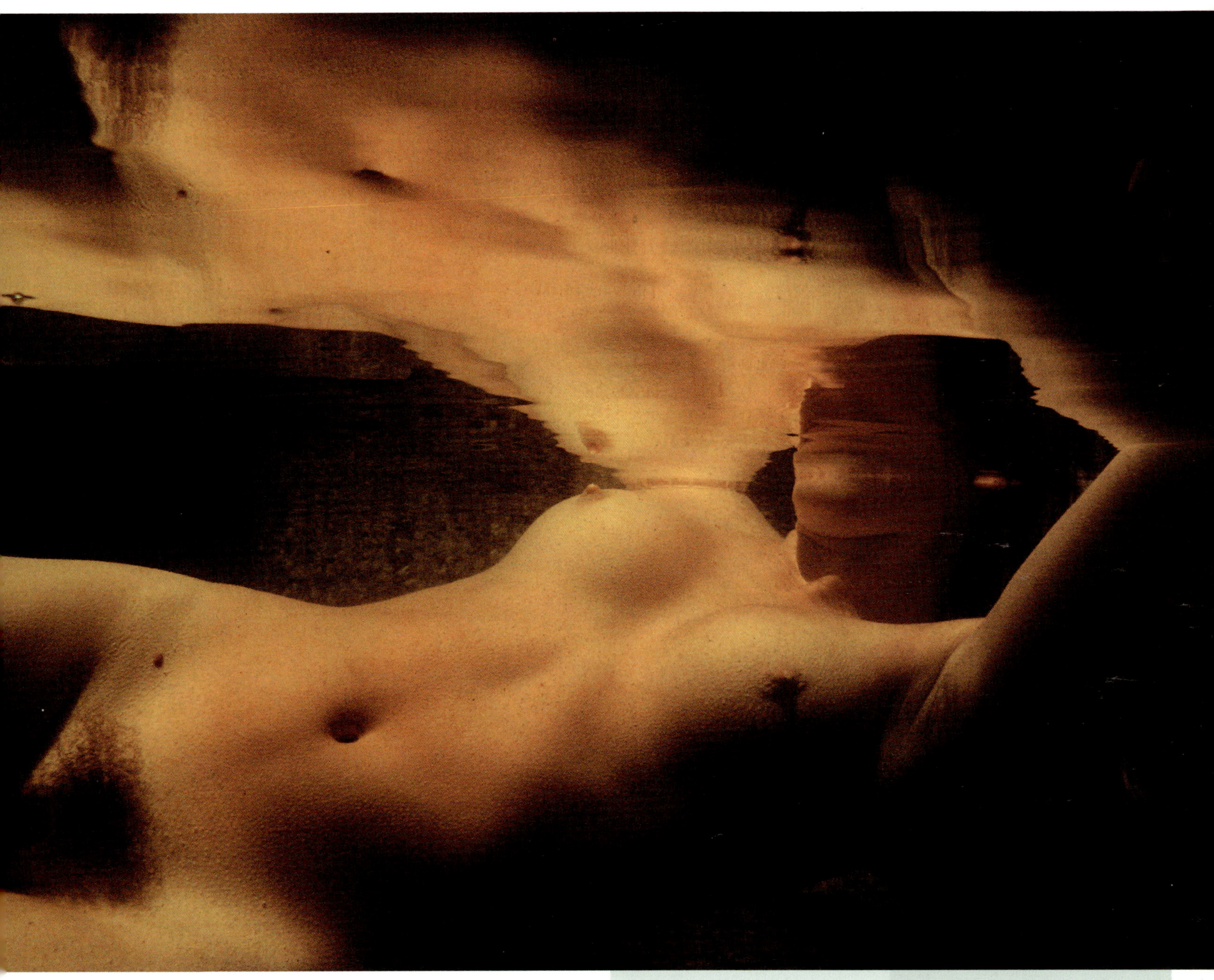

Fact file

Photographer:	Dale Lehmer
Model:	Claire
Location:	Minnawaska State Park, New York, USA
Time of day:	Midday, July

Technical details

Camera:	Olympus E20n (digital)
Lens:	35mm
Film:	n/a
Exposure:	1sec at f/4

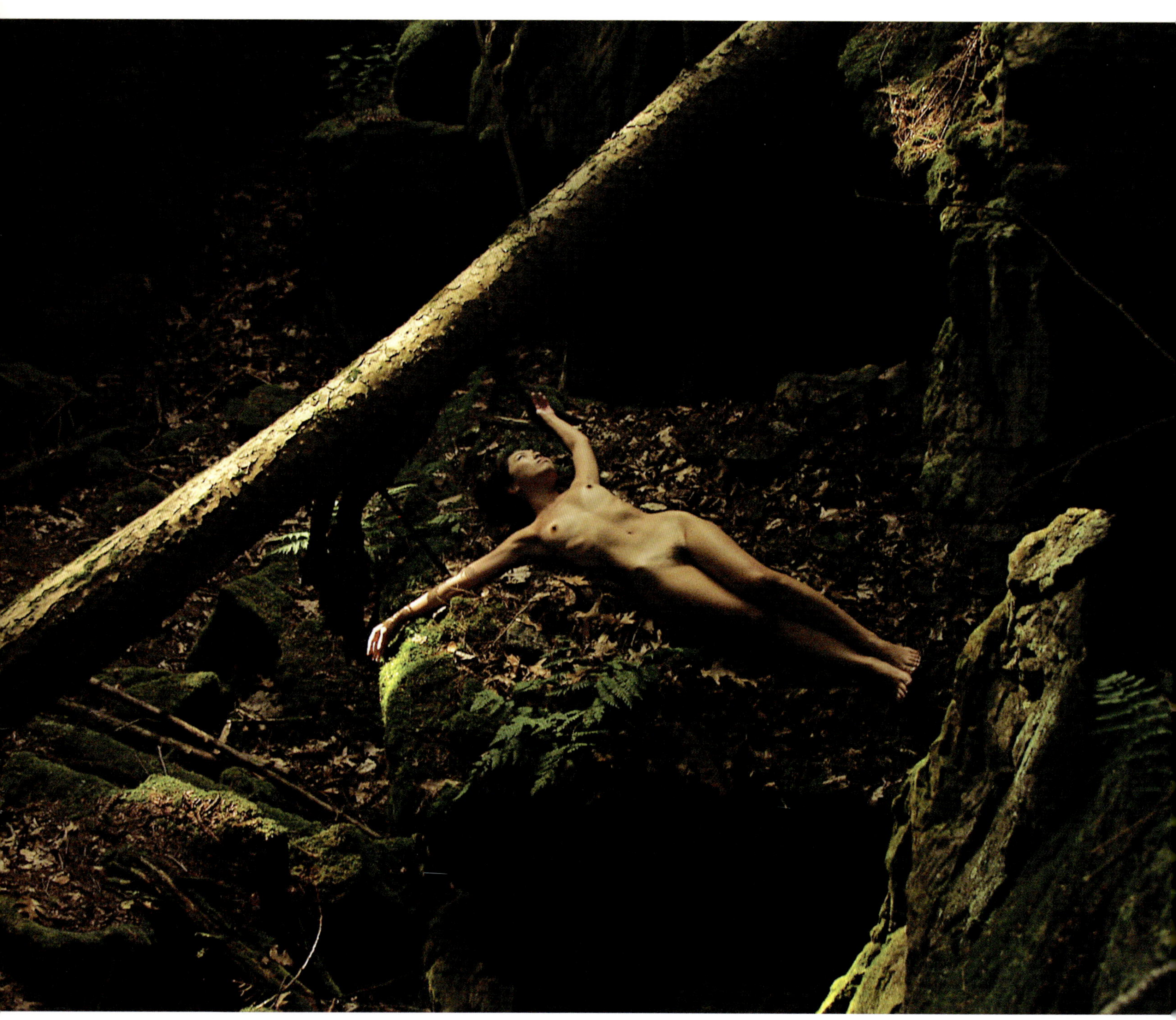

' There is nothing more satisfying to me than to create an image of one of my beautiful models that is elegant, dignified and tender. It's a combination of the model, the landscape and the light.'

Dale Lehmer

The concept

As with all his images, Dale was attempting to capture the female form as a part of nature. He regards his pictures as a way of expressing his appreciation of the beauty of both.

The location

'This is one of my favourite places near my home,' he says. 'Some old concrete caves, made back in the 19th century, have collapsed, creating some really interesting landscapes with textured rock areas and cliffs.'

Composition

Dale took this from a high vantage point because he wanted to convey a sense of depth to the image through a layering effect of parts of the surroundings. The log and rock at the top of the image add to this three-dimensional quality and make the model seem small and vulnerable in the environment.

Lighting and technique

The late afternoon sun, from the left of the camera, was filtered through trees. As he only ever uses natural light, Dale finds these, as well as clouds and mist, an effective way of softening it. He also frequently deliberately underexposes to achieve the quiet, moody feel he is after. Here it helped him produce a deep, warm, forest atmosphere.

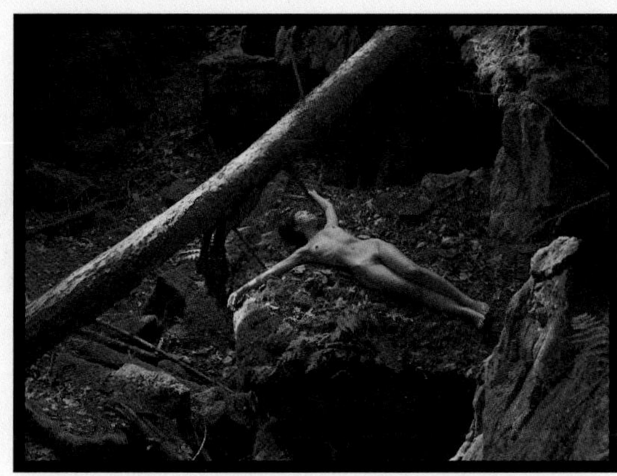

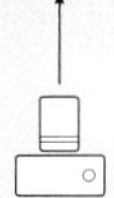

Fact file		Technical details	
Photographer:	Dale Lehmer	**Camera:**	Olympus E10 (digital)
Model:	Akido	**Lens:**	35mm
Location:	Caves, Rosendale, New York, USA	**Film:**	n/a
Time of day:	5pm, August	**Exposure:**	1/80sec at f/3.2

The concept

'My nude photographs are not commissioned works but done for my own, and my models' benefit,' says Blake. 'I like the challenges of photographing nudes outdoors in a landscape and few of my pictures are planned ahead of time.'

The location

This was taken on the coast of Florida, just north of Jacksonville. 'Occasionally I scout a location briefly ahead of the shoot but mostly, and on this occasion, my model and I just wander around promising landscapes and see what we can create,' explains Blake. This spot immediately struck him because of the shape of the trunk, the branch above it and the view of the sea between them.

Composition

The tree trunk and the overhead branch work beautifully as a frame within a frame in a natural and uncontrived way. Blake neatened this up slightly by cloning out a small but intrusive branch with Photoshop on the computer. He kept the composition very simple, placing the model dead centre, with the strongly defined horizon line cutting across, just below the middle of the frame.

Lighting and technique

Blake was working alone with the model on this occasion and, partly for that reason, he kept his equipment to a minimum to avoid lugging too much around while looking for locations. With no reflectors or flash he relied on the existing light, which was almost overhead sunshine, obscured by clouds. The film here was infrared, used in conjunction with a Kodak Wratten 25 red filter which absorbs daylight, allowing just the infrared to reach the film. The effect varies according to the subject but tends to increase grain and contrast. Here it has lightened the model's skin and darkened the sea and clouds. 'It looks as though a storm was brewing but it was just a warm, partly cloudy day in Florida,' says Blake.

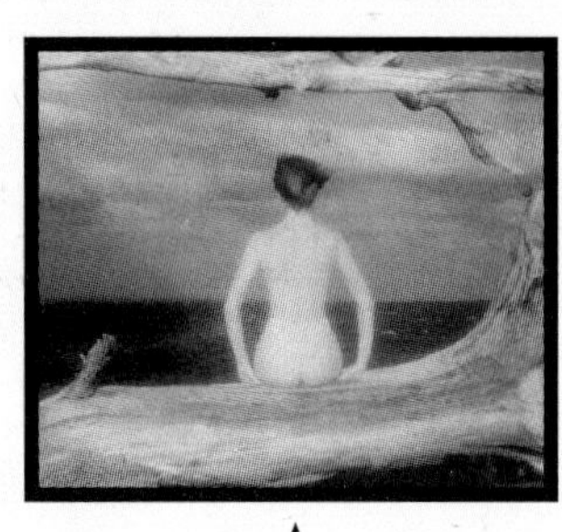

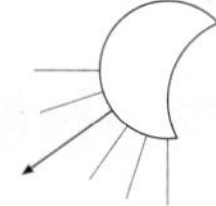

Light cloud

Medium format camera on ground

' The challenge for me is to find interesting shapes in rocks, logs, crevasses, and so on, that I can fit the female form into. I like the contrast of its softness with the rough landscape.'

Blake White

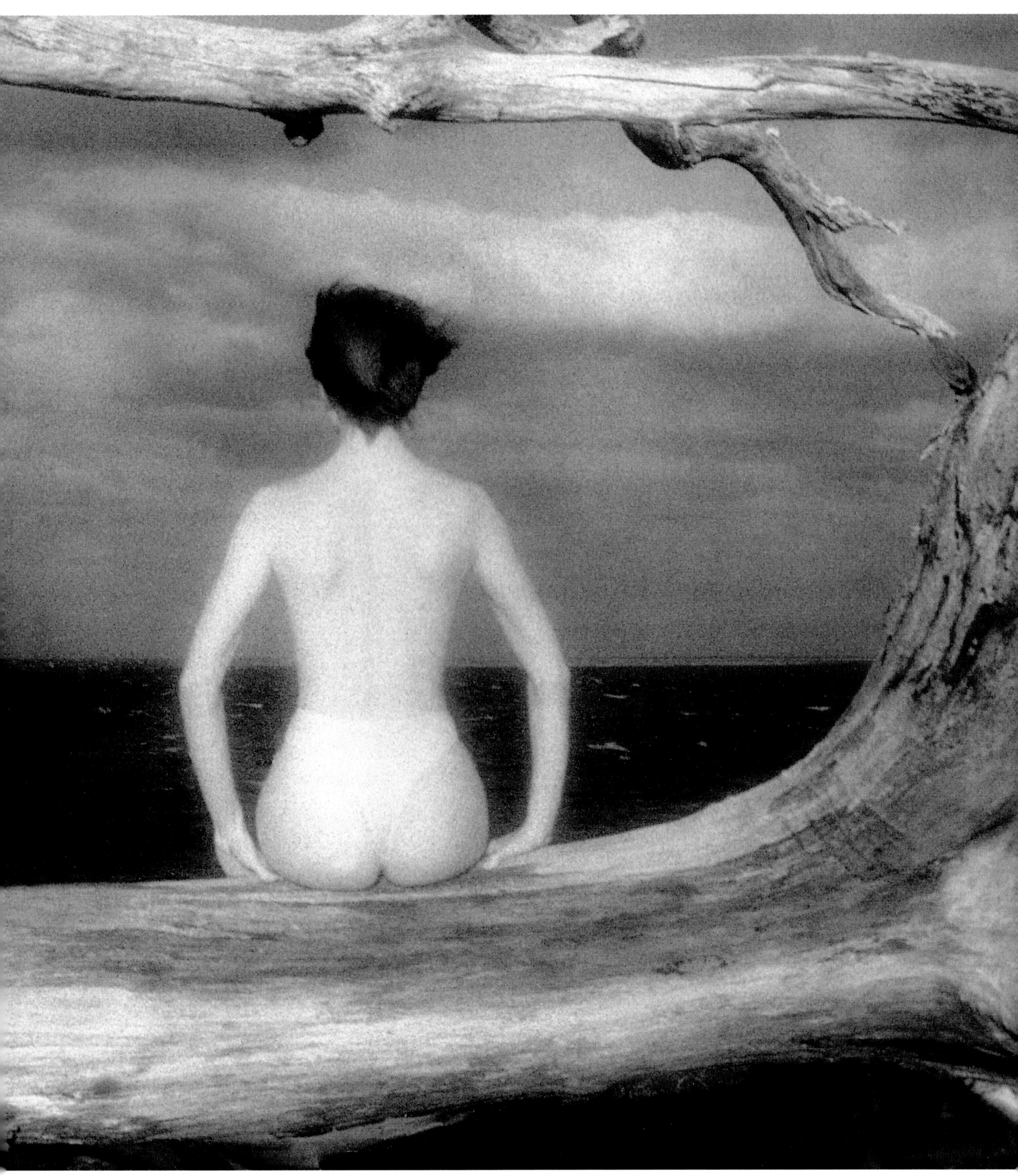

Glossary

Ambient light

The existing light on the scene without any added by the photographer.

Aperture priority

The photographer selects the aperture and the shutter speed is determined automatically.

B setting

Keeps the shutter open for as long as the release remains pressed.

Bracket

To make a series of exposures of the same subject, often at one half or one third stop intervals.

Boom

Extension arm allowing a light to be lifted over the subject.

Burning in

Giving part of a print extra exposure.

Cable release

Flexible cable that screws into the camera shutter release. Allows the shutter to be fired, or held open on 'B', to reduce camera shake.

Differential focus

Using a shallow depth of field to emphasise one part of the picture by showing it sharply focused while other areas are out of focus. Also called selective focus.

Diffuser

Translucent material used to diffuse light.

Fill-in

Light added to an area of shade, often with a reflector, to reduce overall contrast.

Fill-in flash

A burst of flash to illuminate any areas of shadow and reduce lighting contrast.

Filter

A piece of glass or plastic fitted over the lens to modify the light passing through it.

High key

High key pictures concentrate on white or pale tones, often with flat, overall lighting to avoid shadows.

Incident light metering

Using an exposure meter from the subject position, pointing back towards the camera.

Lighting contrast

The difference between the amount of light falling on the shadow areas and the brightly-lit areas of a subject, usually measured in stops.

Medium format

Cameras that use 120 roll film, taking pictures larger than 35mm. Usually 645 (6x4.5cm picture size), 6x6 or 6x7.

Neutral density filter

Grey filter that dims the image by a known amount.

Open flash

Firing the flash manually while the camera shutter is open.

Panning

Moving the camera to follow a subject moving across the picture. Produces a relatively sharp subject against a blurred background.

Reflector

A rectangular or round sheet of white, silver or gold material or card, used to bounce light on to the subject. Also refers to a dish-shaped surround to a flash head.

Ring flash

A circular flash unit that fits around the lens to provide shadow-free lighting.

Scrim

Metal mesh attachment to a lighting unit to reduce intensity.

Slow-sync flash

Combining a blurred effect from a long exposure with the freezing of motion with flash.

Softbox

A box diffuser of varying size placed over the light source to produce a large area of soft, even lighting.

Strobe

An alternative term for electronic flash.

Tungsten-balanced film

Colour film balanced to suit light sources of 3200K. Gives a blue cast when used in daylight.

Umbrella

A special umbrella covered with highly reflective, semi-transparent material and attached to the flash unit. The flash is fired through the umbrella to soften or diffuse it and into the umbrella for reflected light.

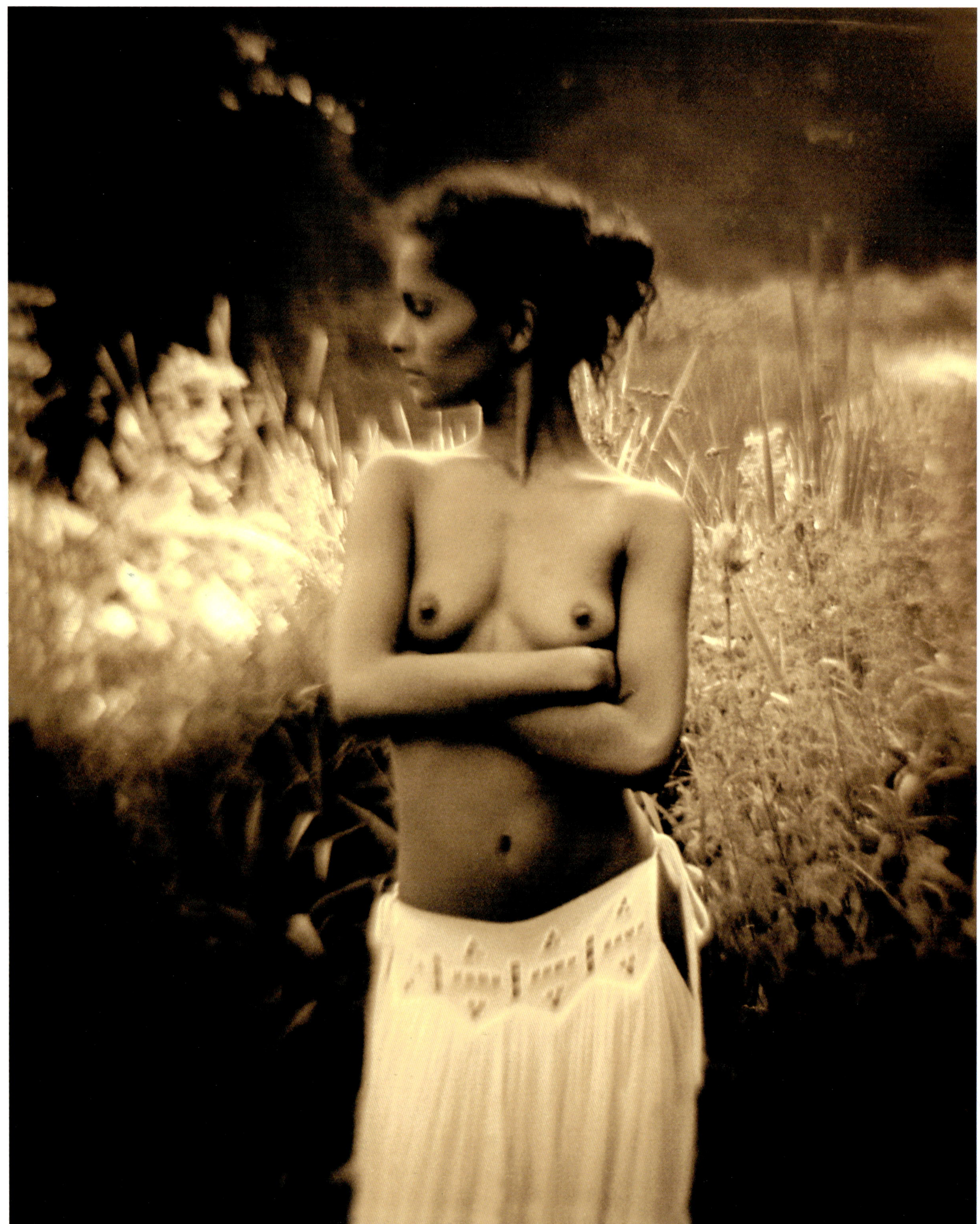

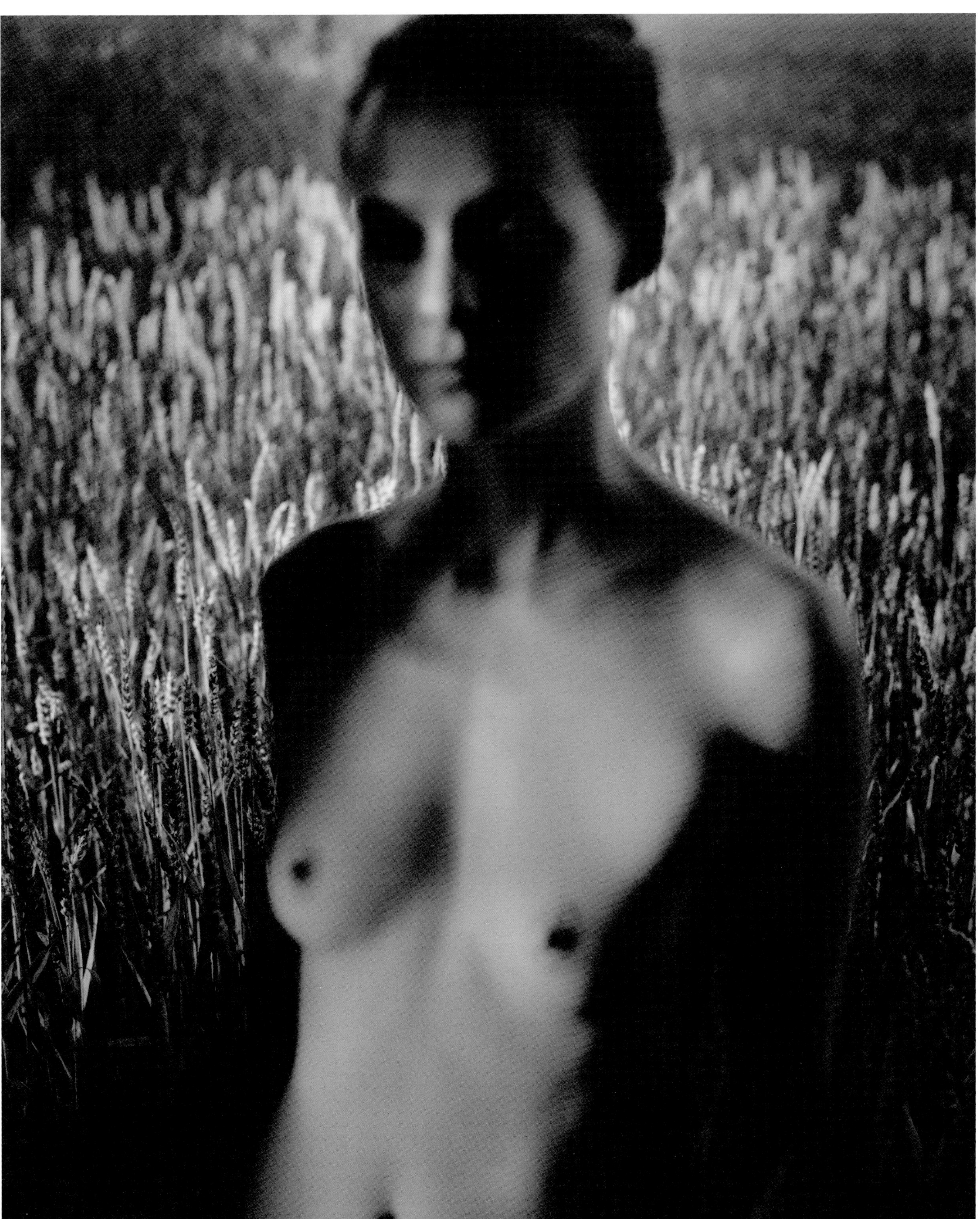

Contacts